Social Theory and Education

Although education researchers have drawn on the work of a wide diversity of theorists, a number of these have been of particular significance to education. While the likes of Karl Marx, Antonio Gramsci, John Dewey and Paulo Freire influenced previous generations of educational theorists, much of the more contemporary theory building has revolved around a quartet of well-known and much-debated thinkers – Michel Foucault, Jürgen Habermas, Pierre Bourdieu and Jacques Derrida. However, while the influence of these thinkers has grown considerably over the last number of years, both their original work and its application to education can prove challenging to the educational practitioner. The challenges they pose to educators are exacerbated by a lack of suitable reading material that can appeal to the advanced practitioner, while also providing a sufficiently in-depth overview of the various theories and their applications in educational research.

This edited book expertly rectifies this omission in the educational literature, and delivers a text that is both advanced and accessible, offering the education practitioner/researcher a suitable guide to assist their acquisition and application of social theory. The chapters included in this collection are designed to illustrate the diverse ways in which continental theory of whatever stripe can be applied to educational issues. From school surveillance to curriculum, social theory is used to shed light on 'practical' issues facing the sector, helping to widen and deepen discussion around these areas when they are in danger of being over-simplified.

This book will be very useful to post-graduate student-teachers who wish to develop their capacity to engage with these debates at an advanced level. It will also prove of great interest to anyone involved in education policy and theory.

Mark Murphy is Reader in Education at the University of Glasgow, UK. He is the creator of www.socialtheoryapplied.com, a website designed to provide a platform for discussion around the relationship between theory and educational research.

Social Theory and Education Research

Understanding Foucault, Habermas, Bourdieu and Derrida

Edited by Mark Murphy

Routledge
Taylor & Francis Group

LONDON AND NEW YORK

First published 2013
by Routledge
2 Park Square, Milton Park, Abingdon, Oxon OX14 4RN

Simultaneously published in the USA and Canada
by Routledge
711 Third Avenue, New York, NY 10017

Routledge is an imprint of the Taylor & Francis Group, an informa business

British Library Cataloguing in Publication Data
A catalogue record for this book is available from the British Library

Library of Congress Cataloging in Publication Data
Social theory and education research : understanding Foucault,
Habermas, Bourdieu and Derrida / edited by Mark Murphy.
      pages cm
   ISBN 978-0-415-53013-2 (hardback) — ISBN 978-0-415-53014-9
   (pbk.) — ISBN 978-0-203-55768-6 (e-book)
   1. Educational sociology.   2. Foucault, Michel, 1926–1984—Political
   and social views.   3. Habermas, Jürgen—Political and social views.
   4. Bourdieu, Pierre, 1930–2002—Political and social views.
   5. Derrida, Jacques Political and social views.   I. Murphy, Mark
   (Mark T. F.), editor of compilation.   II. Allan, Julie (Julie E.) Foucault
   and his acolytes.
   LC189.S6695 2013
   306.43—dc23

                                                                    2012038624

ISBN: 978-0-415-53013-2 (hbk)
ISBN: 978-0-415-53014-9 (pbk)
ISBN: 978-0-203-55768-6 (ebk)

Typeset in Galliard
by RefineCatch Limited, Bungay, Suffolk

Printed and bound in the United States of America by Edwards Brothers Malloy

Contents

List of contributors   vii
Acknowledgements   xi

PART I
Introduction   1

1   Social theory and education research: an introduction   3
    MARK MURPHY

PART II
Foucault   19

2   Foucault and his acolytes: discourse, power and ethics   21
    JULIE ALLAN

3   Foucault, panopticism and school surveillance research   35
    ANDREW HOPE

4   Foucault, confession and reflective practices   52
    ANDREAS FEJES

PART III
Habermas   67

5   Jürgen Habermas: education's reluctant hero   69
    TERENCE LOVAT

6   The politics of school regulation: using Habermas
    to research educational accountability   84
    MARK MURPHY AND PAUL SKILLEN

7 Applying Habermas' theory of communicative action in
   an analysis of recognition of prior learning   98
   FREDRIK SANDBERG

PART IV
Bourdieu   115

8 Bourdieu and educational research: thinking tools,
   relational thinking, beyond epistemological innocence   117
   SHAUN RAWOLLE AND BOB LINGARD

9 Research in the new Christian Academies:
   perspectives from Bourdieu   138
   ELIZABETH GREEN

10 Bourdieu applied: exploring perceived parental
   influence on adolescent students' educational
   choices for studies in higher education   153
   IRENE KLEANTHOUS

PART V
Derrida   169

11 Derrida and educational research: an introduction   171
   JONES IRWIN

12 'Derrida applied': Derrida meets Dracula in
   the geography classroom   184
   CHRISTINE WINTER

13 Engaging with student-teachers on reflective
   writing: reclaiming writing   200
   DUNCAN MERCIECA

   Index   212

Contributors

Julie Allan is Professor of Equity and Inclusion at the University of Birmingham. She is also Visiting Professor at the University of Borås, Sweden. Her most recent books are *Rethinking Inclusive Education: The Philosophers of Difference in Practice* (Springer, 2007), *Doing Inclusive Education Research* (with Roger Slee; Sense, 2008) and *Social Capital, Professionalism and Diversity* (with Jenny Ozga and Geri Smyth; Sense, 2009).

Andreas Fejes is Professor of Adult Education Research at the Department of Behavioural Sciences and Learning at Linköping University, Sweden. His research draws particularly on post-structuralist theory to explore issues of post-compulsory education, workplace learning and education policy. He has edited *Foucault and Lifelong Learning: Governing the Subject* (with K. Nicoll; Routledge, 2008) and co-written *The Confessing Society: Foucault, Confession and Practices of Lifelong Learning* (with M. Dahlstedt; Routledge, 2012). His articles have recently appeared in the *British Journal of Sociology of Education*, *British Educational Research Journal*, *Journal of Education Policy*, *Educational Philosophy and Theory*, *Journal of Advanced Nursing*, *Studies in Continuing Education* and *Studies in the Education of Adults*. He is also the editor of the *European Journal for Research on the Education and Learning of Adults* (RELA).

Elizabeth Green is Director of the National Centre for Christian Education Research at Liverpool Hope University. She gained her doctorate in education from the University of Oxford, Green Templeton College and her ethnographic research into a City Technology College and Academies sponsored by a Christian foundation was the first such study in the UK. Previously she has worked as a history teacher and pastoral head in UK secondary schools. Her publications include articles in journals such as *British Journal of Sociology of Education* and *Cambridge Journal of Education*.

Andrew Hope is an Associate Professor in the School of Education at the University of Adelaide. His current research interests include social aspects of the internet, school surveillance and risk. He has published the book *Internet*

Risk @ School: Cultures of Control in State Education (Lambert Press, 2011) and has also published articles on school surveillance in various journals, including the *British Journal of Sociology of Education, British Educational Research Journal* and *International Studies in Sociology of Education*.

Jones Irwin is a Lecturer in Philosophy and Education at St Patrick's College, Dublin City University, where he is Co-Director of the MA in Human Development. He has published the monograph *Derrida and the Writing of the Body* (Ashgate, 2010) and his book *Paulo Freire's Philosophy of Education: Origins, Development, Impacts and Legacies* (Bloomsbury, 2012). He has specific research interests in philosophy with children and continentalist philosophy of education.

Irene Kleanthous completed her PhD studies in Mathematics Education at the University of Manchester in 2012. She explored adolescent students' dispositions towards mathematics and perceptions of parental influence, applying Bourdieu's theory and using mixed research methods in her thesis. Her doctoral studies were funded by the School of Education (University of Manchester) and the A.G. Leventis Foundation (Cyprus). She was involved in various research projects at the University of Manchester where she worked as a Research Assistant. Irene's most recent academic position was at the European University of Cyprus where she taught educational research methods and didactics of mathematics for the BEd in Primary Education.

Bob Lingard is currently a Professorial Research Fellow in the School of Education and the Institute for Social Science Research at the University of Queensland and a Fellow of the Academy of Social Sciences in Australia. He has also been Professor at the University of Edinburgh (2006–2008), where he held the Andrew Bell Chair of Education, and at the University of Sheffield (2003–2006). He researches and publishes in the areas of sociology of education and education policy. His most recent books include *Globalizing Education Policy* (with Fazal Rizvi; Routledge, 2010), *Changing Schools* (with Terry Wrigley and Pat Thomson; Routledge, 2012) and *Educating Boys: Beyond Structural Reform* (with Wayne Martino and Martin Mills; Palgrave, 2009).

Terence Lovat is Professor Emeritus at the University of Newcastle, Australia, and Senior Research Fellow at Oxford University, UK. He also holds the position of Chair of Theology, Ethics and Education at the Broken Bay Institute, a theological partner of the University of Newcastle. Professor Lovat is a former Pro Vice-Chancellor and Dean of Education at Newcastle and President of the Australian Council of Deans of Education. His research interests span Islam in relation to the Western hegemony, curriculum theory, values education and religion in schools. He has managed funded research worth over two million Australian dollars, written many books, including translations, and over 100 refereed articles and chapters, with many of them making use of Habermasian theory applied to an array of research interests.

From 2003 to 2010, he served as chief investigator of a number of research and practice projects emanating from the Australian Values Education Program. He has been a regular presenter and keynote speaker at conferences associated with this work in countries such as Russia, Ukraine, Belgium, Turkey, China and several parts of Africa.

Duncan Mercieca is a Lecturer in Philosophy of Education in the Faculty of Education, University of Malta. Trained as a teacher, he has had experience teaching in mainstream and special schools. His interests are in the links between education and continental philosophy, particulary in the issues of the *Other* and *becoming*. He has published articles in various journals, including the *Journal of Philosophy of Education* and *Ethics and Education*.

Mark Murphy is Reader in Education at the University of Glasgow. He previously taught at King's College London, University of Chester and the University of Stirling. He has published widely, with numerous articles in journals such as the *Journal of Education Policy*, *Journal of European Public Policy*, *European Journal of Education*, *International Journal of Lifelong Education* and the *British Journal of Sociology of Education*. His most recent book is *Habermas, Critical Theory and Education* (co-edited with Ted Fleming; Routledge, 2010). Mark has recently set up a website devoted to the application of social theory, www.socialtheoryapplied.com, designed to provide a platform for discussion around the relationship between theory and educational research.

Shaun Rawolle is a Senior Lecturer in the School of Education and the Centre for Research in Educational Futures and Innovation at Deakin University. Shaun's research and publications are located broadly in the areas of sociology of education and education policy. Shaun is completing a book with Professor Bob Lingard, *Bourdieu and the Fields of Education Policy*.

Fredrik Sandberg is a Lecturer at the Department of Behavioural Sciences and Learning, Linköping University, Sweden, where he gained his PhD in Adult Learning in 2012. His research explores, but is not limited to, recognition of prior learning in the health care sector and higher education contexts. His main theoretical inspiration is drawn from Jürgen Habermas' theory of communicative action. Recent articles are included in *Vocations and Learning: Studies in Vocational and Professional Education* and *Assessment and Evaluation in Higher Education*.

Paul Skillen is Programme Leader of the Education Studies degree programme in the Faculty of Education and Children's Services, University of Chester. Paul is also completing his doctoral studies at the University of Keele. His doctoral dissertation focuses on comparative education policy, specifically school-based policies in England and the United States.

Christine Winter is a Senior Lecturer in the Department of Educational Studies in the University of Sheffield. Her research focuses on curriculum and curriculum policy analysis, mainly from a Derridean perspective. She is interested in the constitution of curriculum knowledge and its associated responsibilities through the language used in a variety of curriculum texts. Her other research interests are the environmental education curriculum and the concept of globalisation and its influence on school humanities. Christine directs the Centre for the Study of Educational Development and Professional Lives and the Sheffield Doctoral Programme (Ed. D). She teaches a module 'Internationalisation and Curriculum', tutors and supervises students on the MA in Globalising Education and supervises dissertation students for the Advanced Professional Studies in Education Masters Programme.

Acknowledgements

I would like to express my gratitude to the contributors in this collection, all of whom fully appreciated the significance and value of the project from its inception, having themselves spent considerable time applying social theory in their own educational research. This level of accumulated knowledge is strongly evident in the chapters and accounts of their work, providing inspiration for other researchers who look to the likes of Foucault, Habermas, Bourdieu and Derrida for ideas about research design and analytical frameworks.

The idea for the book came after many years of experience conducting my own education research and also supervising education students conducting research on various aspects of professional practice and education policy. Their contribution to this collection should also be acknowledged as they have provided much food for thought when it came to the book's rationale and design. My hope is that the book will be of use to future generations of researchers who wish to make the challenging journey from practice to theory, and back again.

Part 1

Introduction

Chapter 1

Social theory and education research

An introduction

Mark Murphy

Introduction

Ideas relating to educational policy and practice are underpinned by recourse to foundational disciplines, particularly philosophy and the social sciences. Educational research embeds itself in a wide variety of theoretical discourses, using them to explore issues such as professional and cultural identities, forms of educational management, changing work practices and priorities. They also form the basis for numerous debates relating to the user experience, including, for example, differential attainment and achievement, access and inclusion, and the relationship between culture and learning. Although education researchers have drawn on the work of a wide diversity of theorists, a number of these have been of particular significance to education. While the likes of Karl Marx, Antonio Gramsci, John Dewey and Paulo Freire influenced previous generations of educational theorists, much of the more contemporary theory building has revolved around a quartet of well-known and much-debated thinkers – Jacques Derrida, Pierre Bourdieu, Michel Foucault and Jürgen Habermas.

However, while the influence of these thinkers has grown considerably over the last number of years, both their original work and its application to education can prove challenging to the educational practitioner. This is unsurprising, given the manner in which these theories have developed from sometimes arcane debates in continental philosophy, far removed from the modern world of teaching practice that is embedded in concerns over performance, attainment and accountability. The challenge they pose to educators may also result from a lack of suitable reading material that can both appeal to the advanced practitioner market and provide a sufficiently in-depth overview of the various theories and their applications in educational research.

The main purpose of this edited collection is to help rectify this omission in educational theory and provide a text that is both advanced and accessible, offering the education practitioner/researcher a suitable book to assist their acquisition and application of social theory. The work of thinkers such as Derrida and Habermas has often been described as difficult and highly abstract, and can present challenges to those whose prior focus has been professional practice. It can sometimes seem unlikely that their work can be directly related to the kinds of issues faced by the education profession. This book has appeal to readers who have an interest in how theory can be effectively applied to educational problems, helping to illuminate the relationships between theory and practice, in a manner that offers some practically realisable solutions to educational issues.

Alongside the benefits to the individual researcher, there is much to be gained for the educational research community generally from taking advantage of the originality, rigour and intellectual insight of these authors. Their work, while certainly not without its critics of various persuasions, potentially offers such a goldmine of ideas – about power and control, democracy, social organisation, language and communication, selfhood and subjectivities, the state and economy – that they can, when thoughtfully implemented, contribute to the delivery of higher quality educational research.

This is one of the reasons why all four thinkers, to varying degrees, have achieved an increasing level of visibility in educational research (this could also be said to be the case for other professional fields such as health and social work[1]). The chapters included in this collection are designed to provide examples of how this visibility has manifested itself in various aspects of educational research, illustrating the diverse ways in which continental theory of whatever stripe can be used to explore educational issues. From school surveillance to curriculum, social theory can and is adapted to shed light on 'practical' issues facing the sector, helping to widen and deepen discussion around these areas when they are in danger of being over-simplified.

As a preface to these contributions, this chapter is designed to provide a brief introduction to the field of social theory itself, as well as identifying some of the issues faced by educational researchers in applying the work of Derrida et al. This chapter also provides a summary of the core educational questions to which social theory has so far been applied (based on an overview of recent educational research output), finishing with an outline of the book's organisation and content.

What is social theory?

Broadly speaking, social theories are analytical frameworks or paradigms used to examine social phenomena. The term 'social theory' encompasses ideas about 'how societies change and develop, about methods of explaining social behaviour, about power and social structure, gender and ethnicity, modernity and "civilisation", revolutions and utopias' (Harrington 2005, 1). In contemporary social theory, certain core themes take precedence over others, themes such as the nature of social life, the relationship between self and society, the structure of social institutions, the role and possibility of social transformation, as well as themes such as gender, race and class (Elliott 2008).

Alongside the existence of this broad range of issues, there is also a large number of what could be termed social theories – feminist theories of various persuasions could be labelled as such, likewise with critical race theories. Space precludes a more detailed examination of the field of social theory – there are other sources that offer such an overview.[2] Space also precludes the opportunity to explore the ideas of other prominent social theorists, such as Julia Kristeva, Zygmunt Bauman, Judith Butler, Jean Baudrillard and Ulrich Beck. As such, the authors included in this collection are not meant to represent an exhaustive list. Instead they are the focus of this book as they are among the most prominent theorists of the modern age, and have proven popular in the field of educational research. It is also fair to say that their influence on other social theorists, philosophers and the academic world in general is immense, making major contributions to debates across a wide range of disciplines.

This influence has also extended into the broader public sphere, these authors combining the role of social theorist with that of public intellectual. Intellectualising the problems and issues of the day, they provide spaces within which educational researchers as well as others can adopt an intellectual stance to their subjects with some level of legitimation and credibility. It is also evident that their theories are delivered with normative intent, whether it be Derrida's deconstructive approach, the critical theory of Habermas, the critical social science of Bourdieu or the archaeology and genealogies of Foucault. In this way, they could be viewed to some extent as the heirs to the tradition of social philosophy, a tradition that stretches at least as far back as Jean-Jacques Rousseau and his *Discourse on the Origin of Inequality* (1755/2004). This tradition took as its aim the use of philosophy to examine problems in society, an aim not too dissimilar to the social theories included in this collection.

It could also be argued that the work of all four social theorists are influenced in one way or another by the work of a key 'classic' social theorist, Karl Marx. Marx was a pre-eminent social theorist in his own right, his ideas casting a considerable shadow over debates in modern social theory. A great deal of this theory owes some kind of debt to Marx's concepts of capital, class and exploitation, and his re-workings of post-Enlightenment notions of political economy and liberal democracy. This is clearly evident in the work of Bourdieu, for example, whose work on cultural and social reproduction saw him cast as a neo-Marxist, his ideas helping to fill in some of the blanks in Marx's historical materialism (especially around the role of culture) (Fowler 2011). Marxism is a key starting point for Habermas, a figure strongly associated with the Frankfurt School of Critical Theory, which included in its ranks (neo-)Marxists such as Erich Fromm and Herbert Marcuse (Kellner 1989). Habermas' key work, *The Theory of Communicative Action* (1984, 1987), was at base a project designed to reconstruct Marx's theory of historical materialism, in order to provide (in Habermas' opinion) a better diagnosis of the problems facing late capitalist society (Murphy 2009). Foucault, who later in his career moved decisively away from Hegelian dialectics, was 'considerably influenced by Marx' early on (Best 1995, 87); his first book *Mental Illness and Psychology* (Foucault 1976) was immersed in Marxist concepts of alienation and contradiction. Even Derrida, whose post-structuralist approach to deconstruction could never be confused with Marxian political economy, argued at one stage for a return to Marx, publishing his famous text *Spectres of Marx* (1994) to a bemused academic world – the editor arguing that for Derrida, 'deconstruction' 'always already moves within a certain spirit of Marx' (Magnus and Cullenberg 1994, x).[3]

Foucault and Derrida broke more decisively from the Marxist tradition (more so than Bourdieu and Habermas), occupying central positions in the fabric of postmodern and post-structural thought respectively. Their positions as pre-eminent French intellectuals on the post-1968 French Left makes this somewhat inevitable, a context within which post-Marxist social theories proliferated as a form of break with the past (Best and Kellner 1991). For such a diverse set of thinkers, however, it could be argued (strongly) that the legacy of Marx lives on; a common thread in contemporary theory is a fascination, even obsession, with how the dynamics and forms of *power* play themselves out via institutions, linguistic traditions, texts, cultures and forms of selfhood. Above all else, Marx's concern with modern mechanisms of exploitation and how forms of oppression lurk behind the veils of modernisation and capitalist industry provides a strong intellectual and normative backdrop to so much modern theory. His methodology of ideology critique arguably finds an echo in the work of all four theorists and also in the work of those inspired by such theorists (examples of which are included in this collection).

A special mention should be made in this section regarding the interdisciplinary nature of much modern social theory. Central to this nature is the distinction between sociological theory and social theory – while in many cases social theories have a background in the discipline of sociology, they are not one and the same thing. Social theories emanate and draw from a range of disciplines including sociology, but also philosophy, anthropology, history, media and communication studies, psychology and psychoanalysis, linguistics, cultural studies and literary criticism. Social theory is therefore positioned across and between the humanities and social sciences, in particular. The work of the theorists in this collection are utilised across these fields and belong to no one particular discipline, which makes sense given their own interdisciplinary leanings. This level of complexity is often one of the reasons why their work is so influential; it is also one of the reasons why educators can experience difficulty during the act of application, the lack of disciplinary belonging a burden as well as a benefit. Having said that, the fact that education theory draws from a range of disciplines should mean that, at least in principle, the educational researcher should be able to cope in this world of multiple sets of ideas.

Between (social) theory and practice: dilemmas in educational research

As indicated above, the application of these theories brings its own set of challenges. Some of these reflect issues of research design and implementation, including the development of tools such as data measurement and analytical criteria. Just as significant are the difficulties faced when grappling with the core concepts of social theory that already come with a range of contradictory meanings. Notions of 'power', 'culture', and 'practice' are challenging at the best of times, but such challenges are compounded when they are aligned with the core educational concepts of teaching, learning, assessment and curriculum.

All forms of research, regardless of subject, come with a set of issues that need addressing in practical settings. Educational research is no different, its embeddedness in forms of professional practice (in many cases) adding a further layer of complexity. As a result, it should be emphasised from the outset that the movement from practice to theory is as challenging an intellectual journey, if not more so, than the journey from theory to practice. While the latter can often confound researchers who struggle to apply theoretical models and principles in contexts such as health organisations, business and social welfare, the former can often compound the problem for the educational researcher. Many of those engaged in educational research tend to arrive via the linked but distinct field of professional practice. While this can have certain advantages in terms of insight, providing a level of insider knowledge unavailable to the professional anthropologist (for example), it can also mean that intellectual judgement can be clouded by immersion in the hothouse of educational politics. Objectivity can often suffer as a result.

This scenario is also compounded by the nature of professional training. Educators may be well versed in the application of educational theory to educational practice, but rarely are they required in any meaningful way to apply theories from other disciplines. This is a blessing and a curse of being an educational researcher – an *un*disciplined approach to the field of research can have drawbacks as well as benefits – providing professionals with a multidisciplinary grounding while providing a disinclination to belong and to work within the parameters of any specific disciplinary paradigm.

Having said that, it often proves tempting when applying theory to research to try to stay true to the 'authentic' version of the theory being applied. Although the book is organised into four distinct sections exploring the application of each theorist, this is not a reflection of some notion that the work of people such as Habermas and Foucault are and should be kept separate. The book is designed to provide some pointers in terms of introduction and application, but it is certainly not designed to discourage debate and cross-pollination between theories. Nowhere is it written that researchers cannot choose how and in what contexts they apply the work of theory. And while the overzealous might demand the 'pure' use of someone's work, regardless of context, it should not be forgotten that all of these theorists under discussion have, at various stages in their careers, cherrypicked from those who have influenced them. To suggest that there is a 'right' and 'wrong' way to understand and apply these theorists is to misinterpret the role of theory in research – the latter should never be made to bow down to the former. If anything, cherrypicking and cross-pollination should be positively encouraged – for how else do we arrive at original and innovative forms of knowledge, forms that can help us progress through the world of often stale and moribund arguments and paradigms in educational policy and practice?[4]

Another issue in educational research relates to the special status assigned to the concept of power in social theory. Evident in educational research (including contributors in the current collection) is the attraction such thinkers have for those interested in the relationship between education and various mechanisms used to generate and distribute power. But given this close relationship between power and educational research, one needs to be even more careful in the pursuit of research objectives. One does not need to be a Foucauldian to understand that power is omnipresent, and that power and knowledge have a tight bond that is not easily broken. But the workings of power in educational settings should never be taken lightly or over-simplified, given that educational institutions and their assorted sets of practices provide ideal environments for the interplay of multiple forms of power – cultural, social and structural – forms that in many cases are irreducible to the others.

Power is a notoriously difficult concept to pin down, and the researcher can all too easily fall into the trap of looking for power in the wrong places, or worse still, misrecognise their own capacity as power brokers in educational research settings. It is important for the researcher to recognise their own powerful presence in educational settings, while also accepting the fallibility of one theory of power in the face of complex and highly differentiated institutionalised arrangements. Erring on the side of intellectual caution does not do the educational researcher any harm, especially when combined with a recognition of the unfinished debates in social theory that form the backdrop to such forms of research in the first place.

Social theory applied: core topics in educational research

As evidenced in this book, and in the general educational literature, ideas from social theory have been applied across the educational sector, from early years education, to formal schooling, to adult and higher education settings. No field of education has proved immune from the pull of continental philosophy, including the more skills-based 'technical' end of the spectrum.[5] As well as this sector-wide immersion in notions of deconstruction, reproduction, colonisation and performativity, social theory has also been applied in a wide variety of research settings – and while there is considerable overlap between them, social theory has found particular favour in the following key research topics:

- Inequality, inclusion and education
- Notions of educational selves and subjectivities
- Curricular and pedagogical practice
- Governance and management.

Inequality, inclusion and education. The ways in which schooling and learning generally are mediated by, and impact on, issues of class, race and gender have concerned education researchers for decades, with the ideas generated by social theory providing a valuable foundation for innovative methodologies. Much of social theory itself is designed to explore questions of power and privilege, and educational processes, systems and outcomes are intimately connected to these questions. In particular, the work of Bourdieu et al. lends itself well to themes of inequality and inclusion in education, which is unsurprising, as this was one of his research areas.[6] However, there are numerous other examples of educational research on inequality and inclusion that have borrowed heavily from the work of Foucault, Habermas and Derrida.[7]

Notions of educational selves and subjectivities. Questions of identity have recently come to the fore in social science research. In particular, questions of professional identity have received much attention, with the field of education proving a rich source of data. This is because educational identities are open to multiple interpretations, and cover a wide range of professional formations and issues – becoming a teacher, transformations in teacher professionalism, sources of academic identity, the challenges of teacher education, to name but a few. Social theory has been widely applied to these research areas, with ideas from post-structuralism and postmodernism proving especially popular as conceptual schemas.[8] Another area of identity studies to which social theory has been applied is *student* identity. There is a growing body of research literature that examines the relationship between educational processes and forms of selfhood, with questions such as the formation of learner identities receiving a great deal of attention.[9]

Curricular and pedagogical practice. The field of teaching and learning has understandably proven a mainstay of educational research. The field, however, has undergone something of a transformation in the last two decades, moving away from its more psychological and instrumentalist roots to more recently embracing the intellectual traditions of social theorists such as Derrida and Habermas. The application of social theory in this field has been wide ranging, covering topics such as the role of teacher efficacy in learning (Jennings and DiPrete 2010), the metaphorical nature of supervision (Lee and Green 2009), and the role of ethnography in assessment practices (Hill 2009).

Governance and management. Educational governance provides a political and economic context for the previous three thematic areas, but is also an important focus of research in its own right. In education, much of the governance research centres on policies of regulation, marketisation and accountability, and the impact of these on educational values, professionalism, provision and delivery. The ideas of all four theorists have been utilised to explore these themes, but the work of Michel Foucault has proven especially attractive to educators as a way of making sense of changing political imperatives, and the nature of performative and audit cultures.[10] Habermas has also proven to be popular in the field of policy and management studies.[11]

The organisation of this book

In developing the format of this book, a key objective was to present the reader with an overview of the theorists and their influence in education while also providing relevant examples of applied theory in research settings. With this objective in mind, the book is structured around four core sections, each comprising the following:

- A 'general' chapter which introduces the social theorist in question, detailing some of the ways in which the theory has been applied in educational settings, as well as providing a critical commentary on the theory and its application.
- Two applied chapters providing case studies of applied education research using the relevant social theorist as a theoretical framework. Each chapter explores the significance of the theory to the chosen area of study, its influence on research design, while also exploring some of the challenges faced when applying social theory in empirical settings.

The contributors have been carefully chosen so that as wide a range of sectors, subjects and issues as possible are included.

Julie Allan's chapter (Chapter 2) introduces Foucault and explores the interest his work has generated for researchers within education. Allan traces the development of Foucault's ideas, from his initial interest in structures and discourses, through to his archaeologies of knowledge, medicine and madness, in which he demonstrated how discourses produced particular truths. The chapter then charts Foucault's shift of focus onto genealogy, studying institutions such as prisons and schools and the issue of sexuality, and offering a critique of what was considered to be *normal*. His analyses of knowledge and power as interlinked, constructing individuals as objects of knowledge and as subjects who were controlled, even – and especially – by themselves, are explored. The fascination such genealogies have held for educational researchers, and the way in which they have been applied, is examined, Allan finishing her chapter by exploring in more detail Foucault's later writings on ethics.

In Chapter 3, Andrew Hope draws upon empirical research (both his own and the work of others) on internet surveillance devices and Closed Circuit Television (CCTV) use to consider the challenges faced in using Foucault's take on panopticism to examine new surveillance technologies within schools. Using writings on (post-) panopticism, the continued value of Foucault's insights for those studying observational techniques in schools is outlined. The difficulty of exploring student motivations and actions is also considered, as the power ascribed by Foucault to self-policing and wider disciplinary discourses is questioned. Hope argues that issues such as student risk taking and resistance to surveillance provide not only a challenge to the panoptic gaze but also practical challenges for those gathering research data. Suggestions are made as to how the educational researcher can find practical value in Foucault's *Discipline and Punish* (1977) and his related work.

Andreas Fejes in Chapter 4 provides another example of the use of Foucault in applied educational research settings. Drawing on the later work of Foucault and his concepts of governmentality, technologies of the self and confession, Fejes analyses the reflective practices that take place within an in-service training programme for workers in the elderly care sector. Revisiting Foucault's genealogy of confession and how this interconnects with his concepts of governmentality and technologies of the self, the chapter explores how Fejes analysed interview transcripts with care workers, managers and teachers, to illustrate how confession is a prominent part of contemporary educational practices. Fejes concludes by making some reflexive remarks on what he argues is Foucault's major contribution to educational research.

According to Terry Lovat in his introductory chapter on Habermas (Chapter 5), many contemporary educational research agendas, be they in quality teaching, authentic pedagogy, values and citizenship education or service learning, are directed towards re-conceiving and re-constructing schools as transformational learning sites, which potentially entail more holistic developmental experiences for learners. Lovat argues that this is one of the main reasons why Habermas has proven popular in some areas of education research. The chapter claims that Habermas' theories of knowing and communicative action have the capacity to deepen our research understandings in several areas of education, including the role of the teacher and effective pedagogy, as well as the potential of schools to serve as sites of transformational learning. The chapter explores these themes, expounding on Habermasian theory and illustrating its pertinence to educational research through a number of contemporary applications.

Appropriating Habermas and his theory of communicative action, Murphy and Skillen in Chapter 6 explore the impact of accountability mechanisms on the working lives of education professionals. Using qualitative case studies of teachers in the north-west of the UK, the study examines how the new bureaucracy of accountability has impacted, in particular, on forms of communication, support and interpersonal interaction, from the perspective of professionals themselves. As is normally the case when moving from abstract theory to the level of practice, the application of Habermas at the ground level was not a straightforward process, indeed delivering some unintended consequences for the researcher, the findings adding to the complexity already at the heart of Habermas' theoretical construction. The research illustrates that attempts to evidence and understand the limits of political regulation eventually bring to light some of the limitations in Habermas' conceptual apparatus, in particular the existence of other forms of regulation that do not fit neatly into his lifeworld/system construction. The chapter reflects on these limitations while also exploring some other issues highlighted in the research itself.

Drawing on data from a PhD research project exploring processes of recognition of prior learning (RPL) in the Swedish health care sector, Fredrik Sandberg outlines in Chapter 7 the kinds of challenges faced when applying Habermas' theory of communicative action in relation to issues of professionalism and professional accreditation. According to Sandberg, a Habermasian analysis raises issues about how actions and communication shape students' understanding and learning, and how these processes connect to the relationship between system and lifeworld and the risk of colonisation. By reconstructing learning processes it is also possible to criticise actions that facilitate what Habermas terms the systemic 'colonisation of the lifeworld', but also point towards how processes can be developed by using communicative action as an ideal. Sandberg examines the challenges of conducting a critical empirical analysis based on Habermas' normative theory, arguing that, in order to understand how people act, it is necessary to focus on methods that can capture such processes in action.

Shaun Rawolle and Bob Lingard's introductory chapter on Bourdieu (Chapter 8) outlines his 'thinking tools', namely field, habitus, capitals and practices, as well as his theoretical and methodological dispositions and commitment to relational thinking. On the latter, emphasis is given to the rejection of what Bourdieu calls 'epistemological innocence' and the need for a reflexive approach to all research and theorising, what Bourdieu refers to as the capacity for 'socioanalysis'.

In outlining Bourdieu's intellectual *oeuvre*, the chapter also provides a short biographical account of his life, then turns to a consideration of the utilisation of Bourdieu's work in educational research, particularly in the sociology of education and in what has been called policy sociology in education. The chapter outlines the ways in which his work, particularly his concepts of field and habitus, assist researchers in theorising and researching contemporary policy developments in education. These include the emergence of a global education policy field and its cross-field effects into specific national education policy fields.

In Elizabeth Green's applied chapter on Bourdieu (Chapter 9), a strong case is made for his theory of education, reproduction and distinction as a powerful tool in the analysis of faith-based education. Green's example of research in faith-based settings provides readers with an indication of how current educational research is broadening the traditional application of Bourdieu's social theory beyond the study of class. Drawing on empirical research carried out in faith-based academies in the United Kingdom, Green's discussion of Bourdieu's work is grounded in a real and high-profile research context allowing for a discussion of the challenges encountered by researchers in their application of Bourdieu's concepts.

Irene Kleanthous' chapter (Chapter 10) provides a second example of how Bourdieu can be applied in educational research. Drawing on her own work, Kleanthous reflects on the use of Bourdieu's theory in exploring adolescent students' perceptions of parental influence on their educational choices for future studies in higher education. The mobilisation of familial capital from middle-class parents to enhance their children's educational choices is well documented in the literature, and Kleanthous problematises the use of Bourdieu by asking whether capital is adequate as a tool to theorise parental influence. She argues that parental influence is a form of 'symbolic violence' after Bourdieu, which students and their parents 'misrecognise' because parental influence is largely unconscious. This new theoretical conceptualisation of parental influence is discussed in this chapter along with some current debates in the literature about familial habitus and familial doxa.

The final section of the collection is devoted to the work of Derrida, and Jones Irwin uses the introductory chapter (Chapter 11) to explore in detail Derrida's idiosyncratic conception of a philosophy of education, while also connecting his practical work on philosophy in schools with his later re-evaluation of the whole politics of education in *Who's Afraid of Philosophy?* (2002). The chapter also explores the way in which his work has been adapted in educational research settings, particularly in the areas of curriculum and pedagogy. Irwin concludes by evaluating Derrida's very topical defence (in a UK context especially) of the Humanities as part of the vision of a progressivist pedagogy.

In Chapter 12, Christine Winter provides an account of how Derrida can be applied in educational research settings, in this case in studies of the UK geography school curriculum. After providing her own interpretation of deconstruction together with a brief account of the work of researchers who are concerned about 'applying' Derrida in education, Winter details her school-based research project and how Derrida's ideas were engaged in the development, teaching and evaluation of a curriculum unit for a class of students aged 12 to 13 in a state comprehensive school in the north of England. According to Winter, the project was not without its challenges and high points and these are recounted in the third section of the chapter. The conclusion summarises the contribution that Derrida's insights offer to curriculum research and to curriculum itself, in their invitation to strive for a more ethically responsible and inspirational approach to curriculum thinking and practice.

In line with Irwin's and Winter's chapters, the final chapter in the collection sees Duncan Mercieca arguing that Derrida can provide a number of useful concepts for reading the lives of teachers. His chapter does two things in this regard: first, a reading of published and/or produced teachers' narratives from a Derridean perspective with the aim of helping teachers read their own narratives; and second, detailing the possibility of presenting philosophical concepts developed by Derrida to practising teachers. Using Derrida's concept of *aporia* as well as other related concepts such as *trace* and *supplement*, Mercieca focuses on teachers who *wander* on these ideas in relation to their own lives. This is done by teachers through reading/watching other teachers' narratives, seeing moments of aporia in the narratives and in their own work, and through noting that they are 'just' when they engage with 'blind spots' in their work.

Conclusion

It is often the case that books on educational (and other forms of) research emphasise the correct approaches to using specific modes of research tool, such as interviews and questionnaires, or focus on the construction of a dissertation or research report and how the constituent parts are assembled to construct the finished product/project. This of course is invaluable guidance, but nevertheless there is a tendency to pay less attention to the role of theory in the construction of such projects, and the various ways in which social theory in particular can be used to extract *meaning* from the research site under examination. The contributions included in this collection are intended as part of an effort to stymie this tendency and to illustrate what a worthwhile activity it is to engage social theory with educational research, so long as the researchers themselves come armed with an understanding of the challenges that await them.

What the chapters in this collection indicate is not just the complexity of ideas in continental theory but also the varied sets of issues faced when applying such ideas in educational research contexts, a field of complex interwoven imperatives and practices in its own right. These challenges – epistemological, operational and analytical – can be seen to impact on researchers and their attempts to make sense of educational questions, whether these be questions of governance and political regulation, social reproduction, curriculum and pedagogical practices or professional identities. Above all, the contributions indicate that the application of a challenging set of ideas onto a challenging set of practices must be delivered with care and a strong consideration for both intellectual arguments alongside the concerns of the professional researcher.

Having said that, the relationship between theory and practice, in general (and not just in research terms), has never been straightforward. That is as true for policy issues as it is for practical issues faced in teaching and learning contexts. This makes the contributions of the research included in this collection all the more valuable, as they show that such connections can be made, while remaining respectful of both theory and practice as separate entities in their own right.

Notes

1 Useful overviews of the application of social theory to health and social work research can be found in McDonnell et al. (2009) and Gray and Webb (2008) respectively. Specific examples of individual theorists applied to health and social work include Chambon (1999) on Foucault and social work and Scambler (2001) on Habermas and health.

2 An excellent account of modern social theory is provided by Elliott (2008), while a useful summary and analysis of the historical context of contemporary social thought can be found in Callinicos (2007).

3 See also Nancy Fraser's account of Derrida's 'dance' with Marxism (1989), which was published prior to *Spectres of Marx.*

4 Examples of such cross-fertilisation of ideas do exist – see, for instance, the journal *Studies in Philosophy and Education,* a special edition of which explored Habermas 'in conversation with others' – the 'others' including the likes of Derrida and Lacan (Murphy and Bamber 2012).

5 Habermas, for one, has been applied in sectors such as industrial training (O'Donnell 1999), nursing education (Duffy and Scott 1998; Ekstrom and Sigurdsson 2002) and dental education (Whipp et al. 2000).

6 Examples using Bourdieu in this regard include the likes of Ball et al. (2002), Barone (2006), and Macfarlane (2008).

7 The likes of Rasmussen (2002) and Ranson et al. (2004) have applied Habermas in their research exploring issues of inequality, while a good example of Derrida

applied in a similar fashion can be found in Allan et al. (2010). See the work of Douglas (2010) and Liasidou (2008) for applications of Foucault in relation to research on educational inclusion.

8 Weems' research (2003) uses Foucault to explore the professional identities of substitute teachers; Love's work (2008) takes Derrida and applies his concept of the 'quasi-ideal' to critique consumerist academic identities in higher education; while Nelson et al. (2008) apply Habermas in research on what informs the values of novice school principals.

9 A useful example of research linking social theory to student/learner identity is provided in Gorely et al.'s work on Bourdieu and the gendered nature of physical education (2003).

10 See, for examples of 'applied' Foucault, Andersson (2008), Gillies (2008), Morgan (2005) and Vander Schee (2008).

11 Notable examples of educational management research that use Habermas as a theoretical framework include Mabovula (2010), who explores the relevance of communicative action in issues of governance in South African schools; Murphy (2009) who applies Habermas' understanding of bureaucracy to debates over the regulation of higher education; and Smith (2007) who uses Habermas to examine the impact of 'quasi-marketisation' on the world of English further education.

References

Allan, J., N. Moran, C. Duffy and G. Loening. 2010. Knowledge exchange with Sistema Scotland. *Journal of Education Policy* 25, 3: 335–347.

Andersson, P. 2008. National policy and the implementation of recognition of prior learning in a Swedish municipality. *Journal of Education Policy* 23, 5: 515–531.

Ball, S., J. Davies, M. David and D. Reay. 2002. 'Classification' and 'judgement': Social class and the 'cognitive structures' of choice of higher education. *British Journal of Sociology of Education* 23, 1: 51–72.

Barone, C. 2006. Cultural capital, ambition and the explanation of inequalities in learning outcomes: A comparative analysis. *Sociology* 40, 6: 1039–1058.

Best, S. 1995. *The politics of historical vision: Marx, Foucault, Habermas.* New York: Guilford Press.

Best, S. and D. Kellner. 1991. *Postmodern theory: Critical interrogations.* New York: Guildford Press.

Chambon, A. 1999. *Reading Foucault for social work.* New York: Columbia University Press.

Callinicos, A. 2007. *Social theory: A historical introduction.* Cambridge: Polity Press.

Derrida, J. 1994. *Spectres of Marx: The state of the debt, the work of mourning, and the New International.* New York: Routledge.

Derrida, J. 2002. *Who's afraid of philosophy?: Right to philosophy I.* Stanford: Stanford University Press.

Douglas, P. 2010. 'Problematising' inclusion: Education and the question of autism. *Pedagogy, Culture & Society* 18, 2: 105–121.

Duffy, K. and A. Scott. 1998. Viewing an old issue through a new lens: A critical theory insight into the education–practice gap. *Nurse Education Today* 18, 3: 183–189.

Ekstrom, D. and H. Sigurdsson. 2002. An international collaboration in nursing education viewed through the lens of critical social theory. *Journal of Nursing Education* 41, 7: 289–294.

Elliott, A. 2008. *Contemporary social theory: An introduction*. London: Routledge.

Foucault, M. 1976. *Mental illness and psychology*. Berkeley, CA: University of California Press.

Foucault, M. 1977. *Discipline and punish: The birth of the prison*. London: Allen Lane.

Fowler, B. 2011. Pierre Bourdieu: Unorthodox Marxist? In *The legacy of Pierre Bourdieu: Critical essays*, ed. S. Susan and B. Turner, 33–57. London: Anthem.

Fraser, N. 1989. *Unruly practices: Power, discourses and gender in contemporary social theory*. Minneapolis, Minnesota: University of Minnesota Press.

Gray, M. and S. Webb, eds. 2008. *Social work theories and methods*. London: Sage.

Gillies, D. 2008. Quality and equality: The mask of discursive conflation in education policy texts. *Journal of Education Policy* 23, 6: 685–699.

Gorely, T., R. Holroyd and D. Kirk. 2003. Muscularity, the habitus and the social construction of gender: Towards a gender-relevant physical education. *British Journal of Sociology of Education* 24, 4: 429–448.

Habermas, J. 1984. *The theory of communicative action, vol. 1: Reason and the rationalization of society*. Boston: Beacon Press.

Habermas, J. 1987. *The theory of communicative action, vol. 2: Lifeworld and system: a critique of functionalist reason*. Boston: Beacon Press.

Harrington, A. 2005. Introduction: what is social theory? In *Modern social theory: An introduction*, ed. A. Harrington, 1–15. Oxford: Oxford University Press.

Hill, M. 2009. Ways of seeing: Using ethnography and Foucault's 'toolkit' to view assessment practices differently. *Qualitative Research* 9, 3: 309–330.

Jennings, J. and T. DiPrete. 2010. Teacher effects on social and behavioral skills in early elementary school. *Sociology of Education* 83, 2: 135–159.

Kellner. D. 1989. *Critical theory, Marxism and modernity*. Baltimore, MD: Johns Hopkins University Press.

Lee, A. and B. Green. 2009. Supervision as metaphor. *Studies in Higher Education* 34, 6: 615–630.

Liasidou, A. 2008. Critical discourse analysis and inclusive educational policies: The power to exclude. *Journal of Education Policy* 23, 5: 483–500.

Love, K. 2008. Higher education, pedagogy and the 'customerisation' of teaching and learning. *Journal of Philosophy of Education* 42, 1: 15–34.

Mabovula, N. 2010. Revisiting Jürgen Habermas's notion of communicative action and its relevance for South African school governance: Can it succeed? *South African Journal of Education* 30: 1–12.

Macfarlane, K. 2008. Playing the game: Examining parental engagement in schooling in post-millennial Queensland. *Journal of Education Policy* 23, 6: 701–713.

Magnus, B. and S. Cullenberg. 1994. Editors' introduction. In *Spectres of Marx: The state of the debt, the work of mourning, and the New International*, J. Derrida, vii–xi. New York: Routledge.

McDonnell, O., M. Cohan, A. Hyde and S. Porter. 2009. *Social theory, health and healthcare*. Basingstoke: Palgrave Macmillan.

Morgan, A. 2005. Governmentality versus choice in contemporary special education. *Critical Social Policy* 25, 3: 325–348.

Murphy, M. 2009. Bureaucracy and its limits: Accountability and rationality in higher education. *British Journal of Sociology of Education* 30, 6: 683–695.

Murphy, M. and J. Bamber. 2012. Introduction: From Fromm to Lacan: Habermas and education in conversation. *Studies in Philosophy and Education* 31: 103–107.

Nelson, S., M. de la Colina and M. Boone. 2008. Lifeworld or systemsworld: What guides novice principals? *Journal of Educational Administration* 46, 6: 690–701.

O'Donnell, D. 1999. Habermas, critical theory and selves-directed learning. *Journal of European Industrial Training* 23, 4–5: 251–261.

Ranson, S., J. Martin and C. Vincent. 2004. Storming parents, schools and communicative inaction. *British Journal of Sociology of Education* 25, 3: 259–274.

Rasmussen, P. 2002. Education for everyone: Secondary education and social inclusion in Denmark. *Journal of Education Policy* 17, 6: 627–642.

Rousseau, J.-J. (2004/1755) *Discourse on the origin of inequality.* New York: Dover Press.

Scrambler, G. ed. 2001. *Habermas, critical theory and health.* London: Routledge.

Smith, R. 2007. Work, identity and the quasi-market: The FE experience. *Journal of Educational Administration and History* 39, 1: 33–47.

Vander Schee, C. 2008. The politics of health as a school-sponsored ethic: Foucault, neoliberalism, and the unhealthy employee. *Educational Policy* 22, 6: 854–874.

Weems, L. 2003. Representations of substitute teachers and the paradoxes of professionalism. *Journal of Teacher Education* 54, 3: 254–265.

Whipp, J., D. Ferguson, L. Wells and A. Iacopi. 2000. Rethinking knowledge and pedagogy in dental education. *Journal of Dental Education* 64, 12: 860–866.

Part II

Foucault

Chapter 2

Foucault and his acolytes

Discourse, power and ethics

Julie Allan

Introduction

The ideas of the philosopher Michel Foucault have proved seductive to many researchers in education. Alongside the serious scholars who have produced significant analyses of education there are many more who have presented their work with a Foucauldian *lens*. Whilst this latter – often somewhat lazy – appropriation of Foucault's thought is to be regarded with disdain, it is nevertheless remarkable how appealing making reference to Foucault has seemed to so many. Such an observation may, of course, be dated and it may be that the obsession with Foucault has been replaced by a more recent penchant for citing Deleuze, and where previously power was everywhere, now everything is a rhizome. This chapter introduces Foucault and traces the development of his ideas, beginning with his archaeologies of knowledge, medicine and madness, followed by a series of genealogies of discipline and sexuality and concluding with his work on ethics, directed towards the self and including the practice of transgression. This tracing will be accompanied by a consideration of aspects of Foucault's biography and reflection on how some of his own professional and personal experiences may have helped him to develop and refine his ideas. The fascination his work has held for educational researchers, and the way in which they have been applied, with varying degrees of sophistication (or rather levels of engagement with the original concepts), will be examined, as will the dissatisfaction with his ideas expressed by some of his most ardent critics such as Habermas (1986) and Rorty (1986, 1990). The chapter ends with a discussion of whether there is such a thing as a legacy of Foucault, and if so, how this might be constituted.

A fancy for Foucault

> I think I have in fact been situated in most of the squares on the political checkerboard, one after another and sometimes simultaneously: as anarchist, leftist, ostentatious or disguised Marxist, nihilist, explicit or secret anti-Marxist, technocrat in the service of Gaullism, new liberal and so on. An American professor complained that a crypto-Marxist like me was invited in

the USA, and I was denounced by the press in Eastern European countries for being an accomplice of the dissidents. None of these descriptions is important by itself; taken together, on the other hand, they mean something. And I must admit that I rather like what they mean.

(Foucault 1997a, 113)

Foucault sought to defy categorisation of himself as one kind of scholar or another. He is indeed something of a contradiction, issuing enjoinders to study power and knowledge at its roots – for example, in schools and hospitals – whilst remaining largely at a structural level in his own analysis. Furthermore, as Andersen (2003) points out, his concepts are often many sided and often have meaning in terms of what they are not intended to mean. They are presented, according to Andersen, in a rather unsystematic way, often with repetition of similar ideas. Another difficulty with Foucault's work concerns the considerable epistemological and ontological shifts he made from his beginning work, which he termed archaeology, through to genealogy and finally ending (although this work appears to have been far from concluded) with ethics, including the practice of transgression.

The prolific *lensification* of Foucault's work is intriguing. A lens is given by particular concepts, such as 'provided by Foucault's concept of knowledge and power' (Rodriguez and Craig 2007, 739), used as a means of 'complicating power relations' (Fenech and Sumeson 2007, 109) or in order to seek alternative educational possibilities (Butin 2002). Curiously, there is such a thing as an optical device, a microscope, that bears the name of Foucault, its optician inventor, but which was developed to counteract the aberrations caused by imaging by lenses at high power. He also developed a 'Foucault test' for evaluating astronomical mirrors, described as 'cheap and easy to do' (www.myoptics.at/jodas/foucault.html). It may be unfair to suggest that those adopting a Foucauldian lens have been enticed by a similar apparent simplicity, but the limited use made of Foucault's ideas, with lens in many cases serving as little more than a gloss, may warrant such a suggestion. Each of the phases of Foucault's work, and the man who was shaping them, is outlined below.

Archaeology

Foucault's initial interest was in structures and discourses, and particularly in the way in which discourses produced particular truths. Foucault was appointed professor of psychology at the University of Clermont-Ferrand in 1960, having successfully defended his thesis, *Madness and Civilisation*, at the Sorbonne and having had some public success with this text. This was in spite of some questions being raised about whether what he was offering could be considered to be history (Miller 1993). Foucault spent two years, from 1966, in Tunisia, returning to Paris to cement his involvement as a political as well as an intellectual figure with the events of May 1968 and he became a regular public commentator and participant in demonstrations. At the same time, Foucault was engaging with the

French literary world and taking inspiration from the likes of Bataille, Blanchôt and Beckett.

In his archaeologies of knowledge (Foucault 1972a), of medicine (Foucault 1973a) and of mental illness (Foucault 1967, 1976), he demonstrated deftly how discourses produced the '*restitution* of truth' (Foucault 1967, 197; original emphasis). In *The Birth of the Clinic* (Foucault 1973a), Foucault traced the development of medicine, illustrating how the gaze opened up a 'domain of clear visibility' (p. 105) and how the hospital provided a regulated space in which medical knowledge was acquired, recorded and passed on through the rituals of teaching. In his studies of mental illness, *Madness and Civilisation* (Foucault 1967), his doctoral thesis at the Sorbonne, and *Mental Illness and Psychology* (Foucault 1976), he revealed the ways of speaking about mental illness and the way in which psychology made it possible to reveal the conditions of madness, yet was unable to 'tell the truth about madness' (Foucault 1976, 74) because he understood that madness itself possesses the truth about psychology.

Foucault, in this early stage of his work, was intensely interested in structuralism and in how it came to be a central force of so many human sciences including psychoanalysis, in for example the work of Lacan (1982), anthropology (Lévi-Strauss 1996), linguistics (de Saussure 1990) and literary criticism (Barthes 1990). Even Marxism developed a strand that was structuralist under the hand of Althusser (1968). In his analysis of the discourses of structuralism, in *The Order of Things* (Foucault 1973b), he was seeking to refine structuralist principles, having been swept along in the enthusiasm for structuralism within France in the 1970s (Dreyfus and Rabinow 1982). In this work, he was seeking to determine the 'possibilities and rights, the conditions and limitations, of a justified formalization' (Foucault 1973b, 382). At the same time, however, the refinement of his archaeological method effectively undermined structuralist principles by attempting to examine the structural rules that governed discourse. Ultimately, Foucault distanced himself from the structuralist project. Foucault's archeological method has been used to examine negligence in the law (Dent 2002), black consciousness ideology in South Africa (Howarth 2002) and the category of 'mental retardation' in nineteenth- and early twentieth-century Paris (Snigurowicz 2008). Whilst finding archaeology useful and revelatory, these authors caution against using it as a stand-alone method.

Rorty (1986) questions whether Foucault's archaeology represents anything close to a new theory of knowledge and concludes that the way Foucault has set his archaeology up makes this impossible. Furthermore, Rorty argues that Foucault's 'negative maxims' (p. 47) are neither derived from theory nor constitute a method, although he does concede that he offers 'brilliant rediscriptions of the past, supplemented by helpful hints on how to avoid being trapped by old historiographical assumptions' (p. 47). Dreyfus and Rabinow (1982) also pronounce Foucault's archaeology, which they dub a 'quasi structuralist theory' (p. 43), a failure because it runs into the very problems which Foucault had identified in his analyses of the human sciences.

Genealogy

In Foucault's shift from archaeology to genealogy, the focus of his work moved from discourses to institutions such as prisons, schools (1977a), and to sexuality (1978, 1985, 1986). Foucault's political involvement appeared to inspire much of his writing and in 1971 Foucault announced his leadership, together with his long-term partner, Daniel Defert, of the Prison Information Group (GIP), which appeared to be less about gathering information and more about political agitation. Foucault did, nevertheless, collect information about conditions within prisons, 'the only place where power is manifested in its naked state and where it is justified as a moral force' (Foucault 1972b, 6). Foucault also made his first visit to the United States in 1975 at a point when he was writing the *History of Sexuality*, but according to Defert, much of what he had already drafted, on masturbation, incest, hysteria, perversion and eugenics, was shelved following his visit to California (Miller 1993).

In Foucault's genealogies, he uncovered how knowledge and power were interlinked and constructed individuals as objects of knowledge and as subjects who were controlled, even – and perhaps especially – by themselves. His analyses overturned understandings of modern phenomena, driving home the realisation that where we might think we have greater freedom, we are, in reality, more tightly constrained than ever before. We tolerate this exercise of power only because it is hidden in the everyday. In *Discipline and Punish* (Foucault 1977a), a detailed and morbid account of a regicide being hung, drawn and quartered in the eighteenth century is followed by an equally detailed, but apparently more benign, regime of imprisonment almost a century later. Foucault invites us to consider that the removal of the physical punishment as a spectacle has, in fact, led to a more insidious form of control over individuals' bodies and their souls. His analysis is extended to education and the 'disciplinary regimes' which turn young people into 'docile bodies' (Foucault 1977a, 138).

Foucault developed a series of constructs about power and knowledge which he offered as a useful 'box of tools' (Foucault 1977a, 208) for understanding how individuals were controlled and constrained. The most important of these is 'the rather shameful art of surveillance' (p. 172), a disciplinary technique for ensuring individuals were sorted, regulated, normalised and made to behave in particular ways. Foucault identified three ways in which surveillance was undertaken. First of all, hierarchical observation was a means of making it possible 'for a single gaze to see everything perfectly' (p. 173). Physical structures were created, based on Jeremy Bentham's panopticon design, to ensure maximum scrutiny of people:

> to render visible those who are inside it . . . to act on those it shelters, to provide a hold on their conduct, to carry the effects of power right to them, to make it possible to know them, to alter them.
>
> (p. 172)

Hierarchical observation, thus, encompassed a form of supervision of supervisors, with everyone accountable to authority from above. The effectiveness of the supervision was guaranteed by the fact that it was 'absolutely *discreet*, for it functions permanently and largely in silence' (p. 177) and since it was impossible to know when one was being watched, it was necessary to behave as if this was the case.

Normalising judgements are also used, according to Foucault, to justify correction and coercion in teaching and promote standardisation and homogeneity. Individuals can be measured in terms of their distance from their norm and once the extent of their deviance from the norm is established, disciplinary techniques can be used to homogenise and normalise, and, of course, exclusion can be justified as a means to these ends. Foucault regards normalisation as one of the great instruments of power at the end of the classical age, but alerts us to its continued use:

> It is easy to understand how the power of the norm functions within a system of formal equality, since within a homogeneity that is the rule, the norm introduces, as a useful imperative and as a result of measurement, all the shading of individual differences.
>
> (p. 184)

Foucault's third dimension of surveillance, the examination, combines hierarchical observation and normalising judgements in a ritualised form which transforms the 'economy of visibility into the exercise of power' (p. 187). The examination also introduces individuality in order to fix and capture and makes each individual a 'case', capable of being 'described, judged, measured, compared with others, in his very individuality' (p. 191). These mechanisms of surveillance create subjects who are known and marked in particular kinds of ways and who are constrained to carry this knowledge and these marks. The kind of power exercised here, Foucault tells us, is not the negative kind which represses, masks or conceals; rather, he argues, it is the kind which produces 'reality; it produces domains of objects and rituals of truth' (p. 194) in the shape of individuals and what is known about each of them.

Foucault's genealogies of sexuality, substantially rewritten after his US visit, forced a rethink of existing understandings of our relationship with sex. He developed the notion of a 'perverse implantation' (Foucault 1978, 36), in relation to sexuality, a means of naming deviance (and its distinguishing characteristics) in order to then cure or remove them. He described the emergence of an elaborate set of codes for speaking about so-called normal sexuality – between a married couple – and identifying what deviated from this norm. In this 'discursive explosion' (p. 38) in the eighteenth and nineteenth centuries, scrutiny was exercised over:

> the sexuality of children, mad men and women and criminals; the sensuality of those who did not like the opposite sex; reveries, obsessions, petty manias, or great transports of rage. It was time for all these figures, scarcely noticed

in the past, to step forward and speak, to make the difficult confession of what they were.

(p. 38)

Foucault's analyses of subjectification, in which he demonstrated so effectively how individuals were incapable of resistance, have proved seductive to many who have undertaken their own genealogies of educational contexts (Ball 1990; Blacker 1998; Marshall 1989; Fendler 1998). Baker's (1998) 'history of the present' (p. 118) demonstrates how childhood was produced within the public school movement in the United States, although what it meant to be a 'child' was not debated. Special needs and disability have also been seen as ripe for Foucauldian analysis. Tremain's (2005) collection of papers on *Foucault and the Government of Disability* contain a wealth of analyses of epistemologies, ontologies, histories, governmentalities, ethics and politics which reveal 'some of the fascism which still runs round in our heads and still plays itself out in our everyday behavior' (McWhorter 2005, xvii). These studies situate individuals as impotent, heavily constrained and with dismal prospects. Medical, juridical and administrative practices construct and demarcate the disabled subject and the discourses of inclusion are underpinned by a homogenising imperative. In spite of this, however, we are urged to 'think beyond accepted dogmas' (Tremain 2005, 22) and to do what we can:

> The point here, I think, is not to feel bad about the injustice or the suffering in the world . . . The point is to pull up short before the possibility that what you thought was true might not be, that what you thought was normal or natural might be the product of political struggle, and to start – from just that place – to *think*, which means to question, to critique, to experiment, to wonder, to imagine, to try.
>
> (McWhorter 2005, xvii)

Foucault (1982) encourages us to read the 'modern state' (p. 214) of penal institutions, education and even sexuality as creating less, rather than more, freedom and to recognise that the establishment of governmentality ensures that each person is both an individual and part of a totality:

> I don't think that we should consider the 'modern state' as an entity which was developed above individuals, ignoring what they are and even their very existence, but on the contrary as a very sophisticated structure, in which individuals can be integrated, under one condition: that this individuality would be shaped in a new form, and submitted to a set of very specific patterns.
>
> (Foucault 1982, 214)

Whilst Foucault's critique of the way subjects are disciplined has appealed to so many scholars, it has also earned him criticisms that his work is overly pessimistic

(Rorty 1990) and did little to encourage individuals to take action (Shumway 1989). Others have argued that Foucault's depiction of 'docile bodies' (1977a, 138) denies agency and creates a 'fleshless passive body' (Hughes 2005, 84) which is 'dissolved as a causal phenomenon' (Schilling 1993, 80) and with powers which are limited to those invested in them by discourse.

Ethics

Foucault's later work, ethics, contains a much more sanguine view of agency and depicts individuals as capable of working on themselves to achieve new kinds of existence. His turn to ethics arose from his concern with the self and its capacity for both resistance and transformation. It has already been suggested that his genealogies on sexuality had been profoundly influenced by his visits to the United States and his own experience of liberated gay sex. His development of a framework of ethics surfaced in his later volumes on sexuality and he signalled this shift in what he called a 'genealogy of ethics', declaring himself 'much more interested in problems about techniques of the self and things like that than sex . . . sex is boring' (Foucault 1984, 340). Foucault died of complications arising from Aids and, it is suggested, as a result of practising his own 'limit experiences' (Miller 1993, 29).

Foucault's framework of ethics focuses on:

> the forms of relations with the self, on the methods and techniques by which he works them out, on the exercises by which he makes of himself an object to be known, and on the practices that enable him to transform his own mode of being.
>
> (1985, 30)

Foucault gave little advice on how one should undertake transformation of this kind in practice (Smart 1998). He mentions the role of the counsellor, friend, guide or master who will tell you the truth about yourself, but does not discuss the nature of the relationships involved. Bernauer suggests that Foucault provides an invitation to others 'not to renounce the soul . . . but to transgress its borders, to reinvent one's relationship to it' (1999, xiv). This invitation enables individuals to see themselves as the main source of transformation, rather than waiting for a more substantial structural or material change. As Veyne (1997) observes, 'the self is the new strategic possibility' (p. 231), capable of responding to the dangers which are encountered:

> The ethico-political choice we have to make every day is to determine which is the main danger . . . My point is not that everything is bad but that everything is dangerous . . . If everything is dangerous, then we always have something to do. So my position leads not to apathy but to a hyper- and pessimistic activism.
>
> (Foucault 1984, 343)

Foucault (1985) regards ethical practice as having four dimensions, which he elaborates upon in relation to Christianity and sexuality. He points out that the four dimensions of ethics will inevitably overlap and cannot be dissociated from one another or from the actions that support them. The four dimensions are:

1 *Determination of the ethical substance.* This dimension involves the identification of 'this or that part of oneself as prime material of his moral conduct' (Foucault 1985, 26). Individuals decide which aspect of the self is to be worked on or changed and in Foucault's example of Christianity, one's beliefs, intentions or desires might be specified as objects for transformation in order to become a better Christian.

2 *The mode of subjection.* The second of the ethical dimensions concerns the way in which the individual recognises how he or she operates in relation to certain rules and to find other ways of observing these rules. Foucault uses the example of fidelity and contends that there are many ways to practise austerity and 'be faithful' (Foucault 1985, 26). An example of the mode of subjection, provided by Blacker (1998), is the Greek aristocrat who fashions his diet according to certain aesthetic criteria.

3 *Self-practice or ethical work.* This aspect involves what one does 'not only in order to bring one's conduct into compliance with a given rule, but to effect transformation of oneself into the ethical subject of one's behaviour' (Foucault 1985, 26). Thus, sexual austerity in Foucault's example can be practised silently through thought or by a much more explicit and 'relentless combat' (p. 26). It is a form of 'asceticism' (Blacker 1998, 362) through which individuals transform themselves.

4 *The Telos.* The final dimension concerns the ultimate goal which an individual is trying to achieve through ethical work. In Foucault's example, fidelity is identified as part of a journey towards complete self-mastery and he highlights the moral aspect of the transformation of self which is involved. Blacker describes this process as a kind of 'controlled and self-regulated dissemination of the subject into the world, a positive dissolution . . . not self-absorption, but being absorbed into the world: a losing-finding of the self' (Blacker 1998, 362–363; original emphasis).

These practices of the self are not acquired easily but have to be learned through disciplined training and through reading and writing and Foucault (1997b) underlines the importance of writing for oneself and for others:

No technique, no professional skill can be acquired without exercise; nor can one learn the art of living, the *techne tou biou*, without an *askesis* that must be understood as a training of the self by the self . . . writing is regularly associated with 'meditation' and with that exercise of thought on itself that reactivates what it knows, that makes present a principle, a rule, or an example, reflects on them, assimilates them, and thus prepares itself to confront the real.

(pp. 235–236)

Foucault's notion of writing as a form of meditation draws on Seneca and Epictetus and he sees this as proceeding in two different ways. The first is linear, taking the writer from meditation through to the activity of writing and on to *gymnazein*, 'training in a real and taxing situation: work of thought, work through writing, work through reality' (p. 236). The second is circular, going from meditation through to a rereading of notes which provoke further meditation. The reflexive function of writing, particularly in correspondence with others, is emphasised by Foucault: to write is thus to 'show oneself, make oneself seen, make one's face appear before the other' (p. 243). It is a way of 'summoning the gaze of the other' (p. 247). Reading is also seen as implied by the practice of the self because 'one cannot draw everything from one's own funds . . . As a guide or example, the help of others is necessary' (p. 236).

Foucault argues that one should become so accomplished in ethical practice that one engages in it unconsciously:

> You must have learned principles so firmly that when your desires, your appetites or your fears awaken like barking dogs, the logos will speak with the voice of a master who silences the dogs by a single command.
>
> (Foucault 1987, 6)

While Foucault's ethical practice is directed towards a kind of sexual austerity this work is not only ethical but is also a political, social and philosophical endeavour which is put into practice through a kind of 'curiosity' (Foucault 1988, 328), a practice, which he explains:

> evokes the care of what exists and might exist; a sharpened sense of reality, but one that is never immobilized before it; a readiness to find what surrounds us strange and odd; a certain determination to throw off familiar ways of thought and to look at the same things in a different way . . . a lack of respect for the traditional hierarchies of what is important and fundamental.
>
> (p. 328)

Foucault highlights the necessity of establishing conduct which seeks the rules of acceptable behaviour in relations with others, but foregrounds the self as the principle object of care, and as the means through which care for others can occur. Smart (1998) claims that the contemporary version of caring for oneself, which is characterised by self-determination, self-expression and hedonism, has led to indifference towards the other, but this need not be the case.

Although Foucault's ethics still remains a largely neglected work, it has been directed towards the inclusion of children with special needs (Allan 2005, 2008), to strategies for interrupting the exclusion of young people (Youdell 2006) and to the work of the academic (Blacker 1998). Establishing an ethical project in response to educational problems enables the work we each have to do on ourselves to be set out in terms of the determination of the ethical substance, mode of subjection, self-practice or ethical work and a telos. It also allows strategies of transgression to be articulated.

Transgression

Transgression emerged in Foucault's writings on ethics as a subversive tactic which could enable individuals to transform themselves. Transgression is a form of resistance involving the crossing of limits or boundaries. It is not antagonistic or aggressive, nor does it involve a contest in which there is a victor; rather, transgression is playful and creative. Among disabled people, transgression has been a significant means of challenging limits and disabling barriers. It is possible to recognise both collective transgression and more subtle and indirect transgression by individuals.

The development of the concept of transgression was sparked by Foucault's interest in Kant's critique of limits, but represents a more practical (and political) form of engagement. Foucault saw transgression as distinctively different from transcendence or transformation: he did not envisage individuals as gaining absolute freedom from limits, but instead suggested that individuals, in crossing limits or boundaries, might find moments of freedom or of otherness. Foucault's account of where transgression takes place is somewhat complex. In his 'Preface to transgression' (1977b), written as an introduction to the work of Bataille, he argues that 'It is likely that transgression has its entire space in the line it crosses' (p. 34). This implies a boundary that can only be there by crossing it. The limit and transgression depend on each other, but the relationship is not a simple one; rather, the relationship, according to Foucault, is like a spiral, with moments of crossing of the limit appearing as a flash of lightning in the night which give a darkening intensity to the night it obscures. Foucault also describes the interplay of limits and transgression as being regulated by a simple obstinacy. The act of crossing the limit does not violate it, but simultaneously affirms and weakens it. Foucault regards this as a form of non-positive affirmation, which has to be constantly repeated, and likens it to Blanchôt's notion of contestation, which does not imply a generalised negation, but an affirmation that affirms nothing.

Foucault (1977b) acknowledges a difficulty with words which hampers philosophy and sees the absence of a language with which to talk about transgression as inhibiting its practice. Nevertheless, he expresses his hope that one day transgression will be as much a part of our culture as contradiction was for dialectical thought. Bataille also looks forward to the normalisation of transgression whereby silent contemplation would be substituted with language (Foucault 1984). He uses sexuality to illustrate transgression, arguing that since the writings of Sade and, more recently Bataille, sexuality has been a fissure which marks the limit within us and designates us as a limit. Foucault has been criticised extensively for failing to provide empirical examples of his concepts and indeed his discussion of sexuality provides little guidance on the practical pursuit of transgression. His own sexual transgression can hardly be seen as a model for others to follow, given its contribution to his own untimely death (Miller 1993). Transgression has, nevertheless, been viewed as an attractive construct in relation to marginalised and oppressed groups, not least of all because it forces a recognition of exclusion. For those who transgress, according to Boyne (1990), 'otherness lies ahead' (p. 82) and this allows individuals to shape their own identities by subverting the norms which compel them to repeatedly perform as subjects with a particular marginal identity, such as disabled or ethnic minorities. They are not required to – and indeed could not – reject these identities entirely, but can vary the way in which they have to repeat these performances.

There have been few studies of transgression, but researchers studying resistance have uncovered strategies which could be read in this way. In Cooper's (1997) study of religious education, for example, resistance served the function of halting change and involved schools selectively incorporating the religious provisions of the 1988 Education Reform Act, while ignoring others. In Bloor and McIntosh's (1990) study of surveillance and concealment, new mothers avoided both breast feeding and the wrath of the health visitors checking up on them and their resistance was regarded as effective because it enabled 'a way of avoiding control without confrontation' (p. 176). Sullivan's (2005) study of paraplegics in a spinal unit revealed individuals' 'struggle for control of the body' (p. 39). Sullivan found their resistance 'harrowing', but as successful in rejecting the authoritarianism and totalising aspects of control. My own research with disabled students (Allan 1999) highlighted the positive effects of being able to transgress their disabled identities and practise alternative modes of existence.

Foucault's legacy: he makes you think

Whatever Foucault's work constitutes, his critics, among them Rorty, Dreyfus and Rabinow, and Andersen, appear to agree that it is not a major social theory. He has become lodged in epistemological cul-de-sacs because of the very problems with social theory that he himself identifies in his analyses. We can say, however, that Foucault, by inviting new ways of seeing and asking questions about what we think we know, provides 'unforseen untried possibilities in our history' (Rajchman 1995, 14). We should also recognise that Foucault, particularly in his later work, invites us, indeed encourages us, to 'question what is given to us as necessary to think and do' (Burchell 1996, 32) and those who have charged Foucault with pessimism have missed much. Foucault himself argued that it was always his intention 'to show people that they are freer than they feel' (in Martin et al. 1988, 10–11), but perhaps this point was missed as a consequence of believing that Foucault would help us to abandon the truth. Rather, his work helps us find new ways of living today and to 'invent or contrive new ways of saying the truth' (Burchell 1996, 32). This is not an insubstantial legacy.

References

Allan, J. 1999. *Actively seeking inclusion: Pupils with special educational needs in mainstream schools.* London: Falmer.

Allan, J. 2005. Inclusion as an ethical project. In *Foucault and the government of disability*, ed. S. Tremain, 281–297. Ann Arbor: University of Michigan Press.

Allan, J. 2008. *Rethinking inclusive education: The philosophers of difference in practice.* Dordrecht: Springer.

Althusser, L. 1968. *Lire le capital.* Paris: François Maspero.

Andersen, N. 2003. *Discursive analytical strategies: Understanding Foucault, Koselleck, Laclau, Luhman.* Bristol: The Policy Press.

Baker, B. 1998. 'Childhood' in the emergence and spread of US public schools. In *Foucault's challenge: Discourse, knowledge and power in education*, ed. T. Popkewitz and M. Brennan, 117–143. New York/London: Teachers College Press.

Ball, S. 1990. Management as moral technology: A Luddite analysis. In *Foucault and education: Disciplines and knowledge*, ed. S. Ball, 153–166. London: Routledge.

Barthes, R. 1990. *S/Z.* Oxford: Basil Blackwell Publishers.

Bernauer, J. 1999. 'Cry of spirit': Forward to M. Foucault *Religion in culture*, ed. J. Carette, pp. xi–xvii. Manchester: Manchester University Press.

Blacker, D. 1998. Intellectuals at work and in power: Towards a Foucauldian research ethic. In *Foucault's challenge: Discourse, knowledge and power in education*, ed. T. Popkewitz and M. Brennan, 348–367. New York: Teachers College Press.

Bloor, M. and J. McIntosh. 1990. Surveillance and concealment: A comparison of techniques of client resistance in therapeutic communities and health visiting. In *Readings in medical sociology*, ed. L. S. Cunningham-Burley and N. McKeganey, 159–181. London: Routledge.

Boyne, R. 1990. *Foucault and Derrida: The other side of reason.* London: Routledge.

Burchell, G. 1996. Liberal government and techniques of the self. In *Foucault and political reason: Liberalism, neo-liberalism and rationalities of government*, ed. A. Barry, T. Osborne and N. Rose, 19–36. Chicago: University of Chicago Press.

Butin, D. 2002. This ain't talk therapy: Problematizing and extending anti-oppressive education. *Educational Researcher* 31, 3: 14–16.

Cooper, D. 1997. Strategies of power: Legislating worship and religious education. In *The impact of Michel Foucault on the social sciences and humanities*, ed. M. Lloyd and A. Thacker, 147–172. Basingstoke: Macmillan Press Ltd.

de Saussure, F. 1990. *Course in general linguistics.* London: Duckworth.

Dent, C. 2002. *Reflecting on continuity and discontinuity in 'the law': An application of Foucault's archeological method in a reading of juridical decisions of negligence.* Unpublished PhD thesis: Murdoch University.

Dreyfus, H. and P. Rabinow. 1982. *Michel Foucault: Beyond structuralism and hermeneutics.* Brighton: Harvester Press.

Fendler, L. 1998. What is it impossible to think? A genealogy of the educated subject. In *Foucault's challenge: Discourse, knowledge and power in education*, ed. T. Popkewitz and M. Brennan, 39–63. New York: Teachers College Press.

Fenech, M. and J. Sumeson. 2007. Early childhood teachers and regulation: Complicating power relations using a Foucauldian lens. *Contemporary Issues in Early Childhood* 8, 2: 109–122.

Foucault, M. 1967. *Madness and civilisation*. London: Tavistock.

Foucault, M. 1972a. *The archaeology of knowledge*. London: Tavistock.

Foucault, M. 1972b. *Les intellectuels et le pouvour*. Lectures.

Foucault, M. 1973a. *The birth of the clinic*. London: Routledge.

Foucault, M. 1973b. *The order of things: An archaeology of the human sciences*. New York: Vintage/Random House.

Foucault, M. 1976. *Mental illness and psychology*. Berkeley/Los Angeles, CA: University of California Press.

Foucault, M. 1977a. *Discipline and punish: The birth of the prison*. London: Penguin.

Foucault, M. 1977b. A preface to transgression. In *Language, counter-memory, practice: Selected essays and interviews by Michel Foucault*, ed. D. Bouchard, 29–52. Oxford: Basil Blackwell.

Foucault, M. 1978. *The history of sexuality: An introduction*. Harmondsworth: Penguin.

Foucault, M. 1982. The subject and power. In *Michel Foucault: Beyond structuralism and hermeneutics*, ed. H. Dreyfus and P. Rabinow, 208–226. Brighton: Harvester Press.

Foucault, M. 1984. On the genealogy of ethics: An overview of work in progress. In *The Foucault reader*, ed. P. Rabinow, 340–372. New York: Pantheon.

Foucault, M. 1985. *The use of pleasure: The history of sexuality, 2*. Trans. R. Hurley. Harmondsworth: Penguin.

Foucault, M. 1986. *The care of the self: The history of sexuality, 3*. Trans. R. Hurley. New York: Routledge.

Foucault, M. 1987. The ethic of care for the self as a practice of freedom. Interview. In *The final Foucault*, ed. J. Bernaur and D. Rasmussen, 1–20. Cambridge, MA: MIT Press.

Foucault, M. 1988. The masked philosopher. In *Michael Foucault: Politics, philosophy, culture. Interviews and other writings*, ed. L. Kritzman, 323–330. London: Routledge.

Foucault, M. 1997a. Polemics, politics and problematizations. In *Ethics: Essential works of Foucault 1954–1984*, ed. P. Rabinow, 111–119. London: Penguin.

Foucault, M. 1997b. Writing the self. In *Foucault and his interlocutors*, ed. A. Davidson, 234–247. Chicago: University of Chicago Press.

Habermas, J. 1986. Taking aim at the heart of the present. In *Foucault: A critical reader*, ed. D. Couzens Hoy, 103–108. Oxford: Basil Blackwell.

Howarth, D. 2002. Evaluating Michel Foucault's explanation and critique of ideology. *Political Studies* 50: 117–135.

Hughes, B. 2005. What can a Foucauldian theory contribute? In *Foucault and the government of disability*, ed. S. Tremain, 78–92. Ann Arbor: University of Michigan Press.

Lacan, J. 1982. *Ecrits*. London: Routledge.

Lévi-Strauss, C. 1996. *The savage mind*. Oxford: Oxford University Press.

Marshall, J. 1989. Foucault and education. *Australian Journal of Education* 33, 2: 99–113.

Martin, L., L. Gutman and P. Hutton. 1988. *Technologies of the self: A seminar with Michel Foucault*. Amhurst: University of Massachusetts Press.

McWhorter, L. 2005. Foreword. In *Foucault and the government of disability*, ed. S. Tremain, xiii–xvii. Ann Arbor: University of Michigan Press.

Miller, J. 1993. *The passion of Michel Foucault*. London: HarperCollins.

Rajchman, J. 1995. Foucault ten years after. *Michel Foucault: J'Accuse. A Journal of Culture/Theory/Politics* 25: 14–20.

Rodriguez, L. and R. Craig. 2007. Assessing international accounting harmonization using Hegelian dialectic, isomorphism and Foucault. *Critical Perspectives in Accounting* 18, 6: 739–767.

Rorty, R. 1986. Foucault and epistemology. In *Foucault: A critical reader*, ed. D. Couzens Hoy, 41–50. Oxford/New York: Basil Blackwell.

Rorty, R. 1990. Foucault, Dewey, Nietzsche. *Raritan* 9: 1–8.

Schilling, C. 1993. *The body and social theory*. London: Sage.

Shumway, D. 1989. *Michel Foucault*. Charlottesville, VA: University Press of Virginia.

Smart, B. 1998. Foucault, Levinas and the subject of responsibility. In *The later Foucault*, ed. J. Moss, 78–92. London: Sage.

Snigurowicz, D. 2008. The phénomène's dilemma: Teratology and the policing of human anomalies in nineteenth- and early-twentieth-century Paris. In *Foucault and the government of disability*, ed. S. Tremain, 172–188. Ann Arbor: University of Michigan Press.

Sullivan, M. 2005. Subjected bodies: Rehabilitation and the politics of management. In *Foucault and the government of disability*, ed. S. Tremain, 27–44. Ann Arbor: University of Michigan Press.

Tremain, S. ed. 2005. *Foucault and the government of disability*. Ann Arbor: University of Michigan Press.

Veyne, P. 1997. The final Foucault and his critics. In *Foucault and his interlocutors*, ed. A. Davidson, 225–233. Chicago: University of Chicago Press.

Youdell, D. 2006. *Impossible bodies, impossible selves: Exclusions and student subjectivities*. Dordrecht: Springer.

Chapter 3

Foucault, panopticism and school surveillance research

Andrew Hope

Introduction

The panopticon is an architectural design for a prison, which was used by the French social historian Michel Foucault (1977) as an 'ideal type' to explore how discipline was utilised by the state in mid-nineteenth-century France. In this context, an ideal type provides a typification of a phenomenon, constructed by extracting its essential characteristics, and its purpose is to provide a structure against which real examples may be compared. Consequently the concept of the panopticon has broad appeal to social–cultural researchers exploring surveillance practices, as it offers a theoretical framework that aids in the gathering and analysis of empirical data.

This chapter explores academic writing on panopticism, whilst also considering issues and challenges faced by researchers wishing to use this concept to make sense of the social impact of surveillance technologies within schools. Initially Foucault's discussion of the panopticon in his influential text *Discipline and Punish* (1977) is examined, before some contemporary developments of key (post-)panoptic ideas are analysed. These insights are then applied as panoptic themes are developed that could aid researchers focusing upon school observational practices. Finally, some of the practical limitations of the panoptic metaphor are discussed as student resistance to school discipline is pondered.

Foucault's discussion of the panopticon

It has almost become a cliché that any social–cultural work focusing upon surveillance in late modernity should pay intellectual tribute to the work of Michel Foucault. Since its publication in 1975, Foucault's book *Surveiller et punir: Naissance de la prison*, which was printed in English under the title *Discipline and Punish: The Birth of the Prison* (1977), has exerted a strong influence over writings on the social impacts of contemporary surveillance, with regard to both educational institutions and wider society. Indeed, Simon (2005, 2) asserts that there can be no theorisation of the social aspects of contemporary surveillance without reference to this work.

Foucault (1977) asserts that by the mid-nineteenth century there was a punitive change in France, from physical punishment to regimented incarceration, focusing upon the 'transformation of the soul' rather than the torture of the body, with the intent of creating individuals who policed themselves (Mathiesen 1997). Central to this idea of self-surveillance was Foucault's discussion of the panopticon, a prison design wherein exposed, backlit prison cells, situated around the periphery of a building, faced inwards towards a central watchtower. As Foucault (1977, 200) noted '[b]y the effect of backlighting, one can observe from the tower, standing out precisely against the light, the small captive shadows in the cells of the periphery'. Yet the central watchtower is darkened and inside it Venetian blinds and internal partitions are used to avoid the betrayal of movement, so that potential watchers cannot be seen by those in the cells. Power is visible in the form of the central watchtower, the inmate is exposed and the potential watcher is hidden.

Samuel Bentham is credited with the original idea of the panopticon (Boyne 2000, 288), although it was his brother the utilitarian philosopher Jeremy Bentham who published the design in 1791, claiming that it would 'invigorate industry', 'reform morals' and 'facilitate education'. Investing power in light, inspection and architecture, the prisoner in Bentham's design is subject to permanent display; 'the object of information, never a subject in communication' (Foucault 1977, 200). Bentham's design disassociates power from particular people, investing it in a configuration of light, inspection and architecture. Individuals, uncertain that they are being watched, yet fearful of the possibility, start to police their own behaviour. In this context, observation comes to be perceived as continuous. Thus, Bentham's innovation was not just to inspect or ensure an asymmetrical gaze, but also to use uncertainty as a means of social control (Lyon 1994, 65). He maintained that this design had a wider application than prisons, subsequently drawing up plans for a circular nursery as well as designing several schools with semi-circular arrangements to facilitate the influence of the teacher (Markus 1993, 68).

Foucault (1977) drew upon this design as a powerful model for social analysis, suggesting that constant surveillance could encourage individuals to monitor and adjust their own behaviour. Nevertheless, as Norris (2003) notes, care must be taken not to over-privilege the visual aspects of the panopticon. It is noteworthy that Bentham's original design of the panopticon also encompassed 'panauralism' by including metal listening tubes to augment the visual surveillance (Markus 1993), so that guards could listen to prisoners. Furthermore, using the example of the birth certificate, Foucault (1977, 216) draws attention to the importance of keeping records as part of the panoptic mechanism.

Indeed, Foucault is equally concerned with procedures that situate individuals in a disciplinary discourse. Thus he begins his discussion of panopticism by considering measures taken in the seventeenth century to contain the outbreak of plague (Foucault 1977, 195). This illustrates that, for Foucault, surveillance is merely one aspect of panopticism, which includes a much wider discourse on 'disciplinary technology', regimes of control, the labelling of individuals, the keeping of records and attempts to influence self-perception.

Haggerty and Ericson (2000, 607) suggest that the 'disciplinary aspect of panoptic observation involves a productive soul training which encourages inmates to reflect upon the minutia of their own behaviour in subtle and ongoing efforts to transform their selves'. In schools, the keeping of registers, filing of reports, wearing of standardised uniforms, observance of rules, strict use of timetables, regimented examinations and ostentatious punishments can all be seen as fashioning a panoptical discourse of control. Thus the visual element of panopticism can be seen as merely one part of a process of 'corrective training'. Indeed, Foucault (1977, 170) notes '[t]he chief function of disciplinary power is to "train" . . . Discipline "makes" individuals; it is the specific technique of a power that regards individuals both as objects and as instruments of its exercise.' Discourse has a central role in such training, encouraging individuals to behave in a prescribed manner, whilst reproducing the means of control through acceptance and the ongoing replication of normalising judgements. In this context, normalisation refers to processes whereby certain standards of behaviour become hegemonically accepted as naturally the ones that should be adhered to in society. Consequently, emergent discursive constructs act as regulatory forces that have productive power, they demarcate, circulate and differentiate. Foucault (1977) suggests that the successful operation of such power lies in the use of simple instruments such as observation, punishment and normalising discourses. Resultant regimes of control operate discursively through the classification of certain behaviours as 'normal', the labelling of 'miscreant' individuals and attempts to influence self-perception. Consequently, in responding to potential permanent surveillance, individuals may not merely be engaging in self-monitoring but also in a normalisation process, where they come to accept certain types of behaviour as (in)appropriate. Thus students may accept that certain types of activity are examples of misbehaviour in school, never questioning the application of such a label.

Foucault's vision of a panoptical society highlights how a small number of people can exercise control over a large group of individuals, not merely through 'the few watching the many' (both physically and through records) but via self-surveillance and the observed accepting the normalising discourse embedded in the monitoring process, which suggests the 'appropriate' way to behave.

Panopticism in contemporary society

Although some commentators (Lyon 1994; Boyne 2000) assert that the panopticon provides a compelling metaphor for understanding surveillance in contemporary society, there is a growing critique in surveillance studies of the ideas underpinning this concept (Poster 1990; Norris and Armstrong 1999; Hier 2003; Koskela 2003; Yar 2003). Critics argue that Foucault failed to address contemporary developments in surveillance technologies, focusing instead on eighteenth- and nineteenth-century total institutions (Haggerty and Ericson 2000, 607). Hence, Koskela (2003) suggests that panopticism offers a convincing model for 'modern' society, but not for late modernity where power and control have seemingly become more dispersed and fluid. *Surveiller et punir* was first published in 1975 and Foucault died in 1984. Whilst both events preceded the creation of the World Wide Web and the widespread utilisation of wireless digital technologies, critics still argue that his failure to consider surveillance technologies operating in the 1960s and 1970s compromised his analysis. The diversification of media, the subsequent rise of computerised databases, internet connectivity and mobile technologies have led to a recognition that there might be a need to rethink the panoptic metaphor. In particular, critics highlight four elements of contemporary monitoring processes that should be considered in reappraising panopticism. These are the influence of the mass media, the inter-relational nature of surveillance, the growing use of databases and advancements made in the simulation of surveillance. These will each be considered in turn.

Mathiesen commenting upon Foucault's failure to mention the mass media, and in particular television, suggests that '[i]t's more than just an omission; its inclusion in the analysis would necessarily in a basic way have changed his whole image of society as far as surveillance goes' (1997, 219). In an attempt to address this shortcoming, Mathiesen considers the viewer society and the 'synopticon' of the mass media, in which the many watch the few. He points out that the synopticon has a long history from festivals and theatres through to films and television. The synopticon 'directs and controls or disciplines our consciousness' (1997, 230) through mass media. Twenty-four-hour rolling news reports controlled by powerful media interests, reinforced through an obsession with 'celebrity' opinions, may unduly influence how individuals in society think and act. In Foucault's terms this could be seen as part of a normalising mechanism. For example, consider the impact of celebrity chef Jamie Oliver's television series *Jamie's School Dinners*, first aired in the UK in 2005. Criticism in the programme of the unhealthy food consumed by school children resulted in a change of public opinion, the development of new government policy, the banning of many 'junk foods' in school and the introduction of healthier choices. Ultimately, as Doyle (2011) suggests, the synopticon works in parallel with the panopticon, suggesting an amendment to Foucault's analysis, rather than a rejection or radical restructuring of arguments.

Martin et al. (2009) note that much discussion of the panoptic gaze assumes a two-actor model, in which information flows one way from a single source. Yet, in contemporary society, surveillance may be inter-relational in nature, rarely is the observed truly a passive object. Not only do individuals engage in counter-surveillance but they can also be involved creatively in the construction of their own data identity. Haggerty and Ericson (2000) reject Foucault's concepts, instead drawing upon Deleuze to suggest the existence of a 'surveillant assemblage', a 'multiplicity of heterogeneous objects' that work together as a functional entity. 'They comprise discrete flows of an essentially limitless range of other phenomena . . . [are] multiple, unstable and lack discernible boundaries' (Haggerty and Ericson 2000, 608–609). Such analysis draws critical attention to a tendency to treat surveillance technologies discretely, when the reality is that they often act as dynamic, fluid networks. Kuehn (2008) refers to such linking of multiple sources of data from a number of different media as Surveillance 2.0. Kuehn (2008, 87) notes that the monitoring tools used in schooling are still predominantly Surveillance 1.0, each practice operating individually, although he adds that 'one can see all of the pieces coming together that will make it possible to create this totally invasive form of education'.

Whilst encouraging academics to think of 'surveillant assemblage' as 'essentially limitless' could encourage the analysis of new forms of social control that might have been disregarded using a more rigid conceptual approach, practical considerations often dictate that social research focuses on a limited element of social reality. This is not to reject the idea of an assemblage, but rather to note that any analysis will inevitably fail to be all-encompassing. Although Foucault's discussion of the panopticon does suggest a two-actor model, it does not preclude a more complex relationship. Importantly, despite complex social dynamics, much teacher–student interaction might still be best understood with reference to this simple model.

The continuous and automatic monitoring of individuals' everyday lives through digital technologies has resulted in the increased use of classification systems. Lyon (2003, 13) suggests that such social sorting 'highlights the classifying drive of contemporary surveillance', wherein '[t]he resulting classifications are designed to influence and to manage populations and persons thus directly and indirectly affecting the choices and chances of the data subjects'. Indeed, according to Poster (1989, 1995), the development of online technology and complex data handling systems has led to the emergence of a super-panopticon. Whereas Foucault suggested that subjects in the panopticon were conscious of their own self-determination, Poster (1995, 93) argues that with the super-panopticon 'subject constitution takes an opposing course of objectification, of producing individuals with dispersed identities, identities of which the individuals might not even be aware'. Surveillance in this context has gone beyond Foucault's consideration of panopticism. Individuals may no longer be aware that they are the subject of surveillance; furthermore they may be unlikely to understand how information held on networked databases is used to construct consumer, worker or citizen profiles. Information derived from mundane activities such as using a store loyalty card when shopping, booking leisure activities with a credit card or even surfing on the internet can be used to construct such personal data profiles. For Poster (1989), this development has led to dissolution of distinctions between public and private spheres and the construction of a range of new disparate 'identities' that, unknown to the individual, may have a very real effect on everyday life. Yet it is questionable whether the creation of 'data doubles' online will have a panoptic impact. After all, if an individual is denied access to resources without being told that this is a consequence of their covertly observed actions, it is unlikely that they will modify their behaviour and engage in self-surveillance.

Bauman (1992) rejects Poster's notion of the super-panopticon, arguing that whereas the panopticon was meant to instil discipline, databases merely confirm credibility. Yet as Lyon (2001) notes, Bauman underestimates the power of contemporary classification and social sorting systems, which 'make surveillance automatic across all socio-economic strata' (pp. 92–93). Thus publicly accessible databases such as school league tables can impact on students' educational choices and the resources that are subsequently available to schools (Selwyn 2000). Whilst Foucault (1977, 192) recognised the importance of data gathering, the 'turning of real lives into writing . . . as a procedure of objectification and subjection', he could hardly be criticised for failing to anticipate the size, scope and speed of such information flow in late modernity. Yet significantly, Poster sees this development as an extension of the panoptic metaphor, rather than something radically different.

The growing use of databases has led some commentators to suggest that surveillance in contemporary society is no longer merely about recording information or deterring certain actions but is also concerned with prediction. In a classic study of undercover police work in the United States, Gary Marx (1988) noted how 'categorical suspicion' led to pre-emptive surveillance. Computer matching of lists generated categories of likely offenders that could blemish an individual's reputation without due cause. Such surveillance techniques have been introduced into educational establishments, most notably in the form of student violence risk assessment databases. Drawing on the work of Baudrillard on simulation, Bogard (1996) argues that 'the technological enlargement of the field of perceptual control . . . has pushed surveillance beyond the very limits of speed towards the purest form of anticipation' (p. 76). Here Bogard is concerned with the anticipation of the real, aided by forms of diagnostic surveillance. While prediction may add an element to panopticism, simulation of the actual process of surveillance is nothing new. Indeed, Bogard seems to imply that an element of simulation is present in the panopticon, albeit he argues that the perfection of surveillance, through simulation, will lead to the elimination of the panopticon itself. This somewhat misses the point that surveillance has broader outcomes than those met by simulation. Although simulation can encourage social order and self-policing, it cannot hold individuals accountable for acts committed.

Despite these criticisms, Boyne (2000) argues that contemporary developments in screening and surveillance require the retention of elements of Foucault's (1977) work. Although some of the key ideas surrounding panopticism might be flawed, outdated, descriptions of ideal types, this does not mean that they are without contemporary value as analytical tools. After all, Foucault and Deleuze (1980, 208) note that social theory should not be approached as something to genuflect before but rather as a toolkit that is used selectively depending on the analytical task at hand. Having maintained that there remains much of critical value in Foucault's writings on panopticism, some suggestions as to how the concept might be utilised in undertaking research into school surveillance will now be explored.

Panoptic themes and surveillance in schools

Schools have a long history of monitoring students through physical observation, attendance registers, examinations, student progress reports and searches (of desks, lockers, clothes and bags). Such surveillance has recently been augmented through the introduction into schools of computer databases, internet tracking devices, plagiarism software, CCTV cameras (inside institutional grounds as well as on school buses), metal detectors and biometrics (iris, fingerprint or face recognition devices). Observational practices are rife in contemporary schools, spilling beyond the classrooms into new territories. Thus, a media arts college in Brighton was one of the first educational institutions in the UK to utilise CCTV in the circulation areas of student toilets (BBC News 1999). In Sunderland (UK), a school installed a camera using iris recognition software in the cafeteria, enabling students to automatically debit a lunch account (BBC News 2003). A school near Manchester in the UK piloted fingerprinting technology, requiring students to register for classes by pressing their index finger on a scanner system, which then logged the attendance data on a website that parents could access (Manchester Metro News 2008). A London school installed a computer system that registered everything on a student's lunch tray and sent this information to a website that parents could access to check their child's diet (UK Press Association 2009). Such technologies exert an influence, they seek to 'operate as political agents that produce social relationships . . . [they] embody rationalities and engender forms of life' (Kupchik and Monahan 2006, 624). Increasingly, students learn to watch and be watched, expecting surveillance and accepting it as a norm, as they become socialised into a 'culture of observation'.

Yet, a degree of wariness should be adopted in suggesting that such new technologies represent a radical change in surveillance practices. For, as Feeley (2003, 118) notes with reference to CCTV, it may 'represent a dramatic increase in situational social control and crime prevention, but they may be functional equivalents of other forms of informal controls that [previously] operated'. Furthermore, it should not be assumed that new observational technologies simply result in the burgeoning of school surveillance. After all, 'technological systems themselves are neither the cause nor the sum of what surveillance is today' (ICO 2006, 9). Rather there is a need to understand how such devices work, how they are used and how they influence individuals in the contexts in which they are embedded. Nevertheless it can be argued that there has been a quantitative and qualitative expansion in school observational practices in recent years, which signifies not just a 'deepening' of elements of the surveillance but also the emergence of new social processes. Given such changes, it is necessary to consider in what manner panopticism can still provide a useful framework for those researching surveillance in schools, through considering observation by others and of the self, discourse and simulation. Focusing on these areas will not only offer further theoretical insights but also provide some practical indications as to how social researchers might benefit from drawing upon panopticism in undertaking school-based research.

Observation by others and the self

Traditionally, teachers exercised social control over students through physical observation of presence, behaviour and academic output (Hall 2003). Insofar as monitoring was necessary to ensure that students had engaged with and understood key topics, such practices were embedded in the curriculum and not merely part of a disciplinary regime. In considering whether school surveillance can be described as panoptic, Gallagher (2010, 268) notes that 'the teacher's surveillance, as a discontinuous process, could not guarantee the docility of bodies in the classroom . . . surveillance was a strategy, only ever partially and temporally effective'. Yet new technologies extend both the temporal and spatial reach of teachers' surveillance practices. For example, in the US, the principal of a Biloxi elementary school declared that digital cameras in her classrooms acted like a 'truth serum', with the threat of consulting the recordings encouraging students suspected of misbehaving to 'fess up' (*New York Times* 24 September 2003). Hope (2011, 151) notes how school technicians occasionally trawled through student internet accounts and website logs to ensure that unsuitable online material had not been accessed. Furthermore, Casella (2010) describes how some US schools track students outside the institution through radio frequency identification (RFID) chips implanted in identity cards.

Whilst Foucault (1977, 201) suggests that an 'invisible' observer is a guarantee of order, with the result that 'if they are schoolchildren, there is no copying, no noise, no chatter, no waste of time', this ignores that school surveillance is rarely continuous and ubiquitous, or that students respond in a 'disciplined manner' to potential observation. Yet new surveillance technologies contain the promise of constant, albeit not omnipresent, monitoring. It is this possibility of observation that encourages students to engage in self-surveillance. Students become socialised into a culture of monitoring within schools, encouraging them to behave as a compliant subject. Central to Foucault's discussion of panopticism and power is the potential to encourage people to engage in observation of the self. Fostering the practice of self-surveillance means that external monitoring becomes 'permanent in its effects, even if it is discontinuous in its action' (Foucault 1977, 201). Thus, students who suspect that their actions are being recorded by a CCTV camera stationed in the corner of a classroom might reflect upon their own behaviour and modify it appropriately. The motivation to engage in self-surveillance should not be over-stated, however. Simon (2005) asserts that for self-policing to occur individuals must comprehend 'the rules', make 'appropriate' judgements and recognise the signs of a possible spectator. The blind, ignorant, irrational or carefree could be immune to the effects of such panoptic power. Thus the social researcher needs to consider not only how power operates through surveillance but also its limitations and the opportunities created for resistance.

Surveillance in schools does not merely focus on the body of the student. The development of online technology and complex data handling systems has led to an increase in classification systems and social sorting of information, enabling what Clarke (1992) labels as 'dataveillance'. As Selwyn (2011) infers, the increasing use of management information systems, attendance databases, online student records and Virtual Learning Environments in schools have extended institutional surveillance capabilities. The extent to which such technologies embody panoptic power is open to question. Bauman (1992) argues that databases merely confirm credibility, rather than instilling discipline. Yet in schools, databases are often linked to other disciplinary devices and practices. For example, McCahill and Finn (2010) describe how in some schools an absence in the attendance database triggers an automated text messaging system to notify parents of their child's absence. Indeed, as school databases are often connected to broader disciplinary practices, students will be aware of such monitoring and may consequently engage in self-surveillance, adjusting their behaviour to avoid drawing unwanted attention. Consequently, it can be argued that the panopticon provides a useful metaphor when considering such surveillance via school databases.

Yet, it is not only students who are confronted with this controlling gaze. Teachers are increasingly exposed to new surveillance technologies. Selwyn (2011, 478) notes how senior managers made routine use of online systems to render individual teachers' lesson plans 'open' for 'editing' and 'adjusting' by more experienced and specialised colleagues. Thus, rather than being hidden, watching from a darkened watchtower, teachers are equally on display, subjected to panoptic scrutiny. This suggests that those researching school surveillance should resist the temptation to focus exclusively on students. After all, school staff are also subject to the operation of panoptic power, ranging from student feedback forms to formal school inspections.

With regards to physical surveillance by oneself and others, the panopticon offers educational researchers a useful model in exploring how observation is exercised in schools and its extent. Perhaps more importantly it draws attention to the manner in which self-surveillance can be engendered in institutional settings. Thus a key issue for those seeking to apply Foucault's ideas would be not merely how students and staff are monitored but how such processes then encourage individuals to reflect upon and monitor their own behaviour.

Normalising discourses

The panopticon involves more than the possibility of direct supervision in an enclosed institutional setting. Foucault (1977, 195) asserts that any analysis of physical surveillance needs to be equally concerned with procedures that situate individuals in a disciplinary discourse. In schools, the wearing of standardised uniforms, observance of rules, strict use of timetables, regimented examinations and ostentatious punishments can all be seen as part of panopticism, fashioning a discourse of control. Before secondary school students are allowed to use the school internet, they are often required to sign an Acceptable Use Policy. Whilst such documents give guidance on what constitutes (un)acceptable online behaviour, they can also be seen as constructing a disciplinary discourse, seeking to influence how students perceive school cyberspace. Yet, the discourses in which observational tools become embroiled may be complex, contradictory and contested. For example, uniforms operate as instruments of control, enforcing conformity, making schools 'more orderly' as the former US president Bill Clinton famously declared. Yet in Malaysia an Islamic student group condemned uniforms worn by girls at state schools as 'sexy', declaring that such clothes encouraged rape and pre-marital sex (*Toronto Star* 2008).

Drawing upon panopticism to explore surveillance practices in schools, social researchers might consider the discourses surrounding such activities. In this context discourses can be defined as a collection of related statements that seek to control and channel behaviour. Such discourses might be found in signs, such as those in libraries requesting silence, or within school documents. They may also be aural or embodied in repeated actions, passed from one individual to the next. Focusing upon school lunches, Pike (2008, 419) noted that 'no child could scrape food into the bin and exit the dining room without being subject to surveillance by the lunchtime supervisor. Packed lunch eaters were generally required to take their waste food home in their lunchbox so that it might be monitored by parents later in the day.' In this situation, not only are students being subjected to surveillance, but there is also an underlying discourse that children should eat all the food provided and avoid waste. Thus surveillance practices can be seen as embedded in broader discourses of appropriate behaviour. Reflecting upon Foucault's work, it is important that educational researchers make such normalising discourses explicit. Only by doing so will the broader social complexities start to be exposed, giving rise to deeper, more critical understanding. Indeed, some discourses may be so deeply enshrined that individuals do not reflect on the choices that led to their acceptance. Thus, with regards to the example of school lunches, it might be asked why leaving food waste is seen as problematic. In some cultures such actions might be seen as a display of wealth or the exercise of restraint. Yet increasingly in the UK it has become accepted that schools can regulate what students eat, with teachers often confiscating junk food. Consequently, to gain a deeper understanding of school surveillance practices it is necessary to expose and explore the underlying normalising discourses.

Simulation of surveillance

Within contemporary schools, panoptic simulation of surveillance operates through simulacra and predictive data systems. Harrington (2005, 328) notes that a simulacrum can be broadly defined as a superficial, but untrue, likeness.

Thus, fake CCTV cameras in schools can encourage individuals to behave as if the technology is 'real'; at least until the deceit is exposed. At the heart of the panoptic metaphor is the idea of simulated surveillance. Although the underlying suggestion is that actual physical surveillance by others will occur intermittently, much of the power of Bentham's design rests in this uncertainty and the subsequent, at least partial, simulation of surveillance. With regards to school internet use, Hope (2011, 154) relates how a student explained that 'if you go on the internet all the time the Head he like checks it on the server. So he knows which one you've been on.' Whilst staff subsequently denied that this was the case, it was accepted that the threat that such action could be taken was sufficient to encourage students to monitor their own behaviour (Hope 2011). Such simulation lies at the heart of panoptic surveillance techniques in schools. Subsequently, researchers should consider not just the school surveillance practices that do occur but also ones whose possibility of occurrence leads to an adjustment in behaviour.

Bogard (1996) suggests that surveillance has been pushed towards simulation, anticipating reality, aided by forms of diagnostic surveillance. Such predictive systems have long existed in schools, albeit relying on teacher intuition and knowledge of students rather than complex databases. Yet, developments in computer technology and data handling software mean that the speed and reach of such systems has greatly increased. Staples (2000) observes that in 1999 the US Federal Bureau of Alcohol, Tobacco and Firearms working in association with a 'threat evaluation' company piloted a program called Mosaic 2000. This software aimed to confidentially vet and rate potentially violent students based on a series of questions drawn from case histories. In effect, such predictive processes combine all three elements of panopticism discussed above. Thus they include the monitoring of activities/data by the self/others, privilege the normalising discourse to the extent that intervention is acceptable based on probability of inappropriate behaviour rather than the action itself and ultimately seek to simulate a likely reality.

Some limitations of the panoptic model: student resistance to surveillance

Insofar as surveillance has become a characteristic of everyday life in late modernity, then so too has resistance towards it (De Certeau 2002). Whilst Foucault (1982, 245) argues that regardless of the social system 'there always remain the possibilities of resistance, disobedience and oppositional groupings', his arguments regarding resistance in the panopticon are underdeveloped. Consequently, researchers exploring panoptic surveillance practices in schools may be tempted to focus on the institutional exercise of power, ignoring how students seek to resist it. Addressing this shortcoming, this section explores student resistance to observational practices through false conformity, avoidance, counter-surveillance and playful performance. The following discussion is best understood as a development of notions that are central to a critical understanding of panopticism, rather than an outright rejection of the theory.

As schools breed cultures of resistance that have a purpose in wider society (Willis 1977), resisting school surveillance might be 'integral to the educational process' (Martin et al. 2009, 221), equipping students for future life in a surveillance-saturated society. Resistance can take diverse forms, from action that hinders or challenges unequal power relations to moments of relative freedom when the apparently powerless step outside the realities of oppression (Spencer 1996, 489). Although the resultant lack of conceptual consensus might be seen as problematic, certain common properties of resistance can nevertheless be discerned, including its socially constructed nature, its interactional character, the central role of power and its complex dynamic (Hollander and Einwohner 2004, 548). Such considerations suggest that the study of resistance should be situational, contextual and historically specific (Fernandez and Huey 2009, 200).

For the social researcher, intentional feigned conformity is not easy to identify or differentiate from similar responses arising from apathy. Yet, faked compliance might mask resistance to institutional observation, after all 'refusal is a broad term that . . . may also involve feigned participation' (Marx 2003, 382). Hence, Bash et al. (1985) argue that it is possible to resist through conformity, suggesting that such an action would be passive rather than active. Moreover, Simon (2005) notes that if individuals perform compliance, surveillance may not be able to distinguish between acceptance and refusal. Panoptic technologies are challenged by feigned conformity and the limitations of observational systems to facilitate social integration exposed (Simon 2005). There exist empirical difficulties in exposing such strategies, particularly if the primary data collection method is some form of observation. Thankfully if anonymity is guaranteed, students can often be forthright with researchers in interviews. Nevertheless, the researcher needs to engage with this issue and consider whether what looks like conformity with school surveillance practices is actually feigned compliance.

Avoidance of surveillance in schools is much easier than it would be in Foucault's model of the panopticon. In educational institutions, surveillance coverage is unlikely to be universal or constant. Hence, certain school spaces may be less monitored, particularly outside lesson times. For example, over the course of a week Hope (2011, 157) watched three Year 8 students utilising the internet in a secondary school Learning Resource Centre (LRC). On a Friday evening, when the LRC was unsupervised, the students were seen exploring a website called Poo III, which featured verse and pictures 'dedicated to defecation'. This illustrates that students might wait for windows of opportunity in which to misbehave. Of course, there is the possibility that such overt resistance strategies might be avoided if the students are aware that a researcher is observing them. Nevertheless, as the above example aptly illustrates, once students have established that any observer will not intervene or punish them, then they often do not adjust their behaviour.

Referring to the growing potential to use new surveillance technologies to observe those in authority, Man et al. (2003) draw attention to what they refer to as 'sousveillance', the use of observational devices to mirror and confront the monitoring processes undertaken by institutions. This strategy is not concerned with circumventing surveillance but rather directly confronting it through ostentatiously watching the watchers. Websites such as Rate My Teachers provide an online area in which students can post material, potentially exposing staff to a worldwide gaze. Steeves (2010, 94) relates two incidents in Quebec Province, Canada, where students provoked teachers into losing their temper, recorded the occurrence on their mobile phones and uploaded the images onto *YouTube*. Furthermore, Weiss (2010) draws attention to students writing about their experiences of school surveillance, arguing that such creative practices can work as a vital form of sousveillance. Insofar as such material may be published on the internet – for example, on Facebook or other social networking sites – it could be argued that observation and online discussion of school staff surveillance activities may become increasingly significant as a form of resistance. In the panopticon, the prisoner is merely an object to be surveilled. Yet in schools the observer is often also on display. In this context, the educational researcher should not just focus on the 'controlling gaze' of those in authority but also on students watching staff. This highlights the importance of considering the complex 'surveillant assemblage' in schools and not merely restricting analysis to a simple two-actor model.

While the metaphors of both panopticism and the synopticon are useful in considering contemporary power relations and offer an account of why people are 'surveillance tolerant', they also highlight a purpose of surveillance that is absent from much discussion of Foucault's work. Namely, that surveillance is not just concerned with discipline and control but also with performance, entertainment and play. Driven by the popularity of reality television programmes, there has been a growth in the contemporary culture of surveillance, generating 'a new savvy, even blasé attitude to surveillance, which sees its potential entertainment value' (Bell 2009, 209). Thus, rather than trying to become invisible to surveillance, many people are actually seeking to increase their exposure 'playing with, goading and yes, even flirting with surveillance' (Bell 2009, 211). Students may playfully confront surveillance in schools, seeking to be seen. Hope (2010, 330) relates how a female Year 10 student used a camera phone to record herself and a friend drinking alcopops in the toilets of a local shopping centre. This video was then posted by the student on the YouTube website. In publicly displaying her actions, the student was arguably seeking to construct a particular identity, one that was in conflict with the character that school surveillance discourses might seek to foster. This reflects Bell's (2009) argument that a 'hijacking' of the dominant uses of surveillance is possible, with voyeurism and exhibitionism acting as forms of resistance, raising the possibility of new and varied ways of (re)configuring the 'algebra of surveillance', allowing individuals to perform surveillance in ways that seek to take back control. Whilst surveillance can be playful, so too can the act of resisting it. As Marx (2009, 299) suggests, defying observation can be 'a dynamic adversarial social dance involving strategic moves and counter-moves, it has the quality of an endless chess game mixing old and new moves'. Indeed, young people might feel the need to draw attention to and celebrate their inappropriate behaviour, sating their need to flaunt these acts of resistance. Incidents of students 'playing' with school surveillance abound. In one UK secondary school a Year 12 male student discovered a friend's internet password, used it to log on to the school network, found an unfiltered pornographic website, printed an explicit image and left it for a member of staff to find, before ultimately confessing to the deception (Hope 2007, 94). In such instances playful public performance becomes more important than avoiding punishment. After all, without the engagement of an audience the whole experience might prove less gratifying. Whilst such acts of resistance may share certain outcomes with risk taking, namely engendering excitement, fostering identity formation, facilitating skilled performance and traversing boundaries, they might also have a significant symbolic function. Thus the panoptic gaze may be offered up as an object for critical public contemplation, whilst existing power relations are mocked. Consequently, educational researchers should consider the entertainment value of both surveillance and resistance to it.

Conclusion

Although critics suggest that the panopticon has come to exert an oppressive influence as the dominant model of surveillance, its value cannot be contested. As an ideal type it offers numerous insights for educational researchers studying school surveillance practices. It highlights the importance, not merely of the act of watching, but also of self-surveillance, normalising discourses and simulation. Whilst Foucault's discussion of the panopticon is underdeveloped in certain areas, such as on the topic of resistance, it nevertheless provides a convincing analysis of the operation of disciplinary power, which continues to assist and inspire social researchers.

References

Bash, L., D. Coulby and C. Jones. 1985. *Urban schooling: Theory and practice.* London: Holt, Rinehart and Winston.

Bauman, Z. 1992. *Intimations of postmodernity.* London: Routledge.

BBC News. 1999. School puts spy cameras in toilets. 5 November. http://news.bbc. co.uk/1/hi/education/506140.stm.

BBC News. 2003. Eye scan school opens doors. 17 September. http://news.bbc. co.uk/1/hi/england/wear/3115428.stm.

Bell, D. 2009. Surveillance is sexy. *Surveillance and Society* 6, 3: 203–212.

Bogard, W. 1996. *The simulation of surveillance.* Cambridge: Cambridge University Press.

Boyne, R. 2000. Post-Panopticism. *Economy and Society* 29, 2: 285–307.

Casella, R. 2010. Safety or social control? The security fortification of schools in a capitalist society. In *Schools under surveillance: Cultures of control in public education,* ed. T. Monahan and R. Torres, 73–86. New York: Rutgers University Press.

Clarke, R. 1992. The resistible rise of the national personal data system. *Software Law Journal* 5, 1: 25–59.

De Certeau, M. 2002. *The practice of everyday life*. Berkeley: University of California Press.

Doyle, A. 2011. Revisiting the synopticon: Reconsidering Mathiesen's 'The Viewer Society' in the age of Web 2.0. *Theoretical Criminology* 15, 3: 283–299.

Feeley, M. 2003. Crime, social order and the rise of neo-Conservative politics. *Theoretical Criminology* 7, 1: 111–130.

Fernandez, L. A. and L. Huey. 2009. Is resistance futile? Thoughts on resisting surveillance. *Surveillance & Society* 6, 3: 198–202.

Foucault, M. 1977. *Discipline and punish: The birth of the prison*. London: Allen Lane.

Foucault, M. 1982. Space, knowledge and power. In *The Foucault reader: An introduction to Foucault's thought*, ed. P. Rabinow, 239–256. London: Penguin.

Foucault, M. and G. Deleuze. 1980. Intellectuals & power: A conversation between Michel Foucault and Giles Deleuze. In *Language, counter-memory, practice: Selected essays and interviews by Michel Foucault*, ed. D. F. Bouchard, 205–217. Ithaca, NY: Cornell University Press.

Gallagher, M. 2010. Are schools panoptic? *Surveillance & Society* 7, 3–4: 262–272.

Haggerty, K. D. and R. V. Ericson. 2000. The surveillant assemblage. *British Journal of Sociology* 51, 4: 605–622.

Hall, N. 2003. The role of the slate in Lancastrian schools as evidenced by their manuals and handbooks. *Paradigm* 2, 7: 46–54.

Harrington, A. ed. 2005. *Modern social theory: An introduction*. Oxford: Oxford University Press.

Hier, S. 2003. Probing the surveillant assemblage: On the dialectics of surveillance practices as processes of social control. *Surveillance & Society* 1, 3: 399–411.

Hollander, J. A. and R. L. Einwohner. 2004. Conceptualizing resistance. *Sociological Forum* 19, 4: 533–554.

Hope, A. 2007. Risk-taking, boundary-performance and intentional school internet 'misuse'. *Discourse: Studies in the cultural politics of education* 28, 1: 87–99.

Hope, A. 2010. Student resistance to the surveillance curriculum. *International Studies in Sociology of Education* 20, 4: 319–334.

Hope, A. 2011. *Internet risk @ school: Cultures of control in state education*. Saarbrucken: Lambert Press.

ICO (Information Commissioners Office). 2006. A Report on the Surveillance Society. www.ico.gov.uk/upload/documents/library/data_protection/practical_ application/surveillance_society_full_report_2006.pdf.

Koskela, H. 2003. 'Cam era' – the contemporary urban panopticon. *Surveillance & Society* 1, 3: 292–313.

Kuehn, L. 2008. Surveillance 2.0: The 'information panopticon' and education. *Our schools/our selves*. 1 July, 81–91. www.policyalternatives.ca/sites/default/files/ uploads/publications/Our_Schools_Ourselve/10_Kuehn_surveillance_2.pdf.

Kupchik, A. and T. Monahan. 2006. The new American school: Preparation for post-industrial discipline. *British Journal of Sociology of Education* 27, 5: 617–631.

Lyon, D. 1994. *The electronic eye: The rise of surveillance society*. Cambridge: Polity Press.

Lyon, D. 2001. *Surveillance society: Monitoring everyday life*. Buckingham: Open University Press.

Lyon, D. 2003. Surveillance as social sorting: Computer codes and mobile bodies. In *Surveillance as social sorting: Privacy, risk and digital discrimination*, ed. D. Lyon, 13–30. London: Routledge.

Man, S., J. Nolan and B. Wellman. 2003. Sousveillance: Inventing and using wearable computing devices for data collection in surveillance environments. *Surveillance & Society* 1, 3: 331–355.

Manchester Metro News. 2008. *Fingerprint scheme launched by school*. 15 February.

Markus, T. A. 1993. *Buildings and power*. London: Routledge.

Martin, A. K., R. E. van Brakel and D. J. Bernhard. 2009. Understanding resistance to digital surveillance: Towards a multi-disciplinary, multi-actor framework. *Surveillance & Society* 6, 3: 213–232.

Marx, G. 1988. *Undercover: Police surveillance in America*. Berkeley, CA: University of California Press.

Marx, G. 2003. A tack in the shoe: Neutralising and resisting the new surveillance. *Journal of Social Issues* 59, 2: 369–390.

Marx, G. 2009. A tack in the shoe and taking off the shoe: Neutralization and counter-neutralization dynamics. *Surveillance & Society* 6, 3: 294–306.

Mathiesen, T. 1997. The viewer society. *Theoretical Criminology* 1, 2: 215–234.

McCahill, M. and R. Finn. 2010. The social impact of surveillance in three UK schools: 'Angels', 'devils' and 'teen mums'. *Surveillance & Society* 7, 3–4: 273–289.

New York Times. 2003. *Cameras watching students, especially in Biloxi*. 24 September.

Norris, C. 2003. From personal to digital: CCTV, the panopticon, and the technological mediation of suspicion and social control. In *Surveillance as social sorting: Privacy, risk and digital discrimination*, ed. D. Lyon, 249–281. London: Routledge.

Norris, C. and G. Armstrong. 1999. *The maximum surveillance society: The rise of CCTV*. Oxford: Berg.

Pike, J. 2008. Foucault, space and primary school dining rooms. *Children's Geographies* 6, 4: 413–422.

Poster, M. 1989. *Critical theory and poststructuralism: In search of a context*. Ithaca, NY: Cornell University Press.

Poster, M. 1990. *Mode of information: Poststructuralism and social context*. Cambridge: Polity Press.

Poster, M. 1995. *The second media age*. Cambridge: Polity Press.

Selwyn, N. 2000. The National Grid for Learning: Panacea or panopticon? *British Journal of Sociology of Education* 21, 2: 243–255.

Selwyn, N. 2011. 'It's all about standardisation' – Exploring the digital (re) configuration of school management and administration. *Cambridge Journal of Education* 41, 4: 473–488.

Simon, B. 2005. The return of panopticism: Supervision, subjection and the new surveillance. *Surveillance & Society* 3, 1: 1–20.

Spencer, J. 1996. Resistance. In *Encyclopedia of social and cultural anthropology*, ed. A. Barnard and J. Spencer, 489. London: Routledge.

Staples, W. G. 2000. *Everyday surveillance: Vigilance and visibility in postmodern life*. Oxford: Rowman & Littlefield Publishers Inc.

Steeves, V. 2010. Online surveillance in Canadian schools. In *Schools under surveillance: Cultures of control in public education*, ed. T. Monahan and R. Torres, 87–103. New York: Rutgers University Press.

Toronto Star. 2008. *School Uniform Sexy Says Group*. 22 May. http://thestar.com. my/news/story.asp?file=/2008/5/22/nation/21326822&sec=nation.

UK Press Association. 2009. *School dinners spy website launched*. 8 October. http:// latestnews.virginmedia.com/news/tech/2009/10/08/school_dinners_spy_ website_launched.

Weiss, J. 2010. Scan this: Examining student resistance to surveillance. In *Schools under surveillance: Cultures of control in public education*, ed. T. Monahan and R. Torres, 213–229. New York: Rutgers University Press.

Willis, P. 1977. *Learning to labour: How working class kids get working class jobs*. Farnham: Ashgate.

Yar, M. 2003. Panoptic power and the pathologisation of vision: Critical reflections on the Foucauldian thesis. *Surveillance & Society* 1, 3: 254–271.

Chapter 4

Foucault, confession and reflective practices

Andreas Fejes

[T]he confession became one of the West's most highly valued techniques for producing truth. We have since become a singularly confessing society . . . Western man has become a confessing animal.

(Foucault 1998, 59)

In this chapter, I will argue that the contemporary society can be conceptualised as a confessing society by drawing on Foucault's writing on confession, technologies of power and technologies of the self (cf. Fejes and Dahlstedt 2012). One of the primary arguments made by Foucault (1998) is that verbalisation has become a central method through which people make themselves visible to themselves and to others and that people come to know who they are through verbalisation. In his writing, psychoanalysis is used as an example of how previous Christian practices of confession have become appropriated by a secular *scientia sexualis* (Foucault 1998), which has spread to most aspects of private life. In this context, confession does not specifically limit itself to the confession taking place in church, but also signifies the most private and intimate relationships that we have with our lovers, family, friends, and with ourselves. Confession has become scientised.

By drawing on a research project focused on the ways in which care workers within elderly care are fabricated through different technologies that operate within an in-service training programme, I will illustrate how confession is a powerful technology that shapes the self. I will specifically focus on how confession, as a technology of the self, operates through reflective techniques and reflective practices mobilised within and constructed by the in-service training programme.

In the following section, Foucault's genealogy of confession is introduced which will serve as a starting point in a discussion about how confession operates within reflective techniques used within the in-service training programme. The chapter ends with a discussion.

Foucault and confession

In this section, I will present Foucault's (1998, 2003a, 2003b, 2005) genealogy of confession. A genealogy questions the constant search for origins and beginnings or for truths about human nature or the world; it questions the search for essence and stability. The starting point is rather to destabilise and question the taken-for-granted ways in which we think and go about doing things in the present day. A genealogy acknowledges that histories are not objective and that the author cannot detach herself from the discourses in which she is part.

Authors conducting genealogical analyses provide one possible story to tell about our present, which aims to illustrate how the present is not a logical or deterministic effect of the past. The present is rather an accidental construction composed of diverging elements with different historical trajectories. The focus of the genealogist is to trace the descent and emergence of the ideas that are taken for granted in the present so as to disrupt, question and destabilise the present and so that people '"no longer know what to do", so that the acts, gestures, discourses which up until then had seemed to go without saying become problematic, difficult, dangerous' (Foucault 1991, 84). This ambition is political because the aim is to open up a space to live the present otherwise. Such ambition of the author does not mean, however, that the genealogist is aiming to provide another universal truth or meta-narrative of the present or to define what is good or bad; rather, the aim is to provide alternatives to the present.

Foucault argued that the focus of his genealogical work was to

> create a history of the different modes by which, in our culture, human beings are made subjects. My work has dealt with three modes of objectification that transforms the human beings into subjects. The first is the modes of inquiry that try to give themselves the status of sciences . . . In the second part of my work, I have studied the objectivizing of the subject in what I shall call 'dividing practices' . . . Finally, I have sought to study – it is my current work – the way a human being turns him-herself into a subject.
>
> (Foucault 2003d, 126)

Thus, for Foucault there is no project of trying to construct a general history of the human subject. People have been represented as subjects in a whole variety of ways throughout history. Instead, the focus is to try to map out and to make visible the discursive conditions which make possible the emergence of specific subjectivities, the technologies which operate to shape such subjectivities and the practices in which we turn ourselves into what is deemed desirable – to govern ourselves – the conduct of conduct. In his writing, the focus was on analysing the technologies of power and domination and technologies of the self. The former concerns the practices through which the self is objectified and shaped through dividing practices while the latter concerns the ways in which the self constitutes itself as a subject:

> Technologies of power, which determine the conduct of individuals and submit them to certain ends or domination, and objectivising of the subject . . . technologies of the self, which permits individuals to effect by their own

means, or with the help of others, a certain number of operations on their own bodies and souls, thoughts, conduct, and way of being, so as to transform themselves in order to attain a certain state of happiness, purity, wisdom, perfection, or immortality.

(Foucault 2003a, 146)

These technologies seldom function separately; rather, the encounter between the two is what Foucault called governmentality. Thus, the researcher needs to consider both types of technologies, although Foucault turned his attention to the technologies of the self in his later writing. In the next section, I will turn to the issue of the technologies of the self and, specifically, to the technology of confession.

Confession

The confession is a ritual of discourse in which the speaking subject is also the subject of the statement; it is also a ritual that unfolds within a power relationship, for one does not confess without the presence (or virtual presence) of a partner who is not simply the interlocutor but the authority who requires the confession, prescribes and appreciates it and intervenes in order to judge, punish, forgive, console and reconcile.

(Foucault 1998, 61–62)

A central focus in Foucault's writings was on games of truth. In his later writing (e.g., Foucault 2005), games of truth were seen as ascetic practices of self-formation. 'Ascetic' means 'the subject's attainment of a certain mode of being and the transformations that the subject must carry out on itself to attain this mode of being' (Foucault 2003c, 36). Here, it is not about the liberation of the 'true' self because this would mean that there is a hidden self that can be found through practices of liberation. Instead, it is about ontology, that is, the processes of self-formation. Therefore, the interest in analysing games of truth is related here to the practices of self-formation. As a way to analyse self-formation, Foucault conducted a genealogy of the care of the self, where he turned his attention to the Greco-Roman period and to the emergence of Christianity (Foucault 2005).

In his genealogy of the care of the self, the relationship between the Delphic statement *know yourself* and the Greek practice of *care of the self* is important. During the Greco-Roman period, the former was seen as a consequence of the latter while, in the case of Christianity, the former has obscured the latter. Self-renunciation came to be the condition for salvation. To renounce oneself, one had to know oneself. Foucault (2003a, 149) argued that: '"know thyself" has obscured "take care of the self" because our morality, a morality of asceticism, insists that the self is that which one can reject'. From Descartes to Husserl, the subject of thinking is the first step in the theory of knowledge. Therefore, in the modern world, knowledge of the self becomes the fundamental principle in a theory of knowledge. In the following, I will first present the idea of the care of the self as construed during the Greco-Roman period, with a particular focus on the Stoics. Second, I will present the emergence of confession within Christianity.

Care of the self during the Greco-Roman period

During the Greco-Roman period, care of the self became a universal philosophical principle. To care for the self was to make life into an object of an art, namely, a tekhne. To care for the self was about existence. Here, the care of the self became the care of the soul, but only insofar as it was the care of the activity and not of the soul as a substance. For example, among the Stoics, the concept of life as an art meant retiring into the self and staying there. The aim was to develop good values in life and not to develop these values aimed at a life after death, as occurred later in Christianity.

Writing became an important technique in this endeavour. Taking notes on oneself and about the activities of the day (to be reread) and keeping notebooks was a way 'to reactivate for oneself the truths one needed' (Foucault 2003a, 153). Through this writing, the subject becomes the object of the writing activity, which indicates that this trait (writing) is not a modern trait. According to Foucault (2003a), writing is one of the most ancient Western traditions. However, this type of activity is not about knowing oneself and finding the truth about oneself as in Christianity. Instead, writing was about finding the truths that one needs to turn life into an art of existence.

With a writing activity, an examination of conscience emerges. For the Stoics, this examination related to a self-examination of the deeds of the day. However, the writer was not looking for bad intentions, as was done later in Christianity. Faults were simply good intentions left undone. Here, people became their own administrators and looked at what they had done correctly with the aim of finding the lack of success instead of finding faults. Errors concerned strategy and not moral character. The goal was to find out how to be successful in one's intentions and not to excavate guilt as in the Christian confession. 'In Christian confession, the penitent is obliged to memorize laws but does so in order to discover his sins' (Foucault 2003a, 157). Among the Stoics, it was not about discovering the truth in the subject but about remembering the truth or recovering a truth that had been forgotten. Subjects do not forget themselves, but forget the rules of conduct and what ought to be done. The recollection of the errors committed measured the gap between what had been done and what should have been done. For example, Foucault referred to the nightly self-examination conducted by Seneca, not with guilt, but with aesthetic pleasure and serenity, aiming to find the truth he needed to turn life into an art. Modern confessants also take pleasure in their confessions, but they are less calm and are often followed by displeasure. Through the use of writing, Seneca managed to reach self-mastery, where he self-monitored without the need of an other. He focused on the truths needed for an art of life, and these truths were not hidden from him or within him as in Christian confession; rather, they were accessible to him (cf. Taylor 2010). Thus, we can see how self-regulation became an important aspect in the art of life where the focus was on the activities and deeds of individuals rather than on their thoughts. As I will illustrate later, this focus is different from that in Christianity, where the focus came to be on thoughts and about verbalising and making visible one's own sins.

Aside from the technologies of writing and self-examination, there was a third Stoic technique for the care of the self, namely, askesis. Askesis was 'not a disclosure of the secret self but a remembering' (Foucault 2003a, 158). The truth is not to be found within the self, but in the teachings of the master. What one hears is memorised and turned into rules of conduct. The aim here was a subjectivation of truth. In Christianity, asceticism instead referred to a renunciation of the self and of reality as a way to find another level of reality. Among the Stoics, there was no renunciation of the self. Instead, askesis was

> the progressive consideration of the self, or mastery over oneself, obtained not through the renunciation of reality but through the acquisition and assimilation of truth. It has as its final aim not preparation for another reality but access to the reality of this world.
>
> (p. 158)

The exercises connected to askesis tested whether the person was prepared to confront events with the truths he/she had assimilated. Melete was meditation that, through dialogue with one's thoughts, resulted in the anticipation of real situations. Meditation tested your preparedness for different situations in life. Gymnasia, 'to train oneself' (p. 159), referred to physical exercise in real situations. Gymnasia could be about 'sexual abstinence, physical privation and other rituals of purification' that had the aim 'to establish and test the independence of the individual with regard to the external world' (p. 159).

In summary, we can see how the Stoics construed care of the self as an activity that required listening and the remembering of rules. These activities were methods of preparing for life as an art as a way to reach self-mastery. The technologies of writing, self-examination and askesis were used as methods to care for the self, which, in turn, trained oneself for life. As will be illustrated in the next section, these techniques were also important in conjunction with the emergence of Christianity, although they were different with different effects in terms of shaping subjectivity.

Christianity and the emergence of confession

With Christianity as it emerged in the third and fourth centuries AD, the care of the self was reconceptualised. The care of the self was no longer about creating the self as an art or as existence. Instead, everyone had a duty to know who they were, to search oneself and acknowledge one's faults, to recognise temptations, and to locate desires, for example; one needed to disclose these things either to God or to the others in the community and thus bear public or private witness against oneself. 'The truth obligations of faith and the self are linked together. This link permits a purification of the soul impossible without self-knowledge' (Foucault 2003a, 162). Although there are many differences between the Catholic and the Reformist traditions, both consist of the need for the purification of the soul as a consequence of self-knowledge and as a condition for understanding the Holy Text.

Among the Stoics, the problem of aesthetics concerned existence. With the emergence of Christianity, the problem of aesthetics became linked to the question of purity. The reason for care of the self was to keep the self pure. Physical integrity rather than self-regulation became important. The self was no longer something to be created (art of living) but rather something to be renounced and deciphered. In Christianity, writing became a test that 'brings into light the movements of thought, it dissipates the inner shadow where the enemy's plots are woven' (Foucault 2003b, 121). In other words, in Christianity, writing was used to find the truth about one's self as a way in which to access the light, which was accomplished by making one's inner thoughts visible (disclosing one's self). For the Stoics, writing was used to constitute the self by writing down the truths of the masters and by keeping notebooks on the deeds of the day, which were then the subjects of meditation.

During early Christian times, disclosure of the self was conducted through the ritual of exomologesis, which 'was a ritual of recognising oneself as a sinner and penitent' (Foucault 2003a, 162). The bishop was asked to impose the status of a penitent upon the individual. This act in relation to the bishop was not a confession but only a ritual whereby the status of the sinner was made public and confirmed. Thus, exomologesis was a status, rather than an act. The sinner was then, over a period of several years, required to make visible her/his sins through self-punishment, suffering, shame and humility. Here, we can see that what was private among the Stoics (meditating about the activities of the day) became public. Through the ritual of exomologesis, the sinner erased her/his sins and restored the purity acquired through baptism at the same time as her/his status as a sinner was confirmed. Exomologesis 'was not a way for the sinner to explain his sins but a way to present himself as a sinner' (p. 163). Exomologesis thus has similarities with the relationship between a physician and a patient, where the patient needs to show his/her wounds to acquire the status as wounded before healing can take place.

This paradox of confirming one's status as a sinner and erasing one's sins at the same time was most commonly explained by the model of death, torture and martyrdom. Within this model, the sinner would die rather than abandon her/his faith. The sinner demonstrates being able to renounce both life and the self.

The difference between the Stoic and Christian traditions is that in the Stoic tradition examination of self, judgement and discipline show the way to self-knowledge by superimposing truth about self through memory, that is, by memorising the rules. In exomologesis, the penitent superimposes truth about self by violent rupture and disassociation. It is important to emphasise that this exomologesis is not verbal. It is symbolic, ritual and theatrical (Foucault 2003a, 164).

During the fourth century, exagoreusis emerged as another technology for the disclosure of the self. Exagoreusis was a form of self-examination that was related to two principles of Christian spirituality: obedience and contemplation. Obedience for the monk was the total obedience to the rules and to the master, in comparison to the instrumental and professional relationship between the master and the disciple among the Stoics. In exagoreusis, every act that was conducted without the permission of the master was seen as a theft. Exagoreusis was about the sacrifice of the self, of the subject's own will, which was a new technology of the self. 'The self must constitute itself through obedience' (p. 165).

The second aspect of exagoreusis was contemplation, which was seen as the supreme good. It was the obligation of the monk to turn his thoughts continuously to that point that was God and to make sure that his heart was pure enough to see God. The goal was the permanent contemplation of God. This contemplation was directed towards present thoughts and not on the past actions of the day as with the Stoics. The monk needed to scrutinise his thoughts to see which thoughts were directed towards God and which were not:

> The scrutiny of conscience consists of trying to immobilize consciousness, to eliminate movements of the spirit which diverts from God. That means we must examine any thought that presents itself to consciousness to see the relation between act and thought, truth and reality, to see if there is anything in this thought which will move our spirit, provoke our desire, turn our spirit away from God. The scrutiny is based on the idea of a secret concupiscence.
> (Foucault 2003a, 165–166)

Thus, we can see how the emergence of Christianity led self-examination to be construed differently from how it had been construed by the Stoics. Among the Stoics, self-examination concerned the way in which thoughts related to the rules and to actions of the day. Among the Christians, the examination of self was focused on the relationship between hidden thoughts and an inner impurity. 'At this moment begins the Christian hermeneutics of the self with its deciphering of inner thoughts. It implies that there is something hidden in ourselves and that we are always in a self-illusion that hides the secret' (p. 166).

As a way of conducting this type of scrutiny, we had to 'care for ourselves, to attest to our thoughts this kind of scrutiny' (p. 166). One way to attest to our thoughts was to be the permanent moneychanger of ourselves, and the changer was conscience. Our inner thoughts needed to be scrutinised to determine whether they were good or bad in the same way in which the moneychanger examines coins, that is, where did the coin come from? Do the thoughts come from God or the Devil? What is the quality of the coins/thoughts? There was only one way to discriminate between good and bad thoughts: 'to tell all thought to our director, to be obedient to our master in all things, to engage in the permanent verbalisation of all our thoughts' (p. 166). Confession can thus be seen as a mark of truth, and it allows the master to discriminate between good and evil. Even if the master did not respond, 'the fact that the thought has been expressed will have an effect of discrimination' (p. 167). By verbally confessing, the Devil might leave the person who confesses. Without verbalisation, we cannot truly discriminate between good and evil.

As has been illustrated, there is a big difference between exomologesis and exagoreusis; however, what they have in common is that the person cannot make a disclosure without renouncing. The practices of exomologesis and exagoreusis continued until the seventeenth century. However, as argued by Foucault (2003a), the relationship between the disclosure of the self and the drama of the verbalised renunciation of the self is important throughout Christianity. However, today, he argued, verbalisation has become the most important action.

> From the eighteenth century to the present, the techniques of verbalization have been reinserted in a different context by so-called human sciences in order to use them without renunciation of the self but to constitute, positively, a new self. To use these techniques without renouncing oneself constitutes a decisive break.
>
> (Foucault 2003a, 167)

Thus, in contemporary times, we can see how confession has become linked to science and thus has become scientised 'through clinical codifications, personal examinations, histological techniques, the general documentation and data collection of personal data, the proliferation of interpretative schemas and the development of a whole host of therapeutic techniques for "normalization"' (Besley and Peters 2007, 16). Verbalisation has become linked to science and reinvented as a 'scientific' practice that promises to help us live a better life. This scientisation construes confession as an interface between the public and private domains where confession always requires an other, either real or virtual, to whom one confesses (cf. Foucault 1998).

Confession, reflection and reflective practices

Reflection and reflective practice have become a conspicuous part of education and work life, in part due to the publication of two books by Donald Schön, namely, *The Reflective Practitioner* (1983) and *Educating the Reflective Practitioner* (1987). Schön offered a specific epistemology of practice that draws on examples of practitioners within different professional fields. Schön's work has given rise to a wide debate regarding the concepts of reflection and reflective practices. He has been criticised for providing a concept of reflection that is too vague, and the practical applicability of his theory has been questioned (cf. Erlandsson 2006). Other researchers have provided alternative theories on reflection (cf. Boud et al. 1985; Handal and Lauvås 1987) even though they recognise Schön as an important figure in the development of these alternative theories (Erlandsson and Beach 2008). Despite these critiques, Schön's work is part of a wider discourse that has spread across a range of different practices during recent decades within education and work.

We can see how reflection and reflective practices were an important part of an in-service training programme within elderly care work in Sweden, where the goal was to raise the formal competencies of those people working in the elderly care field to allow them to be employed as licensed practical nurses (LPNs) instead of as care workers through the recognition of prior learning (RPL). During work time, care workers participated in the programme where their knowledge was recognised by teachers working within formal adult education. To recognise prior learning and to create spaces for further learning, two pedagogical techniques were mobilised in the programme: learning conversations and log-books. These techniques will serve here as examples of how technologies of power and of the self are at play, with a specific focus on the technology of confession. The data consists of interview transcripts from interviews with managers, supervisors, teachers and participants in the programme. The interview data draws on a larger research project focused on analysing how subjects are shaped in the intersection between work and education, specifically elderly care work (for more information about the project and the empirical data see Fejes 2008, 2010, 2011, 2012; Fejes and Nicoll 2010, 2011).

Learning conversations and technologies of power

Learning conversations were a central pedagogic practice used in the training programme as a method of developing the care workers' abilities to reflect on their work experiences. These conversations were designed in the following manner: five to eight care workers participated in a one-hour seminar that was led by a teacher or a supervisor (a person who worked in the same nursing home as the participants but who was engaged to support them in their assessment and learning process). At the beginning of the seminar, the teacher or the supervisor would raise a problem of current interest in the nursing home. Each person was then invited to reflect on this problem for five to ten minutes and to take notes about their reflections.

This activity was followed by an invitation to share their reflections with the rest of the group. After each person had shared his/her reflections, a discussion took place. During these learning conversations, there was also a passive person present (one of the supervisors or teachers who was not leading the seminar) who took notes about the discussions. At the end of the seminar, he/she provided a reflection on the similarities and differences between the experiences and opinions raised during the discussions. The main aim of these conversations was to engage the care workers in reflection about how to develop their work practice while also assessing them in relation to the curriculum of the health care programme. The goal was also to implement these conversations as a tool that the nursing home could use in the future to develop quality of care and the competencies among its employees.

The focus on the experiences and reflections of the care workers is emphasised by one of the supervisors in the following quotation, where she describes her role as the seminar leader:

> The important thing is to be neutral in the discussions, at the same time as being active. That is my role during learning conversations. Then it is not about my opinions and beliefs but about what others believe and think and to raise their knowledge and make it visible. And that is what I believe we have – that kind of strength. I'm very grateful to have learnt this technique of learning conversation.
>
> (Megan)

In this mobilisation of learning conversations, reflection is construed as a desirable activity that should produce better care work and nursing performance. As we can see, reflection is also construed as desirable both by groups and by individuals themselves because each individual needs to prepare on their own at the beginning of the seminar, and they need to make their reflections visible in relation to other individuals' reflections. This reflective practice is seen as making it possible to discuss and solve the problems faced at work. The idea is that people can learn from each other and that learning conversations are seen as a tool that can enhance work practices in the future, as explained by one of the managers:

> I was thinking, that in some way you could – through supervision, through these techniques – through them create those opportunities for the reflection we often lack. With a deeper cultivation of these questions which are problematic – questions that we have here every day at our nursing home. It is a way of raising the issues . . . the knowledge which is actually here already. Instead of searching for it outside.
>
> (Miriam)

Here, the idea is to use the knowledge that is already available at the nursing home, that is, the knowledge that the care workers already have. To use this knowledge, it needs to be made visible, and a learning conversation is one practice where this happens. Through this reflective practice, the individual is encouraged to contribute his/her knowledge. By making one's knowledge visible by verbalising themselves to others, the health care assistants (HCAs) are objectified and made visible for scrutiny and assessment, that is, they make their experiences available for others to engage in. The process is constitutive; by the act of reflecting, the HCA becomes constituted as a reflective practitioner.

The learning conversation encourages verbalisation to others. The care workers identify problems at work and propose solutions based on their experience. However, there is no deciphering of the self in which the participants gaze towards their inner selves and make the truth about their selves visible to others; rather, they are encouraged to state facts about problems and to identify solutions. The conversations are monitored by a teacher, and the participants know that they are being assessed on the basis of what they say. There is an examination of the participants, and they are encouraged to draw on their experience to provide good examples and the correct solutions to problems. Drawing from their own experience might provide remuneration in passing the course and getting a good grade. The carers are here objectified, measured and assessed by others and by themselves; thus, technologies of power and, to some extent, technologies of the self are in play. Learning conversations, however, might move into a confessional mode if the participants feel obliged and encouraged to speak of their true inner self to the others. This mode might occur if they raise issues from their log-books, which is further elaborated in the next section.

Log-books and technologies of the self

All the HCAs participating in the programme were encouraged to keep a log-book in which they took notes about how they perceived what they were doing during the programme. These notes could include any reflections they had, and they were not required to share the log-books with anyone else. As expressed by one of the teachers:

> We encouraged them to write a log each week. Just to write what they think about the past week, personal things.
>
> (Sandy)

However, the teachers also encouraged the participants to raise issues from the log-books during the learning conversations, although this was voluntary. One of the supervisors explained the uses of the log-book as follows:

> We have a log-book that everyone should take notes in. And if someone believes they have written something good or if they have any queries about, then they can raise that during our sessions . . . there are questions in the log-book that you can. Or, think! Thoughts, so you can think really. Write your thoughts in the log-book concerning things you can do to pay attention to your own way of communicating and collaborating in the job. So, then you need to think and then write.
>
> (Helen)

What is emphasised is every individuals' ability to reflect on their own progress in the training programme or on any other issue related to their learning process.

Through the log-book, the care workers are encouraged to take responsibility for their own learning, which is made possible through individual reflection. Here, the log-book is mobilised as a confessional technique in which the participants verbalise to themselves in relation to themselves. The participants are expected to keep a log-book that contains 'personal things' and encompasses 'their own way of communicating'. It is not expected that what is written will be read by anyone else if the participants do not wish to raise any issues from their own log-books. However, the participants know that they can raise issues from the log-book at forthcoming learning conversations and thus increase their chances of receiving a good grade. Thus, the contents of these books are addressed not only to themselves but could also be addressed to their teachers and colleagues.

This writing is then similar to autobiographical writing in the sense that one writes the self in connection with the presence of a virtual other. In this case, the virtual other takes the role of the master or the priest to compel us to speak (reflect on) the truth about ourselves and to interpret and assess this truth in relation to the norm. Here, we can see how technologies of the self are operating and how an ontological definition of reflection is mobilised. By confessing the true self to virtual others, a modification of behaviour is expected. This modification is not coerced, but rather elicited and fostered. The participants reflect about their inner selves through their own freedom. The log-book is thus part of a wider discourse on learning and governance, where the desirable norms produce subjects at the same time as the subjects produce the desirable norms. Writing the log-book is about writing the self, namely, about becoming a new and improved self.

Relating the log-books to Foucault's genealogy of confession, log-books represent a quite different writing practice from that seen among the Stoics, although there are similarities to the writing practices among the early Christians. Among the Stoics, keeping notebooks was a way 'to reactivate for oneself the truths one needed' (Foucault 2003a, 153). The focus was on documenting actions in order to fulfil good intentions according to the rules. By taking notes about which actions were successful and which intentions were not fulfilled during the workday, one could find the truths that were needed to help turn life into an art (a tekhne). In contrast, the truth sought after by the care worker is the truth about the self. Who am I? What are my weaknesses? How can I better myself? This practice is similar to the Christian practice of finding faults in the self and making them public to a confessor. By disclosing the truth about who they are, the workers can change. However, this activity is not about a renunciation of the self as it was with the early Christians; it is about creating a new and improved self.

Ontological and epistemological forms of reflection

Even though all of our examples of reflection and reflective practices from elderly care are related to power and the shaping of subjects, not all of them can be seen as confessions. Rather, it is possible to identify at least two different definitions of reflection at play, namely, an ontological definition and an epistemological one (Rolfe and Gardner 2006). The former concerns reflection whereby the focus is on knowing and changing oneself while the latter focuses on the improvement of practice. The former type of reflection could be seen as a 'way of being' (Johns 2005) while the latter could be seen as the use of reflection on experience in order to change practices. The epistemological definition is relevant when the carers are expected to reflect about their problems at work and propose solutions, as was done during the learning conversations. Then, the reflection is about improving their work practices by drawing on their knowledge and capacities for change. However, when invited and when being compelled to speak the truth about the self, as illustrated with the log-books, an ontological definition of reflection is mobilised. Reflection then becomes about shaping and improving the self.

Rolfe and Gardner (2006) argued that the epistemological definition of reflection is immune 'from the Foucauldian critique of repressive self-surveillance, but also that it is actively emancipatory'. By drawing on the experiences of the carers themselves, rather than basing actions on large-scale research studies, practitioners are promoted 'to the status of researchers and theorists in their own right' (p. 599). I, however, do not agree with these statements. As my analysis has illustrated, it is useful to speak about reflection as either epistemological or ontological. However, even when epistemological reflection is mobilised, there are technologies of power at work that aim to normalise and shape desirable subjects. Knowing that everything that the participants say about their problems and solutions at work is being assessed and monitored, the participants are shaped into self-scrutinising subjects who should aspire to become normal, well-behaved carers. Thus, the type of emancipatory practice that is outlined by Rolfe and Gardner, rather than being a practice of emancipation, becomes instead a normalising practice in which the knowledge and the experience of the carers becomes the vehicles for how governing operates. The experiential knowledge of the carers is incorporated within the governing discourses that privilege scientifically based knowledge (cf. Fejes 2012). Economising theoretical and science-based knowledge is no longer sufficient. Through the reflective practices and the in-service training programme that are analysed here, the local experiential knowledge is reconfigured into codified forms so that it can work together and/ or be included with science-based knowledge, thereby enabling it to be better mobilised and applied (cf. Nicoll and Fejes 2011).

Living the present otherwise

As Foucault's genealogy of confession illustrates, there have been other modes of governing and other ways through which we construe the relation of the self to the self. Among the Stoics, the focus was on turning life into an art – focusing on caring for the self and through this one would gain knowledge of the self. This is quite different from the ways confession shapes the relation of the self to the self in the present time, where the focus is on deciphering the self in order for the self to be improved. Through such genealogy, the aim is to make the taken-for-granted-ness of the present visible in order to open a space to live the present otherwise (Fejes and Dahlstedt 2012), and to make other power/knowledge constellations possible. However, living the present otherwise will not take us outside power relations. Power is everywhere and it is productive. Rather, living otherwise may traverse power relations that allow for different subjectivities to emerge.

Acknowledgements

This chapter is based on arguments pursued in Fejes (2011) and Fejes and Dahlstedt (2012).

References

Besley, T. and M. Peters. 2007. *Subjectivity & truth: Foucault, education and the culture of the self.* New York: Peter Lang.

Boud, D., R. Keogh and D. Walker. 1985. *Reflection: Turning experience into learning.* London: Kogan Page.

Erlandsson, P. 2006. Giving up the ghost: The control-matrix and reflection-in-action. *Reflective Practice* 7, 1: 115–24.

Erlandsson, P. and D. Beach. 2008. The ambivalence of reflection: Reading Schön. *Reflective Practice*, 9, 4: 409–421.

Fejes, A. 2008. Governing nursing through reflection: A discourse analysis of reflective practices. *Journal of Advanced Nursing*, 64, 3: 243–250.

Fejes, A. 2010. Discourses on employability: Constituting the responsible citizen. *Studies in Continuing Education* 32, 2: 89–102.

Fejes, A. 2011. Confession, in-service training and reflective practices. *British Educational Research Journal* 37, 5: 797–812.

Fejes, A. 2012. Knowledge at play: Positioning care workers as professionals through scientific rationality and caring dispositions. In *Elderly care in transition: Management, meaning and identity at work – a Scandinavian perspective*, ed. A. Kamp and H. Hvid, 83–85. Copenhagen: Copenhagen Business School Press.

Fejes, A. and M. Dahlstedt. 2012. *The confessing society: Foucault, confession and practices of lifelong learning.* London: Routledge.

Fejes, A. and K. Nicoll. 2010. A vocational calling: Exploring a caring technology in elderly care. *Pedagogy, Culture & Society* 18, 3: 353–370.

Fejes, A. and K. Nicoll. 2011. Activating the worker in elderly care: A technique and tactics of invitation. *Studies in Continuing Education* 33, 3: 235–249.

Foucault, M. 1991. Questions of method. In *The Foucault effect: Studies in governmentality*, ed. G. Burchell, C. Gordon and P. Miller, 73–86. Chicago: University of Chicago Press.

Foucault, M. 1998. *The will to knowledge: The history of sexuality: 1.* London: Penguin Books.

Foucault, M. 2003a. Technologies of the self. In *The essential Foucault: Selections from the essential works of Foucault 1954–1984*, ed. P. Rabinow and N. Rose, 145–169. New York: The New Press.

Foucault, M. 2003b. On the genealogy of ethics: An overview of work in progress. In *The essential Foucault: Selections from the essential works of Foucault 1954–1984*, ed. P. Rabinow and N. Rose, 102–125. New York: The New Press.

Foucault, M. 2003c. The ethics of the concern of the self as a practice of freedom. In *The essential Foucault: Selections from the essential works of Foucault 1954–1984*, ed. P. Rabinow and N. Rose, 25–42. New York: The New Press.

Foucault, M. 2003d. The subject and power. In *The essential Foucault: Selections from the essential works of Foucault 1954–1984*, ed. P. Rabinow and N. Rose, 126–144. New York: The New Press.

Foucault, M. 2005. *The hermeneutics of the subject: Lectures at Collège de France 1981–1982*. New York: Palgrave-Macmillan.

Handal, G. and Lauvås, P. 1987. *Promoting reflective teaching: Supervision in practice*. London: Society for Research into Higher Education/Open University Press.

Johns, C. 2005. Expanding the gates of perception. In *Transforming nursing through reflective practice*, ed. C. Johns and D. Freshwater, 1–12. Oxford: Blackwell Publishing.

Nicoll, K. and Fejes, A. 2011. Lifelong learning: A pacification of 'know how'. *Studies in Philosophy and Education* 30, 4: 403–417.

Rolfe, G. and L. Gardner. 2006. 'Do not ask who I am. . .': Confession, emancipation and (self)-management through reflection. *Journal of Nursing Management* 14, 8: 593–600.

Schön, D. 1983. *The reflective practitioner: How professionals think in action*. New York: Basic Books.

Schön, D. 1987. *Educating the reflective practitioner: Towards a design for teaching and learning in professions*. San Francisco: Jossey-Bass.

Taylor, C. 2010. *The culture of confession from Augustine to Foucault: A geneaology of the 'confessing animal'*. London: Routledge.

Part III

Habermas

Chapter 5

Jürgen Habermas
Education's reluctant hero

Terence Lovat

Introduction

In spite of them not being designed with educational research in mind, Habermas' theories of knowing and communicative action nonetheless have the capacity to deepen our research understandings in several areas of education, including the role of the teacher and effective pedagogy, as well as the potential of schools to serve as sites of holistic learning. In his theory of knowing, beyond the well-worn *techne* of learning, Habermas conceives of more authentic ways of knowing through critical reflection and engagement, or *praxis*, conceptions of learning with potential to challenge the dominant notions of the role of the teacher and the kinds of pedagogy that are most effective. Furthermore, in his theory of communicative action, Habermas builds on this notion of authentic knowing to posit the self-reflective knower as one who comes to see his or her own lifeworld relative to the lifeworlds of others. Through this, the knower develops communicative capacity and ultimately communicative action, whereby transformational learning results in taking a stand for justice and effecting change where it is necessary. Many contemporary educational research agendas, be they in quality teaching, authentic pedagogy, values and citizenship education or service learning, are directed towards re-conceiving and re-constructing schools as more transformational learning sites, entailing more holistic developmental experiences for learners. In any of these research agendas, it would seem that a Habermasian theoretical underpinning might serve as a useful ally. This chapter will explore these themes, expound on Habermasian theory and illustrate its pertinence to educational research through a number of contemporary applications.

Historical background

Jürgen Habermas, born in 1929 in Düsseldorf, Germany, is widely referred to as a sociologist and philosopher. He was the younger member of the so-called 'Frankfurt School', a group of social theorists and philosophers associated with the Institute for Social Research at Frankfurt University that included names such as Horkheimer, Marcuse, Adorno, Fromm and Apel. The Frankfurt School is particularly associated with neo-Marxist post-war reconstruction theory, and among a number of key theoretical positions for which its leadership is acknowledged is the set of perspectives broadly known as 'critical theory' – a radically interdisciplinary field designed to ensure that the best thoughts of scholarship were applied to solving real-life issues. From the mid-1960s until his retirement in 1993, Habermas played a leading role in developing, refining and furthering critical theory and making applications to multiple fields.

For Habermas, critical theory represented a way of repairing what he came to understand increasingly as the corrupt regime of Nazism, a thoroughly shameful moment in German history. For one who grew up in a marginally pro-Nazi family, who joined the Hitler youth (compulsorily) and, at 15 years of age, was sent to man the Western defences as the Third Reich was crumbling, the sense of shame seems to have been personalized to the extent that it has come to drive his critical theory with a particular passion. The passion is around ensuring that, in future, personal, social and political action is so informed with norms of reason and compassion that there could never again be a Third Reich. Arguably, Habermas' single most enduring influence has been in his epistemological work, a theory of knowing that impels the kind of reasoned and compassionate reflection and self-reflectivity that issues in benevolent action. Granted his entire platform of thought rests on a theory of knowing, there would seem to be much for educationists to consider. While, on self-admission, Habermas has paid little attention to the details and niceties of formal education and its paraphernalia, he nonetheless presents as the reluctant hero of education for the power of his epistemology to depict authentic learning as being considerably beyond the *techne* if the goal of learning is to be one befitting being human.

Placing Habermas in the knowing debate

Habermas' perspective on the unity of knowledge is part of the heritage of modern work dating at least to Dewey (1922, 1956a, 1956b) and the attempt to identify the standard patterns that underpin knowing, learning and instruction. Ayer's (1936) logical positivism had tried to ground all authentic knowing in the rational or empirically observable/measurable. In turn, Tyler (1949) generated from this conceptual identification a virtual science around assessment regimes, and Bloom and associates (Bloom 1956; Krathwohl et al. 1964) built further on it in the form of the taxonomies of educational objectives.

Meanwhile, Ferre (1982) had begun the dismantling of the apparatus of logical positivism in declaring that 'facts are never given in isolation from the minds that receive them' (p. 761). Ferre implied that the things we call 'facts' are really theories, and hence less observable/measurable than in the ways that logical positivists held to be determinative. Such a rejoinder was further reinforced by Lakatos (1974) and Kuhn (1970) who coined the notions of 'touchstone' and 'paradigm' respectively to connote the true basis of claims to 'know'. In a word, 'knowing' is not linear, it is complex; nor is it objective in any simple observable or measurable sense because it is infused with the subjectivity of the person doing the knowing. Quine (1953) went on to show just how subjective were the assertions of those claiming to be objective and Feyerabend (1975) launched highly critical attacks on education systems for the ways in which they had prioritized certain forms of knowledge over others, on the purported basis that they offered surer knowing (read rational or observable/measurable knowing), while other ways of knowing were relegated to the margins of education.

The response from educationists was to take recourse in various 'forms of knowledge' arguments in order to counter the veritable domination of logical positivism in practical systems of education. Phenix (1964) wrote that curriculum comprises 'realms of meaning', rather than a single realm and that each realm (read 'discipline') needed to be understood and dealt with according to its own terms of meaning. Hirst and Peters (1970) agreed, stating that 'in the recent past, education had been conceived . . . too much in terms of a set stock of information, simple skills and static conformity to a code' (p. 37).

The Hirst and Peters' 'forms thesis' held that there were certain 'forms of knowledge' which underlay any claim to 'know'. The seven forms comprised Mathematics and Logic, Physical Sciences, Human Sciences, Literature and Fine Arts, History, Philosophy and Religion. Each of these forms had an appropriate procedure, or methodology, which suited gathering knowledge within its domain. Hence, while empirical observation and measurement might well be appropriate for dealing with forms of knowledge in the physical sciences, the human sciences required a closer, more subjective approach on the part of the one wishing to know, and knowing in the fine arts and religion required something different again. From this perspective, the great error in logical positivism was in supposing that one or two of the forms of knowledge constituted all knowledge.

It is within the terms of this historical moment that Habermas' work comes to have most meaning, including for education. Habermas (1972, 1974) in a sense constructed his own forms thesis but laid it on firmer epistemological and cognitive grounds, a rare but timely conjunction, seeing it resting not on partitioned knowledge sets as ontological reifications but rather on the ways in which the mind works in constructing reality. As an early aside, this construct of knowing, a rare combination of philosophy and science, might yet have greater potential than has been realized so far for conversation with the emerging neurosciences, which will be referred to in a later part of the chapter. Habermas' explanation for apparent divisions in knowledge derives from his belief that knowing is impelled by a series of 'cognitive interests', interests which are part and parcel of the way the human mind works. These interests are threefold. First, there is an interest in technical control which impels an 'empirical analytic' type of knowing. Second, the interest in understanding meanings gives rise to a 'historical hermeneutic' way of knowing, or 'communicative knowledge' (the knowing that results from engagement, interrelationship and dialogue with others). Third, there is an interest in being emancipated, a free agent as it were, which issues in a 'critical', or 'self-reflective' way of knowing (the knowledge that comes ultimately from knowing oneself).

As far as Habermas is concerned, all three cognitive interests are operative regardless of the discipline area. Whatever the subject matter, our interest in technical control will lead us to want to know all the facts and figures associated with the subject at hand; this is where the quest for empirical–analytic knowing originates and is of use in the total quest to 'know'. Similarly, our interest in understanding the meaning behind an event will lead us to explore the inner dimensions, to try to relate one factor to another and to negotiate interpretations with other interested stakeholders; this impels an historical–hermeneutic type of knowing which serves to extend our understanding and the totality of our knowing. Finally, our interest in ensuring our autonomy as a knower will make us reflect critically on our subject matter, our sources and ultimately ourselves as agents of knowing. This is the preserve of critical or self-reflective knowing and where, according to Habermas, the only truly assured, totally comprehensive and authentic human knowing occurs.

At the heart of Habermas' thesis is the notion that the cognitive interest to be emancipated, or free, in our knowing impels an intensive critique of all of the assumptions and sources of our knowing up to that point in time. Among the assumptions and sources are those of both the external and the internal world. Externally, one confronts one's enculturated past, one's corporate beliefs and community values, one's family, school, political and religious heritage. Internally, one confronts one's self: there is no knowing without knowing the knower. Through critical, self-reflective knowing, one is challenged to let go of much of the past and to embrace new futures. The end of critical, self-reflective knowing is *praxis*, practical action for change. One cannot remain in the same place once one has confronted one's past and one's self. In a sense, the ultimate point of the learning game is to be found in knowing oneself and the consequent change of belief and behaviour that inevitably follows. Habermas saw this process as cleansing and purifying one's intentions and actions in ways that were lacking in the germination of the Third Reich and its many followers. It is here that some of his passion to ensure that the Third Reich could never happen again can be seen.

In Habermas' (1984, 1987, 1990) later theory of communicative action, he builds on the theory of knowing, describing the development of 'communicative capacity' as the initial outgrowth of the self-reflective knower and then, moreover, of 'communicative action'. Communicative capacity is when the self-reflective knower comes to see his or her own lifeworld as just one that needs to function in a myriad of lifeworlds, and so comes to possess communicative capacity. It is in a sense the fully flourished result of the historical–hermeneutical or 'communicative' way of knowing when infused with the critical–self-reflective way of knowing, a veritable formula for the modern, globally competent, intercultural communicator.

Beyond this is the notion of communicative action, an action orientation beyond that which can be impelled by historical–hermeneutical knowing, requiring instead the more profound knowing that comes from self-reflectivity.

Herein, the self-reflective knower takes a step beyond mere tolerance of other lifeworlds to take a stand to defend the right of all legitimate lifeworlds to exist and be accommodated within the human community. The stand is both for justice and for oneself because one's new found self, one's own integrity, is at stake. This is a concept about personal commitment, reliability and trustworthiness that impels and demands practical action that makes a difference. It is a refinement and sharpening of the outpouring of authentic knowing, namely *praxis*, as conceived of in Habermas' theory of knowing, the kind of committed action that can only come from the wellspring enshrined in the notion of self-reflectivity, from one who knows who they are, values the integrity of being authentic and commits oneself to establishing the kinds of caring and trusting relationships that bear the best fruits of human interactivity. Again, Habermas' passion to correct the wrongs of the past, especially around German Christian anti-Semitism, and ensure such travesties can never happen again, can be seen in the way this theory is constructed.

In his clear conjoining of knowing with doing, Habermas' fundamental Aristotelian reliance becomes apparent. In being caught between the rationalism of his teacher, Plato, and the pragmatism that always allured him, Aristotle finally settled on a way of knowing that relied on, yet was beyond, both rationalism and pragmatism in their simpler senses. This was a way of knowing that arose partly from the human need to be guided by one's intellect (as in rationalism) and partly from the need to be guided by one's common sense and intuition (as in pragmatism) but, above all, by one's need to be authentic in what one claimed to know. *Eudaemonia* is Aristotle's supreme good, but it is not a good that can be pursued merely by being known or merely by being experienced. It is a good that must be lived. The kind of judgement essential to the pursuit of *eudaemonia* is what Aristotle finally described as a 'practical' judgement, a judgement that leads to practical action or *praxis* in Habermasian terms.

The Aristotelian connection helps us to see how far Habermas has taken us from the postulations of the logical positivists for whom knowing was entirely locked in to the empirical–analytic domain. The potential for Habermasian theory to inform modern quests to 'think outside the square' across a spectrum of fields seems limitless. Among these fields is educational research. Considerable educational research has been expended in making applications of Habermasian theory to a range of issues relevant to educational theory and practice (Van Manen 1977; Young 1989; Doll 1993) and Habermas (2001) acknowledges the validity of this connection in some of his later work. I will focus on just two species of educational research, in which I have been a participant, to illustrate the pertinence and usefulness of Habermasian theory to these projects.

An application to pedagogical research

In earlier work (Lovat and Smith 2003; Lovat et al. 2005), it was proposed that the Habermasian theory of knowing could be used to analyse different moments in the teacher–learner relationship, and the power thereof, so to clarify and sometimes contest the assumptions that sit behind certain curriculum approaches and forms of pedagogy. Empirical–analytic knowing leads naturally to a relationship where the teacher is the 'expert', the learner the novice; the teacher is there to teach and the learner to learn in top-down linear fashion; all power is with the teacher, little to none with the learner. It offers an epistemic justification for a high order didactic approach to pedagogy. Granted the task at hand, such pedagogy might be seen as appropriate but for other kinds of learning, it might be inadequate and even obstructive. For instance, for a learning task that is centred on a skill that the teacher clearly possesses and the learner does not, didactic pedagogy is likely the most efficient way to close the gap, whereas learning focused on historical or sociological understandings and interpretations could render such pedagogy inhibitive in drawing on the learner's interpretive development. Of course, if the learning exercise is encased in a mandatory testing regime wherein it is considered there is only one licit interpretation, then the issue becomes one not so much about the appropriateness of the pedagogy as the ethics of the entire teaching and learning exercise.

Historical–hermeneutic knowing tends more obviously to a conception of the teacher–learner relationship as one of partnership, communicating about meanings and negotiating about understandings; power is shared to an extent. This would impel naturally a more democratic pedagogy, one that allows and indeed encourages a measure of free thought and speech, and to 'make mistakes' (speculate beyond the evidence) along the way. Such pedagogy would seem more appropriate to interpretive learning about meanings and understandings in the humanities and social sciences. The rider on shared power is that the teacher will normally retain some responsibility to guide the learner around interpretations that are better founded in the tradition, better evidenced in the research, etc. Like most phenomena in a democracy, it is not 'anything goes'.

When dealing with knowing of critical/self-reflectivity, impelled by the cognitive interest in being free to think one's own thoughts, so to engage in *praxis*, the relationship between teacher and learner has the potential to attain that measure of symmetry, even power sharing, beyond that which is obtained through historical–hermeneutic knowing. Herein, there is a relegation of power by the teacher to the learner as the learner is endowed with the confidence and the power of being in control of their own knowing. This can even result in roles being reversed, with the teacher, in a sense, sitting at the feet of the structural learner in the role of the veritable learner, or 'listener'. If the listener wishes to know what the learner has learned, and even more so if the listener wants to 'know' what the learner now knows, then she/he will be dependent upon the learner sharing what is known.

The challenge here for any traditional modes of teaching/learning relates to the fairly obvious truth that learners may often 'know' in ways that are outside the knowing of the teacher. In the epistemic world that sits behind empirical–analytic knowing and the resultant didactic pedagogy, it would be intolerable that the learner might be said to know more than the teacher. In the epistemic world of historical–hermeneutic knowing, this is tolerable and able to be negotiated, although not necessarily to be expected. In dealing with critical–self-reflective knowing, however, it is to be expected and indeed celebrated that new knowing, quite beyond the first-hand knowledge of the teacher, has evolved.

Van Manen (1977) may well capture the relationship between the teacher and the learner that is being proffered here when he says the following of the type of learning he sees ensuing from critical–self-reflective knowing:

> The norm is a distortion-free model of a communication situation . . . (where) there exists no repressive dominance, no asymmetry or inequality among the participants of the educational process.
>
> (p. 227)

For Van Manen, like Habermas, it is at this point alone that education becomes distinctively ethical, characterized by a sense of justice, equality and the freedom of individuals to follow their instincts of knowing wherever they might lead. It is also the way of knowing which, it is said, is a necessary precursor to the stretching of the boundaries of knowledge, to genuinely new knowing taking place. If one were to take Van Manen's 'no asymmetry' thesis seriously, one would surmise that the only form of testing and measuring that could do justice to, or perhaps even detect, evolving knowledge of this type would be one which was conducted largely in self-reflective mode.

In other earlier work (Lovat et al. 2008), this thinking was applied to an analysis of doctoral examination reports and it was noted that there were few instances where reports went beyond the didactic pedagogical mode of correction and little evidence of examiners acknowledging the level of 'original contribution' (supposedly the benchmark criterion for doctoral success), even though the vast majority of the theses in question were successful. It was therefore speculated on whether this indicated that the expectations placed on the doctorate were in fact not being met or whether it was indicative of the incapacity of the university teachers, serving as examiners, to break out of didactic pedagogy and the empirical–analytic assumptions sitting behind it, even when dealing with learners at the alleged zenith point of learning.

Of the 2121 examiner reports under analysis, there was only one that seemed clearly to reveal text indicative of an examiner functioning in critical–self-reflective mode. It began with the words, 'There are those pleasant occasions when one is asked to review a paper or examine a thesis and you wish that you had written it. I believe that this is one of those experiences' (Lovat et al. 2008, 71). This comment re-positioned the examiner's relationship with the student away from one of expertise-to-subject, or even of shared negotiability. The relationship established was at least symmetrical and could even be argued to have turned the traditional relationship on its head to become one of awe on the part of the examiner towards the student's 'original contribution', one which the examiner admitted that she/he had not themselves made. In that sense, the student had exceeded the expertise of the examiner and, in a rare display, this examiner was prepared to admit it. The teacher had become the learner.

In this example, the Habermasian theory of knowing allowed for critical gaze to be applied to an area of educational research with potential to assist in unravelling the learning assumptions that sat behind an arguably unhelpful pedagogy, or one at least demanding critical analysis and review, and so to re-conceive how a particular educational regime might function better. In this case, the findings received wide dissemination and have been cited in a variety of academic and policy sites at the international level (cf. Park 2007; Carter and Whittaker 2009). Moreover, the ramifications of such appraisal have potential to go beyond the particular regime being targeted. A wider concern about rigidity of pedagogy was present in the observation that if those responsible for assessment at the PhD level are locked into 'gate-keeping' pedagogy, then what hope for more 'authentic' pedagogy when applied to undergraduate and school levels of learning?

An application to holistic learning and student wellbeing

A persistent concern of education is with the notion of student achievement and whether this is best served for the majority through regular instrumentalist approaches to learning and assessment (e.g., direct instruction, standardized curricula and norm-referenced testing) or whether student achievement is so enmeshed in broader issues of wellbeing that more holistic approaches to learning are required. Midst this debate comes an array of updated evidence that points to the influence of values education on student wellbeing, including academic diligence and improvement (cf. Noddings 2002; Arthur 2003; Rowe 2004; Campbell et al. 2004; Benninga et al. 2006; Carr 2006, 2007; Nucci and Narvaez 2008; Lovat and Toomey 2009; Lovat et al. 2009; Arthur 2010; Lovat 2010a; Lovat et al. 2010a, 2010b, 2010c).

Values education research and practice is not considered by most educational systems to be a regular instrumentalist approach to learning, normally considered to be marginal to the mainstream agenda of academic content and assessment, and even arguably to be a little oppositional to it through its focus on 'beyond the academic curriculum'. Neither is values education organized in a way that would allow it to be an *ipso facto* device for mainstream academic content, not being characterized by a firm set of guidelines so much as a loose alliance of approaches with the common focus of creating, in learning sites, values-rich environments through relationships, modelling and ambience, and inserting values discourse into the overt curriculum. It is therefore not principally concerned with matters of academic development per se, but rather with student wellbeing as a whole, which makes the above research findings all the more interesting. It seems undeniable now that approaches to learning that de-emphasize academic content and assessment, concentrating rather on creating supportive environments of learning and richer and more personalized discourse, impact positively on student behaviour and classroom calm, and in turn lead to students being more attentive to their academic work. This would seem to indicate that, in all likelihood, all dimensions of student wellbeing, including academic learning, might be better served through holistic approaches to learning.

A variety of philosophical and empirical work has been proffered in recent times to explain the inherent connections between the various dimensions of student wellbeing and so to justify more holistic approaches being taken to learning. For example, David Carr (2006) has revived the philosophical case of Dewey and Peters in arguing that there can be no adequate and effective learning without teachers who model integrity and practise their profession in a way that entails sound relationships and moral interchange with their students. It is for him principally a matter of informal logic that teachers who go about their business in a fully professional and ethical way, with all the attachments of more secure environments and richer classroom talk and interchange, will produce better results of all kinds. In a sense, coming at the same issue from a different standpoint are the psychologists and neuroscientists. Ainley (2006) illustrated clearly that student motivation to learn can only be fully engaged when the emotional context is conducive. Damasio's (2003) work in the neurosciences has gone even further in findings that show that the seat of cognition in the brain is not separable from the seats of affect and sociality. Hence, it is not surprising that the environment characterized by healthier relationships and greater affirmation, together with more challenging discourse, will be the one where students are motivated to learn and attend better to their work.

Newmann's (1996) work on the 'pedagogical dynamics' required for quality teaching also provides a clue in that several of the dynamics concern relationships and ambience of learning. For instance, 'catering for diversity' referred to the centrality of the respectful and sensitive relationship between teacher and student, so ensuring an ambience where the student feels accepted, understood and valued. Similarly, 'school coherence' was of the school that is committed unswervingly to the good of the student, a values-rich concept connoting dedication, responsibility, generosity and integrity on the part of all stakeholders. Meanwhile, the ultimate pedagogical dynamic of the 'trustful, supportive ambience' was deemed to be so indispensable that it would render all teaching ineffective if not attended to.

Osterman (2010) speaks in a sense to all the above conclusions in providing evidence of the greater learning capacity instilled by environments where students feel they belong and therefore experience strengthened emotional wellbeing. Furthermore, she illustrates in this evidence the integral connection between teacher relationship and support and the nature of the pedagogy provided by the teacher. It is neither the teacher who merely provides a supportive ambience nor the one who merely instructs well whose practice enhances academic diligence. It is the teacher whose pedagogy is characterized by the integrity of a supportive relationship and best practice pedagogy as one action, rather than two, who brings students to new levels of academic enhancement.

The role that Habermas has played in providing an epistemological explanation and justification for these insights into the holistic nature of learning has been inestimable. While essentially a philosophical perspective, Habermas' insights have rare potential to straddle the various disciplines that are informing the debate. His theories of knowing and communicative action offer, between them, particularly powerful tools for analysing the capacity of values education to transform people's beliefs and behaviours in ways that conform to the evidence. For one thing, they render the notion of values neutrality in education non-viable and therefore challenge the authenticity of any education conceived of solely in instrumentalist terms. In contrast, they lead naturally to the notion that any legitimate education requires a values-laden approach, in terms of both ambience and discourse. Hence, they help to explain why it is that the values education priority of saturating the learning experience with both a values-filled environment and explicit teaching that engages in discourse about values-related content tends towards such holistic effects as have been uncovered in the research. Furthermore, the Habermasian notion that critical and self-reflective knowing issues in emancipation and empowerment, so spawning communicative capacity and communicative action, both justifies and explains the effects of an approach to learning that prioritizes the transaction of values.

Habermasian epistemology therefore is able to be used to justify philosophically and explain the practical effects of an approach to learning that is aimed at the full range of developmental measures in the interests of holistic student learning and wellbeing. Rather than connoting a mere moral or, least of all, religious option, values education is able to be constructed philosophically and pedagogically as an effective way in which learning can proceed in any school setting. Hence, we find Habermas regularly cited among scholars engaged in values education research (cf. Crawford 2010; Crotty 2010; Gellel 2010; Henderson 2010; Lovat et al. 2010a).

Crotty (2010) for instance is able to employ a Habermasian perspective to make sense of the improved academic focus that he saw so clearly demonstrated in the participants in the case studies he observed of values education leading to effective social engagement. This perspective enabled him to name the effect as enhanced higher order thinking leading to emancipatory knowledge:

> This knowledge-guiding interest concerns the human capacity to be self-reflective and self-determining. The knowledge that is produced by interaction with the interest informs human responsibility. The self-reflection makes the individual aware of those ideologies that influence humans and it offers a way for the individual to deal with them. It seems obvious to me that in the four clusters this particular mode of knowledge is shared by teachers and students.
>
> (p. 635)

Crotty goes on to apply this thinking to the effects he observed in each of four case studies. He concludes: 'In short, habits of self-reflection have been fostered, ideologies have been recognized and higher order thinking has been taking place' (p. 636).

The programmes that Crotty was observing involved social engagement, or service learning, as a component of the values education intervention. The work of Billig (2002) shows that service learning is a particularly powerful form of values education and one with some of the most tangible effects on improved academic performance. Again, Habermasian theory has been utilized in trying to understand why this is the case:

> The frame of reference emanates from Habermas's 'Ways of Knowing' and 'Communicative Action' theories. In a word, it is the one who knows not only empirically analytically and historically hermeneutically, but self-reflectively who is capable of the just and empowering relationships implied in the notion of communicative action. In a sense, one finally comes truly to know when one knows oneself, and authentic knowing of self can only come through action for others, the practical action for change and betterment implied by praxis. Habermas provides the conceptual foundation for a values education that transforms educational practice, its actors in students and teachers, and the role of the school towards holistic social agency, the school that is not merely a disjoined receptacle for isolated academic activity, but one whose purpose is to serve and enrich the lives not only of its immediate inhabitants but of its community.
>
> (Lovat et al. 2010a, 616)

In other words, Habermas rests his notion of effective social action (namely, *praxis*) on people reaching the most sophisticated levels of knowing. In this respect and in contrast with more dated thinking about values formation and the role (or lack thereof) of the teacher and formal schooling in such formation, the Habermasian emphasis on knowing as the key to values formation suggests that effective social and moral citizenship is not only educable but that there is an inherent educational component in it. Furthermore, it helps to clarify why it is that attaining such a level of knowing and then committing to concomitant action would logically have an impact on one's powers of knowing generally and so issue in enhanced academic performance.

In a word, Habermasian thought has potential to deepen profoundly not only our understanding of the full human developmental capacities that are implied in effective learning but also to help us in developing the kinds of pedagogies needed to effect them. The employment of Habermas in the context of values education leading to social engagement in the way illustrated above serves as a case in point. Here, we see a line of convergence opening up between his theoretical world and the pedagogy required to produce the kind of values education that leads to effective social engagement, such that new knowing is implied and deeper learning enhanced. In effect, the Habermasian theories constitute an epistemological template for social engagement that is informed by authentic human knowing, at one end, and impels altruistic action, at the other end.

In a word, Habermasian theory determines that effective education can never be focused solely on 'the basics' of technical learning (the *techne*) if it is seriously looking to the good of its clients and society at large. In a Habermasian schema, social engagement that is aimed at developing *praxis* and communicative action is not an added extra or marginal nicety. It is at the heart of what an authentic school will be about, namely, taking a wide-ranging social agency for the good of society and directly for the good of its clients, the students at hand, because it is only the school that provides these forms of pedagogy that can ultimately facilitate the kind of knowing that is most authentically human. In contrast to instrumentalist notions of schooling, a Habermasian notion will impel educational charters that deal with the intellectual, social, emotional, moral and spiritual good of their clientele. This is an education intention directed towards teachers and schools playing a role in the forming of individuals who understand integrity and apply it to their practical decision-making, and furthermore assist in the cohering of those individuals into functional and beneficent societies.

An implication of this education intention is around the removal of any artificial division between knowing and values, since all knowing has an ethical component and is related in some way to human action. With this understanding, Habermas challenges contemporary education to deal with the essentials rather than mere basics of learning. He offers an epistemology that impels holistic and comprehensive pedagogy that engages with the full array of real-life issues. In a specific example, I have shown how this 'Habermasian' pedagogy can be applied to the very real contemporary life issue of how schools deal with the topic of Islam and set up curricular and pedagogical structures to ensure incorporation into the school of a population that is at increasing risk of being marginalized in school settings (Lovat 2010b; Lovat et al. 2011).

Conclusion

One can see the importance of Habermas to educational thought and practice at almost any level at which one wishes to consider it. This chapter has provided merely a handful of some of the more worked over applications. One senses with Habermas that his influence will continue to be felt for generations. Like the ancient Greeks, Aquinas, Descartes, Voltaire and Dewey, among many others, his insights represent a paradigm shift, promising to shape new futures while, at the same time, to ground us in our heritage. His balanced appraisal of the most sophisticated knowing being one that relies as much on human communication and knowing of self as it does on empirical facts and figures is, as demonstrated above, reminiscent of the moderation of Aristotelian thought about human virtue, whereby one knew what was right, cared about one's fellows and knew how to translate this knowing and feeling into practical action. So, to be introduced to Habermas is to be introduced to Aristotle and through this, all of the foundations of thought relevant to an agency of human service, like teaching, become available to it along with the most fortified philosophical basis on which to build a stronger human service for the future. In a word, I believe Habermas is in for the long term as a hero of education, perhaps ultimately not so reluctantly.

References

Ainley, M. 2006. Connecting with learning: Motivation, affect and cognition in interest processes. *Educational Psychology Review* 18, 4: 391–405.

Arthur, J. 2003. *Education with character: The moral economy of schooling.* London: Routledge.

Arthur, J. 2010. *Of good character: Exploration of virtues and values in 3–25 year-olds.* Exeter, UK: Imprint Academic.

Ayer, A. J. 1936. *Language, truth and logic.* London: Victor Gollancz.

Benninga, J., M. Berkowitz, P. Kuehn and K. Smith. 2006. Character and academics: What good schools do. *Phi Delta Kappan* 87, 6: 448–452.

Billig, S. H. 2002. Support for K-12 service-learning practice: A brief review of the research. *Educational Horizons* 80, 4: 184–189.

Bloom, B. ed. 1956. *Taxonomy of educational objectives: Book 1 cognitive domain.* London: Longman.

Campbell, R. J., L. Kyriakides, R. D. Muijs and W. Robinson. 2004. Effective teaching and values: Some implications for research and teacher appraisal. *Oxford Review of Education* 30, 4: 451–465.

Carr, D. 2006. Professional and personal values and virtues in education and teaching. *Oxford Review of Education* 32, 2: 171–183.

Carr, D. 2007. Character in teaching. *British Journal of Educational Studies* 55, 4: 369–389.

Carter, B. and K. Whittaker. 2009. Examining the British PhD viva: Opening new doors or scarring for life. *Advances in Contemporary Nurse Education* 32: 169–178.

Crawford, K. 2010. Active citizenship education and critical pedagogy. In *International research handbook on values education and student wellbeing*, ed. T. Lovat, R. Toomey and N. Clement, 811–824. Dordrecht, Netherlands: Springer.

Crotty, R. 2010. Values education as an ethical dilemma about sociability. In *International research handbook on values education and student wellbeing*, ed. T. Lovat, R. Toomey and N. Clement, 631–644. Dordrecht, Netherlands: Springer.

Damasio, A. (2003). *Looking for Spinoza: Joy, sorrow and the feeling brain.* New York: Harcourt.

Dewey, J. 1922. *Human nature and conduct: An introduction to social psychology.* New York: Modern Library.

Dewey, J. 1956a. *The child and the curriculum.* Chicago: University of Chicago Press.

Dewey, J. 1956b. *The school and society.* Chicago: University of Chicago Press.

Doll, W. 1993. *A post-modern perspective on curriculum.* New York: Teachers College Press.

Ferre, F. 1982. *Language, logic and god.* New York: Harper & Row.

Feyerabend, P. 1975. *Against method: Outline of an anarchistic theory of knowledge.* London: Humanities Press.

Gellel, A. 2010. Teachers as key players in values education: Implications for teacher formation. In *International research handbook on values education and student wellbeing*, ed. T. Lovat, R. Toomey and N. Clement, 163–178. Dordrecht, Netherlands: Springer.

Habermas, J. 1972. *Knowledge and human interests* (trans. J. Shapiro). London: Heinemann.

Habermas, J. 1974. *Theory and practice* (trans. J. Viertal). London: Heinemann.

Habermas, J. 1984. *Theory of communicative action* (trans. T. McCarthy) (vol. I). Boston: Beacon Press.

Habermas, J. 1987. *Theory of communicative action* (trans. T. McCarthy) (vol. II). Boston: Beacon Press.

Habermas, J. 1990. *Moral consciousness and communicative action* (trans. C. Lenhardt and S. Nicholson). Cambridge, MA: Massachusetts Institute of Technology Press.

Habermas, J. 2001. *The liberating power of symbols: Philosophical essays*. Cambridge: Polity Press.

Henderson, D. 2010. Values, wellness and the social sciences curriculum. In *International research handbook on values education and student wellbeing*, ed T. Lovat, R. Toomey and N. Clement, 273–290. Dordrecht, Netherlands: Springer.

Hirst, P. and R. S. Peters. 1970. *The logic of education*. London: Routledge & Kegan Paul.

Krathwohl, D., B. Bloom and B. Masia. 1964. *Taxonomy of educational objectives. Handbook II affective domain*. New York: McKay.

Kuhn, T. 1970. *The structure of scientific revolutions*. Chicago: Chicago University Press.

Lakatos, I. 1974. Falsification and the methodology of scientific research programs. In *Criticism and the growth of knowledge*, ed. I. Lakatos and A. Musgrave, 91–196. Cambridge: Cambridge University Press.

Lovat, T. 2010a. Synergies and balance between values education and quality teaching. *Educational Philosophy and Theory* 42, 1: 489–500.

Lovat, T. 2010b. Improving relations with Islam through religious and values education. In *International handbook of inter-religious education*, ed. K. Engebretson, M. de Souza, G. Durka and L. Gearon, 695–708. New York: Springer.

Lovat, T. and D. Smith. 2003. *Curriculum: Action on reflection* (4th edition). Melbourne: Thomson.

Lovat, T. and R. Toomey, eds. 2009. *Values education and quality teaching: The double helix effect*. Dordrecht, Netherlands: Springer.

Lovat, T., A. Holbrook and S. Bourke. 2008. Ways of knowing in doctoral examination: How well is the doctoral regime? *Educational Research Review* 3, 1: 66–76.

Lovat, T., M. Monfries and K. Morrison. 2005. Ways of knowing and power discourse in doctoral examination. *International Journal of Educational Research* 41, 2: 163–177.

Lovat, T., R. Toomey and N. Clement, eds. 2010a. *International research handbook on values education and student wellbeing*. Dordrecht, Netherlands: Springer.

Lovat, T., K. Dally, N. Clement and R. Toomey. 2010b. Addressing issues of religious difference through values education: An Islam instance. *Cambridge Journal of Education* 40, 3: 213–227.

Lovat, T., K. Dally, N. Clement and R. Toomey. 2010c. Values education as holistic development for all sectors: Researching for effective pedagogy. *Oxford Review of Education* 36, 6: 713–729.

Lovat, T., K. Dally, N. Clement and R. Toomey. 2011. *Values pedagogy and student achievement: Contemporary research evidence.* Dordrecht, Netherlands: Springer.

Lovat, T., R. Toomey, N. Clement, R. Crotty and T. Nielsen. 2009. *Values education, quality teaching and service learning: A troika for effective teaching and teacher education.* Sydney: David Barlow Publishing.

Newmann, F. and Associates. 1996. *Authentic achievement: Restructuring schools for intellectual quality.* San Francisco: Jossey Bass.

Noddings, N. 2002. *Educating moral people: A caring alternative to character education.* New York: Teachers College Press.

Nucci, L. and D. Narvaez, eds. 2008. *Handbook of moral and character education.* New York: Routledge.

Osterman, K. 2010. Teacher practice and students' sense of belonging. In *International research handbook on values education and student wellbeing,* ed. T. Lovat, R. Toomey and N. Clement, 239–260. Dordrecht, Netherlands: Springer.

Park, C. 2007. *Redefining the doctorate.* London: Higher Education Academy. Available at: www.heacademy.ac.uk/assets/York/documents/ourwork/research/redefining_the_doctorate.pdf.

Phenix, P. 1964. *Realms of meaning: Curriculum and methods in education.* New York: McGraw-Hill.

Quine, W. V. 1953. *From a logical point of view.* Oxford: Oxford University Press.

Rowe, K. J. 2004. In good hands? The importance of teacher quality. *Educare News* 149: 4–14.

Tyler, R. 1949. *Basic principles of curriculum and instruction.* Chicago: University of Chicago Press.

Van Manen, M. 1977. Linking ways of knowing with ways of being practical. *Curriculum Inquiry* 6, 3: 205–228.

Young, R. 1989. *A critical theory of education: Habermas and our children's future.* New York: Harvester Wheatsheaf.

Chapter 6

The politics of school regulation

Using Habermas to research educational accountability

Mark Murphy and Paul Skillen

Introduction

Political stakes are high on the front line of public services. Professionals working in sectors such as education, health and social care function as the interface between the public and the public sector, their capacity to fulfil their duty of care being a key component of modern state legitimacy. The fact that these services occupy the space where public interest meets private concerns means that they represent the state at its most exposed. The success or otherwise of professional practice on the front line has implications for how governments are judged across a range of issues – financial efficiency, political competence and, not least, the promotion of democratic values.

It is unsurprising, then, that modern governments have developed extensive mechanisms of accountability designed specifically to measure the effectiveness of public services. One of the more striking developments of recent years in national and institutional governance is the rise of what Max Travers (2007) calls the 'new bureaucracy' of quality assurance. This is particularly true of the public sector, with areas such as education under increasing pressure to evidence accountability to the public and the public purse. The mechanisms of this new bureaucracy – performance indicators, audit, inspection and evaluation – are designed to increase formal levels of accountability to the state while also making the public sector more accountable to the public via marketisation and the development of a consumer culture. This new bureaucracy of accountability has dramatically altered the landscape of public services since its development in the last several decades. In particular, the implementation of these quality assurance mechanisms has opened up the public sector to ever greater scrutiny.

As a tool of political regulation, however, they are not without their critics, accused of, among other things, undermining professional autonomy, instrumentalising public services and trivialising democracy (Clarke and Newman 1997; Odhiambo 2008; Salter and Tapper 2000; Shore and Wright 2000). Problems associated with political accountability suggest it deserves its 'tricky' reputation (Barberis 1998, 451), a description that extends beyond definitional complexities. Attempts to manage and control outcomes via mechanisms such as audit and inspection face numerous difficulties (Scott 2000) with the gap between the ideal and reality (Bovens 2010) often too wide to deliver satisfactory outcomes. Accountability arrangements, for all their value, 'do not necessarily produce better government' (Bovens 2010, 958).

Given these concerns over accountability, it is inevitable that debates have developed over the usefulness of such a bureaucratic apparatus generally. Increasingly, evidence suggests that these state bureaucratic systems, rather than alleviating issues associated with a lack of public accountability, have unwittingly managed to help facilitate their development in the first place. The evidence from a range of studies indicates that accountability can be a 'double-edged sword' (Papadopoulos 2010, 1032), with a number of unintended consequences arising from the reforms, including risk avoidance (Papadopoulos 2010, 1032) and what Bovens calls the 'accountability trap' (2010, 958), a trap in which public servants achieve success in meeting accountability targets, yet are not 'necessarily performing better in the real world of policy-making and public service delivery' (p. 958).

These unwelcome consequences of the new bureaucracy for the likes of education should be a major concern to policy makers and those interested in the effective functioning of democratic institutions. As Michael Lipsky put it in *Street-level Bureaucracy* (1980), accountability is 'the link between bureaucracy and democracy'. So why is it that the new bureaucracy has these effects? How best to theorise these consequences of political regulation? While academics have certainly made claims for the work of Michel Foucault in particular as a way of understanding modern state governance (as illustrated elsewhere in this collection), it does not take much of a stretch for the imagination to situate the work of Jürgen Habermas at the centre of this debate over educational governance, similar to the way his work has been utilised in other public sector professions such as health and social work (Brown 2008; Cooper 2010; Small and Mannion 2005; Sumner 2001). His *Theory of Communicative Action* (1984, 1987), in particular, lends itself well to an examination of the reaches and limits of bureaucratic regulation in modern liberal democracies (Murphy 2009).

One of the criticisms aimed at Habermas, however, is that the connections to everyday practice, professional or otherwise, have never been satisfactorily outlined (Murphy 2010). According to Blaug (1997, 117), this is because the highly abstract nature of Habermas' work, combined with his own theoretical limits, 'restrict its practical implications'. He goes on to refer to Habermasian theory as like a 'promissory note: fully written, but as yet uncashed' (p. 117). The purpose of the current research is to help facilitate the cashing in of this note. Using qualitative case studies of teachers in the north of England, the current research seeks to examine the impact of quality assurance on the work of professionals on the front line of public services. In particular, it seeks to use Habermas' conceptual apparatus as a way of theorising these effects.

As is normally the case when moving from abstract theory to the level of practice, the application of Habermas at the ground level was not a straightforward process; indeed, delivering some of its own unintended consequences for the researcher, the findings add to the complexity already at the heart of Habermas' theoretical construction. The research illustrated that attempts to evidence and understand the limits of political regulation eventually bring to light some of the limitations in Habermas' conceptual apparatus, in particular the existence of other forms of regulation that do not fit neatly into his lifeworld/system construction. This chapter reflects on these limitations while also exploring some other issues highlighted in the research itself.

Habermas, bureaucracy and political regulation

Pathologies of bureaucratic governance have been a concern of sociologists for some time, and were a favourite theme in the work of the Frankfurt School of Critical Theory to which Habermas is aligned. One of the key books published by the Frankfurt School, Adorno and Horkheimer's *Dialectic of Enlightenment* (1972), envisaged the result of modernisation processes to be a 'totally administered world', a belief that borrowed heavily from Max Weber's famous metaphor of the iron cage. This metaphor reflected Weber's concern that the process of rationalisation, brought about by capitalist modernisation, would inevitably lead to a nightmarish world of all-encompassing bureaucracy, in which individual freedoms would disappear under a mountain of government red tape. Professional life, Weber perceived, was unable to escape the fate of the bureaucratic iron cage of societal rationalisation – a fate that, in his famous words, produced 'specialists without spirit' and 'sensualists without heart' (Weber 1958, 182). The relentless march of bureaucratic rationality in capitalist societies was sweeping everything before it, leaving organisations and cultural activities increasingly devoid of freedom and empty of meaning.

Unwittingly or not, much academic commentary on public sector professions suggests that Weber's iron cage has been realised, with areas such as health and social work apparently over-burdened by the rise of performance mechanisms and other audit measures, in the pursuit of a reformed accountability culture (Exworthy and Halford 1999; Scambler and Britten 2001; Stecher and Kirby 2004). This is also a familiar argument in the context of schooling (Thrupp and Wilmott 2003; Walsh 2006), where the proliferation of audit measures has encouraged the likes of Hoyle and Wallace (2005, 100) to argue that professional autonomy has been, or is being, replaced by accountability as the core principle of school management. The imperatives of bureaucratisation, it is feared, are threatening to usurp the educational values at the heart of the profession, on a relentless drive to account and to measure everything, thereby reducing everything to the status of means to ends.

Habermas certainly has sympathy for such a view, concerned as he is with the process of bureaucratisation, but in his more sociological writings he came to distance himself from such a negative diagnosis of the ills of modernisation. In the *Theory of Communicative Action* (1984, 1987), Habermas took to task Weber's diagnosis, and consequently Adorno and Horkheimer's, arguing that the depiction of modern professional life as an iron cage suffered from a contradiction – how was it possible to provide a rational critique of rationalisation if reason was at fault in the first place? The analysis of Habermas differs in two fundamental respects (Murphy and Fleming 2006). First, Habermas argues that Weber incorrectly conflated modernisation and rationalisation – that is, he equated instrumental rationality with rationality per se. As a result, Weber has no option but to cast reason *itself* as the iron cage, a belief resurrected in the *Dialectic of Enlightenment* (Adorno and Horkheimer 1972). Instead, Habermas argues that modernisation and rationalisation are *not* one and the same thing, and that there exists another form of rationality – communicative rationality oriented to processes of mutual understanding – that is not necessarily tied into modernisation processes.

Second, where Weber utilises an *action* theory of society, one formulated from the perspective of acting subjects, Habermas instead utilises a two-level conception of society, which allows for both an action-theoretic and a systems theoretic understanding of societal rationalisation. Two central concepts are introduced at this stage. The first is the concept of the *lifeworld* – which signifies the background consensus of our everyday lives, the vast stock of taken-for-granted definitions and understandings of the world that give coherence and direction to our lives. The second concept is what Habermas calls 'system', the aspect of society where imperatives of technical efficiency and bureaucracy have precedence, that is, the state administrative apparatus (steered by power) and the economy (steered by money).

This reconstruction enabled Habermas to argue that capitalism has ushered in a process of one-sided (instrumental) rationalisation, and has done so via the state and the market overstepping their own functional boundaries and 'colonising' the lifeworld. Political and economic imperatives, the two main manifestations of instrumental rationality in Habermasian terms, have restricted the potential of communicative rationality to shape decisions and actions that affect the core activities of the lifeworld, namely socialisation, cultural reproduction and child-rearing. In other words, the pursuit and maintenance of state political agendas, alongside the ability of capitalism to exploit new avenues for wealth creation, have resulted in more and more decisions affecting the lives of citizens being based on the 'bottom line' of power and/or money (Murphy 2009).

For Habermas, this restriction on the capacity for communication and the development of mutual understanding is a pathological form of modernisation: 'monetarization and bureaucratization appear to overstep the boundaries of normality when they instrumentalize an influx from the lifeworld that possesses its own inner logic' (1987, 323). As Habermas explains (p. 322), there are aspects of living that are 'tied to lifeworld contexts and cannot be taken over economically or politically as can abstract quantities of labor power and taxes'. Pathological forms of modernisation, therefore, manifest themselves in distorted relations that bear the brunt of dysfunctional forms of bureaucracy. Effectively, for Habermas, bureaucratic mechanisms of accountability are 'tricky' because they have a tendency to overstep their limits, the red tape of political bureaucracy stifling the imperatives of an intersubjective world in which its remit does not govern.

Habermas' theoretical construction is much more complex that can be detailed here,[1] but suffice to state that his argument is well established in the field of social theory, and has sparked a great deal of debate across philosophy, sociology and political science in particular – see Duvenage (2003) and Morris (2001). His theory of colonisation has also been applied in a wide variety of contexts, testifying to its power as a theoretical analysis of modernisation and its discontents.[2] On a more practical level, however, how does it stand up to scrutiny? In the current climate of accountability in the UK public sector reform agenda, the scenario sounds plausible, given the evidence that supports such a notion of a state apparatus overstepping its boundaries, often in the guise of the neo-managerialist state (Newman and Clarke 2009). It may sound plausible, but the question remains: what kind of evidence base exists to support such a colonisation thesis? Just as importantly, if such colonisation has occurred, how does it manifest itself at the level of professional practice? How do political and economic imperatives overstep their boundaries?

As an application of Habermas, the education sector is a powerful field within which to help answer these questions. Education occupies a useful structural position from which to 'test' the validity of Habermas' argument, as it straddles both the lifeworld and system – an essential aspect of public sector work that, in Blaug's terminology, is a 'dual-aspect' activity, with both communicative and instrumental rationalities (ethics of care and efficiency) awkwardly combined (1995, 427). In particular, the work of teachers and their interactions with pupils places them at the front line of professional regulation and its consequences for the public. What follows is an overview and analysis of our research exploring the experience of teachers on this regulatory front line, research that illustrates just how regulated the sector actually is.

A note on methodology

The purpose of the original study, funded by a small grant from the University of Chester, was to examine the impact of accountability mechanisms on the work of public-sector professionals, specifically how mechanisms such as audit and inspection impacted on their relationships with the public. Included among the research subjects were nurses and social workers, as well as teachers. The research focused on the ways in which teachers et al. perceived their work to be affected by the instrumental rationality at the heart of the new bureaucracy of quality assurance – a form of regulation that, at least in the UK, public-sector professionals are very familiar with.

In total, nine interviews and three focus groups were carried out, equally split between the three professions. The focus groups were organised once relevant themes had been identified in the individual interviews. All interviews and focus groups were conducted in the same borough of the north-west of England. Given that three different professional groups were part of the study, it required different strategies to access the respondents. In order for access to be obtained to subjects that could provide adequate narratives around accountability and its consequences, more experienced personnel were requested to take part. This chapter reports only on the research conducted with teachers (real names have been replaced with pseudonyms).

The politics of school regulation: findings from the research

Is there evidence for colonisation? The evidence from the research suggests that, generally speaking, some form of colonisation may have taken hold in the education sector. Certainly, the narratives of the teachers reflect strong and increasing pressure to supply visible and tangible evidence of accountability. The need to document activity and performance for later evaluation and analysis, regardless of context, unites the teachers and places them in a situation where their workloads, subjectively at least, allow little room for manoeuvre. It was apparent from the teachers' perspectives that political regulation has some consequences for the ways in which they related to the public in their various guises. The interviews and focus group were awash with evidence of what Ricardo Blaug calls the 'distortion of the face-to-face' (1995). Although Blaug used the phrase specifically in the context of social work, underpinned by a Habermasian analysis of modernisation, it seems to also apply in the context of education in an age of quality assurance. It was the case that teachers view political regulation, rather than assuring the quality of relationships, having the potential to cause damage to them.

According to respondents, the need to achieve and complete accountability-related tasks, whether in relation to inspections, audits, evaluations or performance indicators, has significant consequences for their ability to complete what they consider core professionals tasks – dealing with the issues and concerns of pupils. A particular concern of the teachers in our study was that they perceived an ever-loosening grip on the capacity to make professional judgements. The (in)capacity to weigh up a situation and make a reasoned and logical decision was a strong theme in the research. What was also evident among the participants was a sense that, while the increasing pressure of instrumental rationality in the form of political regulation had taken its toll, professional values associated with more communicative forms of rationality were never far from the concerns of teachers, at least in this study – they were more than aware of the tension between the two. This was evident in the forms of resistance to strategic thinking witnessed in the data gathering. Not all forms of dissent or conflict have disappeared from professional life in the public sector. While the evidence for resistance was minimal, there were some indications that professionals were not wholly fatalistic in their acceptance of increased workloads:

> If you tried to take on board everything you are asked to do then you would sink. You can't do time management when you have no time to manage.
>
> (Emma)

There was also evidence to suggest that some professionals have developed counter-strategies that work to counteract the effects of accountability – one of these strategies being procrastination:

> Procrastination is always good as well because if you wait, the things which are really important eventually will be done. So procrastination is a way of survival because if you leave it, leave it, leave it and if someone really wants something they will come back to you again and again and again.
>
> (Caroline)

The existence of such forms of resistance indicate that the prevalence of instrumental rationality does not negate the existence of communicative rationality in the professional workplace; it could be the case instead that it tends to push this form of rationality out to the margins of professional life, where it flourishes as forms of muted resistance and 'negotiated' work practices.

As the study progressed, however, it became more apparent that other tensions existed alongside the instrumental/communicative rationality at the centre of Habermas' work – what was also evident was the presence of a conflict over different forms of *regulation*. What increased political regulation appears to have achieved is to highlight the existence of two other forms of regulation that tend to get sidelined or forgotten entirely when it comes to talk of regulatory mechanisms – *temporal* and *legal* regulation. It is important to highlight these as they have the effect, in this study at least, of mediating the effect of political regulation on the working lives of educational professionals.

Accountability and temporal regulation

The pressure on time as a valuable but limited resource eaten up by the demands of accountability, was a recurring theme in the research: As Jane put it: '[W]e are put under a lot of pressure and we are continually monitoring and assessing the children and there is a greater workload because of the paperwork that has to be filled in.' Such temporal pressure, or 'time compression' leads, the evidence suggests, to what Sabelis (2002) has called 'task suppression'. The exclusion of tasks is evident among the teachers; as one of them puts it, targets in reading, writing and maths 'are your be all and end all' (Jane):

> As teachers you are continually under pressure to fit in all the things you have to in a week and sometimes you don't have the time. You are continually thinking I should have fitted in this particular lesson and you are worrying about fitting everything in otherwise perhaps they won't reach their target.
>
> (Jane)

The research suggests that tasks are not always wholly suppressed – what is also present are forms of task *dilution*: 'Inevitably if your time is taken up doing one new thing then you are spending less time on preparation and accurate marking in the time available' (Yvonne). But the principle is the same – the quality of the relationship is impacted by the amount of time available for professional end-user interaction. And while teachers may have extended periods of input over the child's educational career, there is also a sense that their time to 'know' their pupil is under threat:

> There is no depth or quality in the interactions anymore because you have no time to develop quality relationships with the children and the focus on their particular strengths and weaknesses, which is what you're supposed to do as a teacher. We have not got time to develop and nurture a child.
>
> (Maria)

The amassing of this situated and personal knowledge is mostly hidden from view, forms of 'soft' knowledge that professionals often rely on to help them exercise judgement, discretion and most importantly to make the 'right' decision. Without sufficient amounts of this soft knowledge, however, the implications can be profound for both professionals and non-professionals.

The question then becomes: how is judgement related to time? At least part of the answer to this question lies in the intersubjective nature of the work carried out by teachers, the kind of emotion-laden work that is difficult to measure but unavoidable in such encounters. Dealing with other people, the *raison d'être* of Lipsky's street-level bureaucrats, is an essential but fragile aspect of these professional lives. These intersubjective encounters are easily influenced by factors that mediate the relationship between professional and non-professional. And some of these factors were evident in the research, for example, in the kinds of situated knowledge indicated above.

Accountability and legal regulation

In the dynamic world of classroom politics, the presence of temporal regulation as a mediating mechanism of colonisation is joined by the presence of legal regulation. The presence of such a regulatory mechanism can often get entwined with political regulation – the paper-trail culture of quality assurance being the focal point of this entanglement. The paper trail counts not just as evidence of accountability (or lack of), but also, in different circumstances, as *legal evidence*. The evidential appetite of accountability mechanisms is one reason why so much time is devoted to them (as opposed to other activities). Using steering mechanisms such as audit and inspection to regulate professional behaviour results in strong emphasis being placed on measured outcomes, which itself produces a culture of evidential exposure.

The creeping nature of exposure creates a nervous and uncertain professional climate, helping to engender a sense of anxiety in the school environment. This fear on the part of the teachers is to some extent based on historical evidence. As

Andy, one of the teachers in the focus group, stated, 'there is a lot of litigation in schools and I think there is even more which we just don't hear about. I can think of at least 10 cases of litigation in 5 years at my particular school.' The challenges of the modern classroom is enough to strike fear into the heart of many teachers, particularly those that deal with children with special educational needs: 'I have a child with X syndrome who throws things about, and again it's about how you manage that because you are worried that if she injures another child, will I get sued? If I restrain her, then will the parents sue me?' (Caroline).

The effects of evidential exposure on behaviour management in schools, a contested but necessary function of education professionals, suggest that the quality of experience offered to pupils suffers in the crosshairs of these regulatory mechanisms. The encroachment of law into schools via equality legislation and health and safety law, alongside the threat of litigation, has made the management of children in school settings even more problematic. Behaviour management is affected by litigation 'because you are pussy-footing around them all the time and too frightened to discipline them properly' (Brenda).

It appears that a connection between evidential exposure and risk avoidance has taken hold in the school environment. A specific form of risk avoidance situated in the accountability/law nexus relates to direct physical contact with others. Although there are no specific accountability mechanisms that attach themselves to physical space, there was a particular concern that the emphasis on accountability affected teachers' ability both to form meaningful relationships and to take appropriate professional action as they saw fit. As one of the teachers in the focus group put it, 'ten years ago I would have probably picked her [an upset child] up and sat her down next to me and now I worry about doing that' (Brenda). This sense of worry was specifically a concern about how a particular action *might* be legally interpreted.

The fear of risk also surfaced when the potential existed for physical harm associated with particular environments. Arguably, a more significant rationale for litigation and claims for compensation, the dangers of injury to members of the public is a particular concern for front-line professionals, especially those with a duty of care. Although litigation in the medical profession tends to grab most of the headlines, there is an increasing focus on the risks attached to physical behaviour in school settings. The dangers of school trips, for example, has been a recent topic of debate in the UK, with some calling for the bureaucracy to be trimmed back so that schools and teachers can offer more activities outside the school environment (*Guardian* 2011). One of the teachers in our study, however, indicates why some teachers prove reluctant to take pupils on school trips. Andy, the teacher involved, took the school pupils to an indoor football tournament:

> On my way back upstairs I heard a scream and found a child who had cut her head on the railings. This worried me all night because if that parent took the risk assessment word for word I would be picking up my P45 in the morning.

I didn't take the kids to any sports things after that. I stayed at school and did my marking instead.

(Andy)

Discussion

The research tends to support the notion that political regulation in the form of accountability mechanisms has unintended consequences, consequences that impact on the capacity of such mechanisms to carry out their task effectively – that is, to regulate professional behaviour. There is evidence in the findings of impression management, risk avoidance, damage to the face to face, all consequences that could be classified as forms of colonisation. But the research also indicates that other unintended consequences occur, not just for professional behaviour, but for other already existing regulatory mechanisms – the power of which tend to get amplified in the presence of political regulation.

Such a finding suggests that proponents of ever greater accountability exhibit a naive view of what political regulation can achieve at the ground or 'street' level, notions of a cause and effect bureaucratic model being simplistic at best. No form of governance is ever that straightforward, too many factors mediating the end result. The regulation of schools is a much more complicated and multi-faceted activity than commentators give credit for. The research also exposes some of the limitations of Habermas' own theoretical apparatus – a model that suffers from an over-simplistic understanding of the reaches and limits of bureaucratic governance. Habermas has indeed provided a more nuanced understanding of the workings of modernisation than that provided by the overbearing pessimism of the iron cage. By (laboriously) constructing a more elaborate notion of rationality alongside a dual conception of social integration, Habermas provides a strong platform by which 'functional' and 'dysfunctional' forms of bureaucratisation can be separated off.

Nevertheless, while political imperatives via the new bureaucracy may have overstepped their boundaries, the binary model of system–lifeworld interaction neglects to take into account the ways in which this interaction is open to multiple forms of regulation, not just system or lifeworld forms. The absence of this more dynamic world of regulation from his theoretical framework is a significant oversight, as its presence may help to more fully understand how such colonisation occurs in the first place. While the exact processes via which one form of rationality usurps/overshadows/blocks another is very much open to debate (and is undertheorised in the literature), it could be the case that legal and temporal regulation unwittingly act as conduits for colonisation. Their inevitable presence in the working environments of public sector professionals means that professionals have little room for manoeuvre when it comes to balancing their 'dual-aspect' activities – the lower common denominator of instrumentalism the easier choice in a world of legal risk and time compression.

At the same time, communicative rationality is never entirely extinguished from the working lives of teachers, and one recommendation of this research at a policy level would be to place more emphasis on the interplay between various forms of regulation. This aspect of professional life needs to be investigated more thoroughly in order to develop a better understanding of how political regulation can be more 'effective', not just in relation to providing a visible account of outcomes but also in relation to the quality of the professional 'service' afforded to pupils (or patients, clients, etc.). It should also be acknowledged that the accountability of public sector professionals is especially complicated in regulatory terms, their working lives situated in the space between the public and the state, care and control, social democracy and political strategy. Professionals such as teachers deal directly with the public and as a result arguably represent the state at its most exposed to regulatory confusion. Any legitimacy of their work is strongly dependent on fragile layers of trust and respect, the intersubjective nature of their core activity a real testing ground for regulation.

The success or otherwise of these intersubjective relationships is a vital aspect of any analysis of accountability, such relationships having implications for the political legitimacy of the state and its capacity to deliver on its agenda of care. Also, professional relations with the public and the perceived quality of these relations provide a litmus test for notions of relative autonomy in the public sector – that is, the capacity of teachers to make judgements and use their discretion as public sector professionals. While having its drawbacks, it would be wise to more fully consider the implications for Habermas' colonisation thesis for the world of professional practice, especially if accountability is to remain as the link between bureaucracy and democracy.

Alongside these more theoretical and policy-related issues, the project also presented some issues for the researchers. It should be emphasised that the completion of the project has some unintended consequences for the project itself. For a start, it was never envisaged that the regulatory mechanisms detailed in this chapter would ever be so significant to the study. As a result, this meant that the approach to the original question had to be amended and updated as the research progressed, the project itself becoming something quite different from that originally intended. This illustrates how unpredictable research can be, suggesting that sufficient flexibility should be built into research design to allow for such unpredictable results to be considered more thoroughly.

These unintended consequences also highlight the nature of the relationship between the researchers and the theorists who are being applied. It should be self-evident that no theorist, no matter how exalted, is infallible. As with Bourdieu, Foucault or Derrida (or any other social theorist for that matter), Habermas' theoretical framework is not exempt from intellectual scrutiny, a fact that is as true for the educational researcher as it is for the professional philosopher. Habermas' theory of communicative action should not be treated as gospel, as a set of self-evident truths to be shoehorned into professional lives that oftentimes resist simplification at the hands of abstract theory.

This is a significant issue for those engaged in educational research, as it highlights another side to the theory–education relationship that sometimes gets overlooked. What our research illustrates is that the process of knowledge generation can be a two-way street: educational research does not just have to be concerned with the 'application' of ideas from elsewhere, but can also provide a fertile ground on which such ideas can be questioned, refined or even transformed. The knowledge gained at the level of professional practice is often just as useful for the development of theory, if not more so, than that gained through the construction of 'pure' theory. The politics of school regulation, as detailed here, is a good example of such fertile ground, a ground that suggests the theory/practice nexus is as challenging to the educational researcher as ever.

Notes

1 Two excellent overviews of Habermas' work can be found in Ingram (2010) and Outhwaite (2009).
2 To give a flavour of the range of applications, the theory of communicative action has been applied in relation to such issues as diverse as: the future of trade unionism in the UK (Edwards 2009); the role of partnerships in developing national sport policy (McDonald 2005); dilemmas in child protection practice (Spratt and Houston 1999); and the rehabilitation of cancer patients (Mikkelsen et al. 2008).

References

Adorno, T. and M. Horkheimer. 1972. *Dialectic of enlightenment*. London: Continuum.

Barberis, P. 1998. The new public management and a new accountability. *Public Administration* 76: 451–470.

Blaug, R. 1995. Distortion of the face-to-face: Communicative reason and social work practice. *British Journal of Social Work* 25: 423–439.

Blaug, R. 1997. Between fear and disappointment: Critical, empirical and political uses of Habermas. *Political Studies* 45, 1: 100–117.

Bovens, M. 2010. Two concepts of accountability: Accountability as a virtue and as a mechanism. *West European Politics* 33, 5: 946–967.

Brown, P. 2008. Trusting in the new NHS: Instrumental *versus* communicative action. *Sociology of Health & Illness* 30, 3: 349–363.

Clarke, J. and J. Newman. 1997. *The managerial state: Power, politics and ideology in the remaking of social welfare*. London: Sage.

Cooper, B. 2010. Educating social workers for lifeworld and system. In *Habermas, critical theory and education*, ed. M. Murphy and T. Fleming, 169–184. New York: Routledge.

Duvenage, P. 2003. *Habermas and aesthetics: The limits of communicative action*. Cambridge: Polity Press.

Edwards, G. 2009. Public sector trade unionism in the UK: Strategic challenges in the face of colonisation. *Work Employment Society* 23: 442.

Exworthy, M. and S. Halford, eds. 1999. *Professionals and the new managerialism in the public sector.* Buckingham, UK: Open University Press.

Guardian. 2011. Jobsworths misusing rules to ban fun at school, says health and safety chief. 2 July. Online at: www.guardian.co.uk/society/2011/jul/02/jobsworths-health-safety-schools-fun-children.

Habermas, J. 1984. *Theory of communicative action, Vol. 1: Reason and the rationalization of society.* Boston: Beacon Press.

Habermas, J. 1987. *Theory of communicative action, Vol. 2: Lifeworld and system: A critique of functionalist reason.* Boston: Beacon Press.

Hoyle, E. and M. Wallace. 2005. *Educational leadership: Ambiguity, professionals and managerialism.* London: Sage.

Ingram, D. 2010. *Habermas: Introduction and analysis.* Ithaca, NY: Cornell University Press.

Lipsky, M. 1980. *Street-level bureaucracy: Dilemmas of the individual in public services.* New York: Russell Sage Foundation.

McDonald, I. 2005. Theorising partnerships: Governance, communicative action and sport policy. *Journal of Social Policy* 34, 4: 579–600.

Mikkelsen, T., J. Soendergaard, A. Jensen and F. Olesen. 2008. Cancer surviving patients' rehabilitation: Understanding failure through application of theoretical perspectives from Habermas. *BMC Health Services Research* 8: 122.

Morris, M. 2001. *Rethinking the communicative turn: Adorno, Habermas and the problem of communicative freedom.* New York: SUNY Press.

Murphy, M. 2009. Bureaucracy and its limits: Accountability and rationality in higher education. *British Journal of Sociology of Education* 30, 6: 683–695.

Murphy, M. 2010. Forms of rationality and public sector reform: Habermas, education and social policy. In *Habermas, critical theory and education*, ed. M. Murphy and T. Fleming, 78–93. New York: Routledge.

Murphy, M. and T. Fleming. 2006. The application of the ideas of Habermas to adult learning. In *Lifelong learning: Concepts and contexts*, ed. P. Sutherland and J. Crowther, 48–57. London: Routledge.

Newman, J. and J. Clarke. 2009. *Publics, politics and power: Remaking the public in public services.* London: Sage.

Odhiambo, G. 2008. Elusive search for quality education: The case of quality assurance and teacher accountability. *International Journal of Educational Management* 22, 5: 417–431.

Outhwaite, W. 2009. *Habermas* (2nd edition). Cambridge: Polity Press.

Papadopoulos, Y. 2010. Accountability and multi-level governance: More accountability, less democracy? *West European Politics* 33, 5: 1030–1049.

Sabelis, I. 2002. Hidden causes for unknown losses: Time compression in management. In *Making time: Time and management in modern organisations*, ed. R. Whipp, B. Adam and I. Sabelis, 89–103. Oxford: Oxford University Press.

Salter, B. and T. Tapper. 2000. The politics of governance in higher education: The case of quality assurance. *Political Studies* 48: 66–87.

Scambler, G. and N. Britten. 2001. System, lifeworld and doctor–patient interaction: Issues of trust in a changing world. In *Habermas, critical theory and health*, ed. G. Scambler, 45–67. London: Routledge.

Scott, C. 2000. Accountability in the regulatory state. *Journal of Law and Society* 27, 1: 38–60.

Shore, C. and S. Wright. 2000. Coercive accountability: The rise of audit culture in higher education. In *Audit cultures: Anthropological studies in accountability, ethics and the academy*, ed. M. Strathearn, 57–89. Abingdon, Oxon: Routledge.

Small, N. and R. Mannion. 2005. A hermeneutic science: Health economics and Habermas. *Journal of Health Organization and Management* 19, 3: 219–235.

Spratt, T. and S. Houston. 1999. Developing critical social work in theory and in practice: Child protection and communicative action. *Child and Family Social Work* 4: 315–324.

Stecher, B. and S. Kirby, eds. 2004. *Organisational improvement and accountability: Lessons for education from other sectors*. Santa Monica, CA: RAND Corporation.

Sumner, J. 2001. Caring in nursing: A different interpretation. *Journal of Advanced Nursing* 35, 6: 926–932.

Thrupp, M. and R. Wilmott. 2003. *Educational management in managerialist times: Beyond the textual apologists*. Maidenhead, UK: Open University Press.

Travers, M. 2007. *The new bureaucracy: Quality assurance and its critics*. Bristol: Policy Press.

Walsh, P. 2006. Narrowed horizons and the impoverishment of educational discourse: Teaching, learning and performing under the new educational bureaucracies. *Journal of Education Policy* 21, 1: 95–117.

Weber, M. 1958. *The protestant ethic and the spirit of capitalism*. New York: Charles Scribner's Sons.

Chapter 7

Applying Habermas' theory of communicative action in an analysis of recognition of prior learning

Fredrik Sandberg

Introduction

This chapter draws on a research project exploring a process of recognition of prior learning (RPL) in the health care sector, for which Habermas' theory of communicative action was used as an analytical framework. Habermas' critical social theory has been of interest to scholars and researchers in education (Ewert 1991) and recent educational literature drawing on Habermas suggest that this interest is ongoing (Murphy and Fleming 2010). Just as it is possible to divide Habermas' intellectual career into different periods, educational scholars draw from different periods in his career; for instance, earlier writings on knowledge and human interests (1971) to communicative action (1984, 1987) and the more recent focus on deliberative democracy (1996). Habermas' most significant contribution to social theory is nevertheless probably associated with his famous turn to language and the attendant construction of the theory of communicative action (1984, 1987).

The focus in this chapter is on the process of RPL. RPL can be defined as a practice that reviews, evaluates and acknowledges skills and knowledge that adults gain through experiential, formal or self-directed learning and formal education (Thomas 2000). In Sweden, RPL was defined as a process of structured assessment, evaluation, documentation, recognition of knowledge and competences regardless of where this has been acquired (Ministry of Education 2003). Such general and various definitions do not immediately apply to all contexts of RPL. In this chapter, an RPL process for accreditation of prior work experiential learning to qualify for course credits is explored. The context is an RPL process in an in-service training programme at the upper secondary level in Sweden. The purpose of the programme is to provide an opportunity for health care assistants to become licensed practical nurses through RPL and education. Fourteen female health care assistants attended the in-service programme. Most of the assistants work in the elderly care sector. The in-service training programme is at the upper secondary level and lasts for approximately one and a half years. The participants continue to work 80 per cent of the time and invest 20 per cent of their time in coursework. An empirical analysis based on the theory of communicative action brings to the fore, for instance, i) questions of how different kinds of actions and communication influence students' learning and understanding in RPL and ii) although not primarily focused in this chapter, how the tension between the system and the lifeworld influence RPL, education and learning. By rationally reconstructing the RPL process it is, for instance, possible to criticise actions that facilitate the systems colonisation or assimilation of the lifeworld. However, as will be shown here, it can also be fruitful to reconstruct learning processes to see how they fit the norms of communicative action to advance, in this case, RPL practice. In the end of this chapter, challenges of conducting a critical empirical analysis based on a normative critical social theory are also considered. In the next part the main concepts in the theory of communicative action are illuminated.

The theory of communicative action

Educational research began to draw on the work of Habermas at the start of the 1970s (Ewert 1991), and recent work tells us that his work is still gainfully employed in the sector (Murphy and Fleming 2010; Moran and Murphy 2012; Fleming 2011). The work of Habermas has informed several discussions within educational research. In adult educational research, of most relevance here, Mezirow (1981) introduced Habermas when constructing his transformative learning theory. Since then, several researchers in adult education have continued to use Habermas to confer about the purposes of education and learning (e.g., Brookfield 2005; Welton 1995). Even though some recent articles draw on Habermas to explore RPL (Houlbrook 2012; Sandberg 2010, 2012; Sandberg and Andersson 2011), the work of Habermas has rarely been used to explore this phenomenon.

On a macro level, Habermas argues for the need to separate society into system and lifeworld in order to better understand the pathologies of modernity. The system can be viewed as: i) a bureaucracy, where the steering media is power, and ii) the market or economy, where the steering media is money. Systems can be located in areas in which social integration and language are not the main media for reproduction (i.e., bureaucracies, economic institutions, etc.). In the contexts of family and education, social integration is necessary to reproduce the lifeworld. Habermas' lifeworld forms a horizon of interpretative patterns that are implicitly used when people communicate to generate mutual understanding. However, even though education may be observed as part of the lifeworld and as a context in which social integration occurs, education is also a system. Education must therefore be reproduced as both a system and a lifeworld, but the two must be distinctly separate. For instance, the steering media of money and power could colonise the lifeworld within the area of education by focusing on regulation through tests, grades (Sandberg and Andersson 2011) and administrative or judicial oversight (Habermas 1987).

Habermas argues that 'the overbureaucratization of the educational system can be explained as a "misuse" of the media of money and power' (1987, 293–294). When education is formalised through the power of bureacracy and legal interventions, relationships between students and teacher and student in education are also at risk of becoming formalised. One main conclusion that Habermas makes is that, just as the lifeworld of the family in late modernity has been formalised, one can also witness a similar development in education ('School') (ibid.). These issues become salient in RPL for accreditation because RPL processes often focus on assessment and grades as the means-end goal of education, rather than on learning in a social context (Briton et al. 1998). These processes could force the education system to focus on coordinating RPL through grades and administrative control to ensure quality in assessment. Thus, the system might assimilate the lifeworld-grounded work experiences of participants in RPL and re-order them in instrumental ways so that they fit the grades/curricula of the institution. Or, as Habermas puts it, 'Autonomous subsystems make their way into the lifeworld from the outside – like colonial masters coming into tribal society – and force a process of assimilation upon it' (Habermas 1987, 355).

Although the macro-level concepts of the system and lifeworld are useful for a more general analysis, the concepts that structure communicative action must also be explained before it can be used to analyse the empirical data. In his work, Habermas coins several concepts related to communicative action (1984, 1987). Such an idea is the formal world concept. In communication, individuals can refer to exactly three worlds. First, when they raise a truth claim, they are referring to something in the objective world. Second, when they raise a claim to normative rightness, they are referring to something in the social world. Third, when they claim to be truthful or sincere, they are referring to something in their subjective world. At the same time, individuals can also behave in different ways in different worlds. Goal-oriented actions take place in the objective world, normatively regulated actions take place in the social world and dramaturgical actions take place in the subjective world. In communicative action, actors harmonise their individual goals through consensus (Habermas 1984). By raising truth claims and claims to normative rightness and truthfulness – thus referring to the objective, social and subjective worlds – individuals can successfully harmonise their plans for action (Habermas 1987). They thus attempt to reach a mutual understanding of the goals of the process (means-end rationality), to determine how to act in a manner that is normatively correct (normative rationality) and to depict their subjective worlds through dramaturgical action (expressive rationality). Two of the more important features of communicative action are its teleological and communicative aspects. The goals of the ego are linked with those of other individuals, and goals are pursued cooperatively based on a shared definition of the situation. The concepts presented above can be used to analyse, or, as will be the focus in the next part, to rationally reconstruct data on educational processes.

Habermas methodology: from virtual participation to rational reconstruction

Within Habermas' work, and especially in the theory of communicative action, it is possible to trace a methodology. In this part, two concepts will be described: virtual participation and rational reconstruction. Virtual participation is a concept that can describe how a researcher can act when collecting data. Habermas argues that researchers must engage themselves in the communicative structures of the context explored, to understand the meaning of utterances, but this must be done without an involvement in the goal-oriented actions undertaken by actors in the practice system. Habermas' method of rational reconstruction can be seen as an alternative to the approaches found in the empirical–analytical and hermeneutic traditions. Historically, the development of this method progresses as Habermas makes his famous turn to communication and language. It is located somewhere between a transcendental and empirical approach. In a nutshell, it allows a researcher to rationally reconstruct learning processes against the norms of communicative action.

Virtual participation

Before moving into a discussion of how to analyse RPL as communicative action via rational reconstruction, ideas concerning the role of the social researcher as a virtual participant are considered. Researchers must involve themselves in the communicative structures to understand the meaning in a communicative discourse, but without involving themselves in the goal-oriented actions of the practice system explored: thus, they have to become a 'virtual participant'. A researcher:

> participates in processes of reaching understanding and not for the sake of an end that requires coordinating the goal-oriented actions of those immediately involved. The action system in which the social scientist moves as an actor lies on a different plane . . . the social scientist does not pursue any aims of his own within the observed context [i.e., act goal-oriented] . . . the social scientist has to participate virtually in the interactions whose meaning he wants to understand.
>
> (Habermas 1984, 114–120)

When it comes to communication, Habermas distinguishes between three validity claims, that is, truth, normative rightness and sincerity/truthfulness, that in turn connect to three worlds, that is, objective, social and subjective (1984). When a researcher takes on the role of a virtual actor he or she must engage with a performative attitude and thus take a virtual stand on validity claims that are raised in, for instance, participatory observations or interviews. The main purpose of this enterprise would be to reach mutual understanding with the participants in the research process. For instance, if an interviewee raises a truth claim or a claim to normative rightness that is not understood by the researcher, the interviewee may be asked to clarify his or her position. Or if an interviewee engages in a subjective way to explain something truthfully, these expressions may become blurred for a researcher and then s/he might have to ask for further explanations of the subject's experiences. These ideas were adopted when collecting data. Thus, acting virtually is to act communicatively, without passing the fine line of acting-goal oriented within the context explored. These suggestions were used when gathering data. In the next section Habermas' method of rational reconstruction is explored, a method that inspired the analysis of the RPL process in the current research.

Rational reconstruction

Even though Habermas' theories have been deployed to a great extent in education and the social sciences in general, his method of rational reconstruction has unexpectedly not been deployed to the same extent (Pedersen 2008, 2009, 2011). It can be viewed as a method that focuses on an analysis that is theoretical, critical and non-relativistic at the same time. Its aim is to be descriptive and normative, as well as interpretative and explanatory. A concern is that Habermas' method is developed as a way to describe how his own theoretical work emerges. Thus, the theory of communicative action, in itself, is the result of rational reconstruction. Habermas' use of the concept of 'empirical science' and traditional 'empirical analytical research' are, of course, quite different, and Habermas has been the recipient of some criticism on this issue. Concepts used by Habermas are not specified empirically. The hypotheses derived by Habermas are not always empirical but sometimes based on traditional philosophical methods, such as critical explorations of literature, analyses of concepts and more personal reflections. Even though empirical examples are not absent in its entirety, examples and clarification of concepts are continuously not dealt with in satisfactory ways (Pedersen 2009).[1] Of even greater concern, according to Pedersen, is that 'the hypotheses arrived at through rational reconstruction are empirical hypotheses but cannot be tested by empirical means' (Pedersen 2009, 383).

However, (if we sidestep this rather philosophical dilemma) it is still possible to propose a design of how to make use of Habermas' method for empirical explorations (Pedersen 2009). Empirical sources that may be used for reconstructions could include document analysis, observations and interviews. Analyses of documents engaging in observations of participants make it possible to get information and knowledge that can be used to construct interview guides – ideas that were adopted in the research project analysed in this chapter. It is important to note that Pedersen's proposal focuses on empirical investigations in political science. A main difference between Pedersen's use of rational reconstruction and the focus in this chapter is thus that he focuses on 'deliberative democracy'. The focus for the analysis of RPL here is on the possibility for mutual understanding.

The following questions drawn from communicative action were used to reconstruct the RPL process:

Theme 1: Reconstruct the students' understanding of the assessment interview as communicative action.

Questions posed: What consequences do certain actions have for the RPL process and its outcome focusing on the participant's view of the assessment interview? How can the validity claims inform the process? How can the rationalities inform the process?

Theme 2: Reflexively reconstruct the possibilities of communicative action for advancing RPL focusing on the RPL placement.

Questions posed: By which actions does the RPL placement progress? What does a focus on validity claims reveal?

This type of reconstruction can be used to: i) critically appraise processes that do not realise the potential for communicative action; ii) reconstruct examples of processes that are more in tandem with the norms of communicative action; iii) highlight the consequences of a lack of mutual understanding and communication and the resentment, confusion and fragmentation that individuals may feel when the conditions for proper communication are scarce; and iv) look for examples that show potential for changes in practice. Following these suggestions, the next part presents two themes within a research project exploring RPL as communicative action.

A rational reconstruction of a process of recognition of prior learning in the health care sector

In a research project exploring RPL, the theory of communicative action was used for analysis (Sandberg 2010, 2012; Sandberg and Andersson 2011). Many of the procedures in the RPL process included various forms of assessment. Two processes will be focused on in this chapter: i) the assessment interview where the teachers assess the participants' prior learning more generally against courses in the health care programme and ii) a six-week placement in which the participants' prior learning is evaluated in a practical setting. Based on this project, the focus will be on reconstructing the RPL process as communicative action within two broader themes: i) confer about the consequences of a lack of mutual understanding in the assessment interview and ii) reflexively reconstructing the possibilities of communicative action for developing RPL drawing on data from a six-week RPL placement. Within the first theme, the assessment interview focused upon an interview that teachers conducted to be able to map and assess the participants' prior learning against several courses in the health care programme. In the second theme, the focus was on a six-week placement where the participants were assessed in practice by a tutor. During the placement, the health care assistants worked under the supervision of a licensed practical nurse. During the RPL placement, the participants and tutors also engaged in discussions concerning the participants' prior learning. In some cases, these discussions lasted several hours each week, and a form with questions drawn from the health care programme curriculum was completed based on these discussions. These forms were then collected by the teachers and used to assess the more practical content from the curricula of several courses within the health care programme. The data used here was based on interviews with the students, conducted after the RPL process was finalised. The interview guide was constructed based on prior observations of the RPL process.

The consequences of a lack of mutual understanding

The first theme explored is based on a reconstruction of the participants' understanding of the assessment interview. It was quite obvious that these interviews were often not based on mutual understanding. Participants are confused about how the assessment is conducted, how the teachers document their answers and many of them also report a feeling of being blocked during the interview. Mia spent quite some time thinking about how it was possible for the teachers to document her prior learning:

> It must be amazingly hard to take notes and get it out. And we said that several times when we talked afterwards in the group [with the other students], that it is totally amazing that they were able to get what they needed.

In this quote Mia reflects on how the teachers documented her answers and is astonished at how the teachers were able to receive enough information based on her answers. However, she never understood this process. Rose feels the same way and raises several questions:

> What is written down? Is she quoting me correctly? But I guess they write when they have to. It is actually they who are responsible. So you get a true assessment when you step out.

Rose asks herself if the teachers have actually understood her appropriately and documented her prior experiences accurately – that is, if the process is actually based on a mutual understanding of her prior learning. It is evident that both Mia and Rose do not understand how this assessment process works. The teachers document what they think is true in relation to the curriculum of the courses. Thus, the teachers are aware of claims that are true in relation to the curriculum, but this is not communicated to the students during the process. This process does not seem to be based on mutual understanding and thus the participants try to answer the questions posed by the teachers in a subjective and truthful way and the teachers assimilate the knowledge they consider to be true to the system.

This lack of mutual understanding produces a feeling of 'being blocked'. Here one fundamental issue in communicative action is raised: the lack of mutual definitions concerning the purpose of the assessment interview (means-end rationality). Maria presents the following statements about her experiences of the assessment interview:

> Well, during that conversation [assessment interview] I was totally blocked . . . I don't know why but I know we sat down afterwards and talked about it. And if you had been prepared a little it might have turned out differently.

Maria suggests that she felt blocked during the interview. Her suggestion is that she did not reach a mutual definition of the assessment situation with the teachers. If they had reached a mutual definition, she would have been able to perform differently. Juli also felt blocked during her interview:

> Throughout I thought: what was that? Because you thought that you had to prove something here. In a way you probably did, but all the time I was thinking: What is it they want? What are they looking for? You were a bit blocked there, I felt.

Juli wants to prove something in the interview, but it was not clear to her what this was. This shows that the means-end results of the RPL process and prescribed norms of how to act are not mutually defined. Only the teachers know the rationale of the process. This raises concerns about the mutual understanding of what is normatively right; the students should be able to know how to act in relation to the questions given by the teachers. However, this feeling of being blocked also seems to have other consequences for the students. What seems to take place is that the students have not reached a mutual definition of the purpose of the assessment interview or a mutual understanding with the teachers during the interview. It thus becomes unclear what the focus of the process is. One conclusion is that this process is primarily oriented towards the teachers' success in strategically receiving the 'right' answers to questions they ask. At the same time as the students are trying to respond to the teachers' questions, they are trying to understand what is really going on. Sandy discusses this as:

> That phenomenon that arose [during the assessment interview]: at the same time as you answered questions, you frantically reflected and tried to find the knowledge [internally].

Thus, at the same time as Sandy has a conversation with the teachers externally, she is also having a conversation internally. She is trying to figure out what the purpose is. She seems to be alienated.

Many of the students also had problems understanding how their prior learning was supposed to be assessed. When Juli is asked to describe how the teachers assessed her prior learning, she posed several questions internally:

> how could they get anything out of the answers I gave them? But, ok [they said]: we are pleased now. But, what have I said that you [they] can touch upon [grasp]? I thought after these conversations [assessment interviews].

It seems that Juli is trying to understand if and how her answers are true. But this was never communicated to her. It is unclear how her answers were helpful to the teachers. Mandy also felt that the interview was unclear:

> Well, there were quick switches between this and that – from one subject to another. So, alright, was that ok now? If you only started [replying] to the questions, it solved itself. You sat down and talked for an hour. So, alright, an hour has already passed?

For Mandy, the interview did not seem to have a clear thread. Instead, it seemed to jump between different subjects. Like Juli, Mandy also posed questions internally during the interview and accepts that she does not really understand what is going on.

From a Habermasian perspective, the problems raised here reflect the teachers' goal-oriented and strategic actions. The lack of mutual definitions concerning the purpose of the assessment interview and the lack of mutual understanding during the interview seems to have several consequences for the students' understanding of the process. First, the students do not know what the means-end goal of the assessment interview is (or what is true). Second, they do not know how to behave in relation to the prescribed norms in the assessment interview (claim of normative rightness). Because of this, the students are forced to carry on internal conversations. Instead of being a process based on communication between teacher and student, the assessment interview forces the students into internal conversations. These processes also highlight issues concerning the tension between lifeworld and system. It could be seen as a process where the system, through the teachers' goal-oriented and strategic actions, assimilates such experiences that fit the system (curricula). However, this rather instrumental process of the assessment interview that was reconstructed here does not speak for the entire RPL process. In the next section, the focus will be on the RPL placement explained above, a process more in tandem with the norms of communicative action.

Reconstructing the possibilities of communicative action for developing RPL

Another core feature of the RPL process was the six-week placement. In contrast to the rather instrumental process of the assessment interview, the processes taking place in the placements seemed to be more in tandem with the norms of communicative action. It was especially apparent among participants and tutors, who shared similar subjective experiences of caring practice. However, these experiences of the students and tutors were not always the same, and this tended to obstruct engagement between them. Several participants describe their relationships with the tutors as positive. Anna, a participant, reported a positive experience:

> It was so heavenly good, and we connected at once. So, right away it was more like interacting with an ordinary colleague.

Mallory also highlights the collegial character of her relationship with her tutor: 'It was almost like working with a colleague you worked with before. It was really good.' One conclusion that we can draw based on these comments is that because these and other participants and tutors share the immediate lifeworld of caring practice, they also already share a horizon of interpretative patterns, which makes it possible for them to enter into interpersonal relationships and develop mutual understanding of the objective, social and subjective premises of caring practice. However, these individuals may not always agree on the truths, norms and personal experiences associated with working within the field of care work. For example, they may agree that there are normatively correct ways of performing an aspect of care work – but even though they agree that such norms exist, they may disagree that this is the correct way to perform.

The RPL placement and the tutor–student relationship were experienced as positive under certain circumstances. There seem to be two main reasons why this relationship works in terms of communicative action. First, as previously stated, the tutor and candidate share a mutual social context or lifeworld as care workers. They understand each other's context and subjective experience. Second, the tutors on the placement are well informed about its purpose, and third, managers are able to construct a schedule allowing for conversations between tutor and candidate. Ingrid found that she and her tutor could relate to one another because of their common experiences and interests and that they had plenty of time for dialogue:

> My tutor and I cooperated well. We talked a lot. We reflected very much and talked very much. 'What do you think about that?' I think like this. 'Aha, but how do you think?' But I think like this and that. We were able to have a dialogue . . . Then, we talked a lot about other things around care work and our situation . . . Both me and her were interested in union work, and we talked a lot about that – How to raise our salaries, questions of care ethic and care work in general.

It seems as though the process Ingrid describes is based on mutual understanding and that the cooperative work that she and her tutor completed was successful. This quotation can be linked to two of the more important features of communicative action mentioned above: the goal-oriented and communicative aspects – that ego's goals are linked with those of other individuals, and the cooperating parties pursue their goals through a shared understanding of the situation (Habermas 1984). Even though the primary focus of the conversations was to complete a form handed out by the teachers, the dialogue transcended the boundaries of this formal assessment process to include more developmental discussions of the current status of caring practice.

It is important to note that not all students experienced the type of successful conversations and cooperation. Lena, with 25 years of experience with care work, felt very different:

> Ehh, well, it went all right, but she [the tutor] felt that here I am, tutoring you and I have been working here for 2 years as a licensed practical nurse, and you have been working in health care since 1985 . . . We worked – I was there as manual labor. I guess we took some time to sit down and talk, but she did not really understand what it was all about.

This experience draws attention to the problems that arise when the student and tutor are not sharing experiences and an immediate lifeworld and when they are not able to reach a mutual understanding. When the conditions for reaching mutual understanding are not fulfilled, it may be difficult to develop mutual understanding and thus to cooperate to fulfil the goals of the RPL placement. It also shows the importance of reaching consensus of the goal of the process – something that is not possible because of the tutor's lack of knowledge concerning this, according to Lena. In some cases, it is easier to reach a mutual understanding of the situation because the tutor and the student can agree on what is true and normatively right, while considering each other's expressions to be truthful and sincere. In such cases, the student and tutor may almost immediately begin working towards the goals of the placement through a shared understanding of the situation. However, the process also showed potential for making use of prior learning in a critical fashion.

Critical discussions in the social world of caring practice

From a Habermasian perspective, the critical discussions in the placement could be seen as occurring primarily within the normative dimension of care work, where the prescribed norms of caring practice are critically discussed. In some cases, the participants directly address critical issues with care workers at the placement. Many of these issues are raised during the conversations with the tutors. Astrid describes a situation where she reacted to an issue she thought was normatively incorrect:

> There were clients who sat in their wheelchairs a lot. And I was a bit against that because they could walk. So I got my tutor to agree that was wrong . . .

She thought that was good but that she had not thought about it. She thought that we were different [had different views] but that she thought it [my idea] was very good.

Astrid describes a situation in which she thought the staff at the placement acted in a manner that was normatively incorrect. She raises this claim in a conversation with her tutor and offers another claim she considers to be normatively correct for acting in this situation. The tutor agrees that the staff did not address the situation appropriately and agrees with this claim to normative correctness. When norms are mutually justified in this way, the norm becomes 'true' in the sense that the tutor and the participant can now agree that the right norm has been objectively satisfied. Astrid found that the individuals at her placement were behaving in ways that were normatively incorrect. She also communicated her criticism to her tutor. The participant raises concerns regarding how a norm has been violated. This norm also applies to the tutor as an actor in the same context as the student and can thus be further discussed and objectively accepted as true once the two individuals have reached a consensus. Thus, the norm also has the potential to change. Here, the participants thus show that they can use their prior experiences and learning for critical thinking. These types of critical discussions show potential for change, which will be explored next.

Communication and the possibility of change through RPL

There seems to be potential for change of caring practice when participants make critical use of their prior learning. Thus, the RPL placement opens up a possibility to question norms that seem to be unjustified. Lisa discusses this:

I think that there is a need to do that [change the workplace] because you become 'home blind'. You have done this for 20 years, and you are supposed to do this for another 20 years. You have to be open-minded when younger people start working and question. You do not have to take it as criticism; instead try out what they say – because they see it from another view.

Lisa suggests that changing one's workplace can be helpful because it can open the mind to other ways of engaging in caring practice. The RPL placements makes it possible to challenge the status quo that often comes with routinised care work. Lisa promotes the idea that health care assistants would benefit from the experience of changing to another workplace. Seeing things from another viewpoint is a positive outcome when, as in Lisa's example, younger people enter the workplace, and it is also something that seems to happen quite often when the participants enter 'new' workplaces for their RPL placements.

For these individuals, engaging in discussions with tutors and other workers facilitate two change processes. First, participants are able to use their prior learning to think critically about caring practice, in particular thinking about how to perform care work in normatively correct ways. They question and critically use prior experiences and learning to argue for normatively correct ways to perform caring practice. Second, they also experience other ways of approaching caring practice, experiences they bring back to their normal workplaces and which have potential to change these circumstances as well.

Concluding discussion

The objective of this chapter has been on analysing RPL as a form of communicative action. First, a summary and discussion of this analysis will be outlined. Second, a discussion of the challenges of rationally reconstructing the RPL process as communicative action is discussed.

On a more general level, the process analysed above could be seen as a procedure where the education system is focused on coordinating the participants' prior experiences and learning through grades and administrative control. Thus, the system might assimilate the lifeworld-grounded work experiences of the participants and re-order them in instrumental ways so that they fit the grades/ curricula of the institution. However, by a rational reconstruction against the norms of communicative action, two more broad themes were developed. Within the first theme it is possible to return to the three forms of rationalities. What is the goal of the assessment interview (means-end rationality)? How are students' actions supposed to be oriented in relation to the prescribed norms of the RPL process (normative rationality)? How can the participants present a truthful picture of their prior learning and experiences (expressive rationality)? Based on these three forms of rationalities it seems as though the participants: i) do not know how the assessment is conducted or what the goal of the assessment interview is; ii) do not know how to orient their actions towards the normatively prescribed norms in the process (What does it mean to be a participant in the process? How are the participants supposed to reflect so their prior learning can be made visible for the teachers?); and iii) they do not know how to present themselves truthfully. It seems difficult for the students to describe their subjective experiences when they do not know how to describe these experiences. The reconstruction thus draws attention to the problems when mutual definitions of a situation are not reached through consensus and when mutual understanding is not the focus in general.

Within the second theme, a rational reconstruction of the RPL placement as communicative action seemed to provide helpful insights into the development of RPL: i) mutual understanding was important so tutors and participants can reach a mutual definition of their situation so that they can cooperate towards the goals of the process; ii) the students and tutors must agree on the goal(s) of the process and cooperate towards these goals; and iii) they must try to understand each other's subjective experiences and act truthfully towards each other. When these conditions were not met, it was hard for the participants to fulfil the goals of the six-week placement. When assessing prior learning in practice, it is vital to try to match the tutor and participant in terms of their work experiences and work context. If not, the placement may become an aggravating process where the tutor and participant fruitlessly try to develop a mutual understanding. Then it becomes unmanageable for the participants to act based on consensus, which has a bearing on learning and development through RPL. The results based on the rational reconstruction presented here included examples where the participants and tutors seemed to expand their views through communication. It seems that when prior learning is used critically there is a potential for action and thus both learning and changes in practice can possibly occur. Such outcomes would not have been achievable if the tutors and participants had not reached a mutual definition of their situation. Although modestly argued, it seems that critical discussions or discourses were made possible when tutors and participants entered into mutually trusting relationships.

Certainly, there are challenges in rationally reconstructing RPL against the norms of communicative action. Four (but certainly not the only) challenges will be highlighted here: i) finding a balance between the empirical data and the theory; ii) the problem of focusing on the subjective experiences of the participants; iii) communicative action is a normative critical social theory that the participants do not know anything about; and iv) the challenges of presenting a normative analysis to those involved in the study.

The first issue raises a problem concerning how to perform an analysis. Should it be a process where the theory is shoehorned into the data? At first it could be interpreted that a rational reconstruction is merely about taking the theory and making it 'fit' with the available data. However, this would not be something promoted by Habermas. Instead, communicative action is an interpretative framework and the aim of a rational reconstruction is to be descriptive and normative (i.e., critical) on the one hand and interpretative and explanatory on the other. However, it is a challenge to balance these issues.

The second issue here is connected to the data used for the analysis. Habermas' main focus is to develop a theory that moves away from the individualistic and ego focus of phenomenology to a focus on an intersubjective dimension. Thus, the lifeworld is for Habermas a collective horizon that reproduces meaning. It might thus at first seem to be a bit problematic to use interviews when conducting a Habermasian analysis. However, as discussed before, it has been promoted that an analysis based on the theory of communicative action can be used to highlight the resentment that individuals feel when they are denied access to proper communication. Even though this is a challenge, the interview guide used in the analysis in this chapter was structured based on observations of processes in real time. When conducting interviews, there is also a need to engage as a virtual participant and based on this role reach mutual understanding with interviewees.

The third issue draws attention to power issues between a researcher and those persons involved in the study. It could even be seen as elitist to reconstruct a process against norms that individuals in the study know little or nothing about. However, as the fourth issue points to, presenting the final results to those involved in the study could partly redeem this problem. However, if the reconstruction focused on critically appraising the process, this could become a tough experience for both researcher and participants partaking in the study.

Using Habermas' theory of communicative action to rationally reconstruct RPL also shows potential for analysis of other educational processes. Hopefully this chapter will help inspire educational researchers to proceed with such endeavours.

Note

1 Although Habermas draws on research that is empirical.

References

Briton, D., W. Gereluk and B. Spencer. 1998. *Prior learning, assessment and recognition: Issues for adult educators.* Paper presented at the CASAE Conference Proceedings, University of Ottawa, Ontario, Canada.

Brookfield, S. 2005. Learning democratic reason: The adult education project of Jürgen Habermas. *Teachers College Record* 107, 6: 1127–1168.

Ewert, D. G. 1991. Habermas and education: A comprehensive overview of the influence of Habermas in educational literature. *Review of Educational Research* 61, 3: 345–378.

Fleming, T. 2011. Fromm and Habermas: Allies for adult education and democracy. *Studies in Philosophy and education* 31, 2: 123–136.

Habermas, J. 1971. *Knowledge and human interests.* Boston: Beacon Press.

Habermas, J. 1984. *The theory of communicative action, Volume 1. Reason and the rationalization of society.* Cambridge: Polity.

Habermas, J. 1987. *The theory of communicative action, Volume 2. Lifeworld and system: A critique of functionalist reason.* Cambridge: Polity.

Habermas, J. 1996. *Between facts and norms: Contributions to a discourse theory of law and democracy.* London: Polity.

Houlbrook, M. C. 2012. RPL practice and student disposition – insights from the lifeworld. *Journal of Education and Work* 25, 5: 555–570.

Mezirow, J. 1981. A critical theory of adult learning and education. *Adult Education Quarterly* 32, 1: 3–27.

Ministry of Education. 2003. *Validering m.m. – fortsatt utveckling av vuxnas lärande.* Stockholm: Utbildningsdepartementet.

Moran, P. and M. Murphy. 2012. Habermas, pupil voice, rationalism and their meting with Lacan's objet petit a. *Studies in Philosophy and Education* 31, 2: 171–181.

Murphy, M. and T. Fleming, eds. 2010. *Habermas, critical theory and education.* New York: Routledge.

Pedersen, J. 2008. Habermas' method: Rational reconstruction. *Philosophy of the Social Sciences* 38, 4: 457–485.

Pedersen, J. 2009. Habermas and the political sciences: The relationship between theory and practice. *Philosophy of the Social Sciences* 39, 3: 381–407.

Pedersen, J. 2011. *Habermas' method: Rational reconstruction. Dissertation.* Bergen: University of Bergen.

Sandberg, F. 2010. Recognising health care assistants' prior learning through a caring ideology. *Vocations and Learning* 3, 2: 99–115.

Sandberg, F. 2012. A Habermasian analysis of a process of recognition of prior learning. *Adult Education Quarterly* 62, 4: 351–370.

Sandberg, F. and P. Andersson. 2011. RPL for accreditation in higher education: As a process of mutual understanding or merely lifeworld colonisation? *Assessment and Evaluation in Higher Education* 36, 7: 767–780.

Thomas, A. 2000. Prior learning assessment: The quiet revolution. In *Handbook of adult and continuing education*, ed. A. Wilson and E. Hayes, 508–522. San Fransicso: Jossey-Bass.

Welton, M. R. 1995. In defense of the lifeworld: A Habermasian approach to adult learning. In *In defense of the lifeworld: Critical perspectives on adult learning*, ed. M. R. Welton, 127–156. Albany: State University of New York Press.

Part IV

Bourdieu

Chapter 8

Bourdieu and educational research

Thinking tools, relational thinking, beyond epistemological innocence

Shaun Rawolle and Bob Lingard

Introduction

The French sociologist Pierre Bourdieu (1930–2002) was perhaps the pre-eminent sociologist of the late twentieth century. The impact of his work is evident in social theory, sociology of art, culture and the media, sociology of education and in respect of important issues of research methodology and epistemology in the social sciences.[1] In this chapter we consider Bourdieu's *oeuvre* and draw implications for education researchers today. Specifically, Bourdieu's work seeks a way through some of the central conundrums facing all social science researchers and we are thinking of educational research here as framed within social science research. Bourdieu's work also provides a way through a range of sticking points that present themselves in the form of conceptual dualisms, such as the structure and agency relationship, and micro and macro binaries. At a broader level, Bourdieu presents a social science that rejects 'theoreticism' (theory not informed closely enough by empirical data and not open to challenge) and 'methodologism' (a narrow concern with methods and techniques to the neglect of epistemological and ontological issues about data collection and knowledge claims) (Bourdieu and Wacquant 1992). In practice, Bourdieu emphasised the necessity of putting both theory and data to work together, and his accounts emphasise the social world as being the product of social constructions, yet also more than such constructions. The effects of social science were, for Bourdieu, located both within the relative autonomy of the academic field, and more broadly within the polity, including other social fields such as education, journalism and politics. Bourdieu also rejected what might be seen as a *substantialist* account of social phenomena that were the focus of social science research; as such, he rejects individualism and holism. Instead, Bourdieu recognised the *relational* workings of the social arrangement, seeing all social phenomena in relation to their location in a given field and in relation to others in the field.

It is interesting in this respect to consider *Sketch for Self-Analysis* (2004a) in which Bourdieu applies his thinking tools to his own life. Bourdieu states emphatically in a frontnote to the book that 'this is *not* an autobiography', and that he is interested in understanding his own habitus and dispositions in terms of the times and places in which he lived. Bourdieu's account mirrors C. Wright Mills' 'sociological imagination', which stresses the need to understand the interweaving of individual agency with structure through time.[2] An element of potential human agency against structural determinism for Bourdieu is the possibility we as human beings have for what he calls 'socio-analysis', our capacity for reflecting on what has made us who we are; the capacity to reflect upon, and to be reflexive about, our habitus in Bourdieu's terms. It is just such a set of dispositions or habitus that Bourdieu sees as necessary for good sociological research (see Brubacker 1993; Grenfell 2008). We view such a research habitus as central to good research in the sociology of education; this is a research habitus which is able to reflexively understand the positioning of the researcher in respect of what is being researched and in relation to the intellectual field in which the research is located.

The main aim of this chapter then is to provide an introduction to the theoretical work of Pierre Bourdieu, and to outline different ways in which Bourdieu's work is influential and has been engaged with in education research and to suggest implicitly the usefulness of this work for educational researchers. In order to do this, we draw on a range of Bourdieu's own writing published singly or with colleagues, emphasising in particular his engagements with education. Part of our treatment also deals with his wider writing that has subsequently been influential for education researchers, and in particular Bourdieu's anthropological writing and account of practice (Bourdieu 1977, 1990), his approach to social class and cultural issues, his account of the judgement of taste and distinctions (Bourdieu 1984), and his later politically focused writing (Bourdieu 1989/1996, 2003, 2004c, 2005a).

Running through the account presented is an overarching argument that Bourdieu's work has developed a global influence, utility and continued importance to educational research. There is a case to be made, as Santoro (2009) has argued, for 'putting Bourdieu in a global field' (p. 1). In this chapter, we expand on this account to argue a pluri-scalar case in relation to education research: that Bourdieu's theories are important for understanding a global field of education research, different national fields of education research, and cross-field effects between these two scales of fields. Here we are recognising the necessity of understanding the impact on his work of the national field of research in which it was produced, but also stress the need to understand its playing out and cascading effects in different national fields of consumption. This reciprocal looping shares a family resemblance with Giddens' (1993) concept of a *double hermeneutic* that recognises both the fields of production and the fields of consumption. Such recognition is necessary for understanding the impact of Bourdieu's work (Wacquant 1993, 235).

Bourdieu's theoretical work can be understood as the complementary development of three interlinked foci, each of which has been developed, tested and honed through empirical work. It is these three foci that will be explored in the remainder of this chapter. First is the focus of Bourdieu's research on specific empirical cases, to which he returned with different elaborations and theorisations at various stages of his writing. These include his writing on Algeria, on education and on art and cultural production. Our focus will be Bourdieu's writing about education in its various forms. This work on education is linked specifically to understanding reproduction and change in societies. Wacquant (1993, 235) argues that Bourdieu's *oeuvre* can be seen as 'a generative anthropology of power with special emphasis on its symbolic dimension', especially the misrecognitions involved in the workings of power in social and cultural reproduction. We also note the ways in which Bourdieu returned throughout his research career to some earlier foci and in this reprise conceptualised things differently, as indicative of the reflexivity of his account and the openness of his concepts to re-interrogation via the empirical. Second is the development of intellectual resources such as specific conceptual tools (Bourdieu's 'thinking tools') that were developed over the course of his work and tested and applied between different cases. This is considered separately in that as these tools were products of the practice of Bourdieu's intellectual work that were generated over time, they did not emerge as fully formed and complete conceptual tools at the beginning of his career. For example, Bourdieu's (1958/1962) earliest works on Algeria present no direct account of practice or *habitus*, or fields, yet do present an initial account of capital in ways consistent with later work, though not differentiated into forms. Third is the development of theoretical resources that elaborate methodological, epistemological and researcher approaches and stances to the study of the social world.

In education research, these three broad foci have been engaged to differing degrees, with a variety of commitments to these kinds of theoretical resources. We use this basic analytic distinction as a way of structuring the next sections, but note that this distinction is a specific device designed to add some focus for understanding both the different reception of Bourdieu's work and the differential potential that his work and theoretical approach hold for educational researchers.

The production, consumption and reception of Bourdieu's research on education

This section is structured as an account of the reception (or 'consumption') of Bourdieu's works about one specific area of study: education. Our central argument in this section is that the utility of Bourdieu's work lies in the multifaceted theorising of all aspects of research, which therefore provide a range of connections with different elements of research in education.

Engagements with education

[A] truly rational pedagogy, that is, one based on a sociology of cultural inequalities, would, no doubt, help to reduce inequalities in education and culture, but it would not be able to become a reality unless all the conditions for a true democratization of the recruitment of teachers and students were fulfilled, the first of which would be the setting up of a truly rational pedagogy.

(Bourdieu and Passeron 1964/1979, 76)

The main contribution of Bourdieu's initial works in education lay in the development of a broad theory to explain the reproduction of cultural and social inequalities through education, and the legitimation of these inequalities through misrecognition. For Bourdieu, education acted as a sorting institution that functioned to divide groups primarily through the valuing of cultural capital. This cultural capital was implicit in school curricula and pedagogy, and was aligned with, embodied, assumed and possessed by certain classes. This implicit cultural capital became the mechanism of selection, which, with pedagogic action, helped to reproduce inequalities and led to the misrecognition of these cultural differences as differences in individual ability. What was largely contentious about this account was the implication that the reproduction of such inequalities was inherently embedded in the structure and functioning of institutions of education, in their curricula and pedagogies, and that such reproduction occurred largely in spite of the (good) intentions of teachers. Theories in the 1970s premised the identification of education as a major site of change and reform of broader social institutions. It is therefore understandable that Bourdieu's contributions, particularly as outlined in the publication of *Reproduction* (Bourdieu and Passeron 1970/1977) and *The Inheritors* (Bourdieu and Passeron 1964/1979) were viewed with some suspicion.

At the time of the publication of these books, Bourdieu's argument was heavily criticised as either being conservative or implying the need for a revolution to challenge such reproduction. On that very point Bourdieu later noted:

The paradox I have to recall is that it's precisely the law of gravity that enables us to fly: that is what I always said, from *The inheritors* onwards, particularly in the conclusion on 'rational pedagogy', which some people saw as reformist [see quote above]. It is by knowing the laws of reproduction that we can have a chance, however small, of minimizing the reproductive effect of the educational institution.

(Bourdieu 2008, 52–53)

Despite this suspicion, initially by those of all political persuasions, Bourdieu's and colleagues' contributions to reproduction theories of education have been influential and have continued salience to a range of researchers in education.

The consumption and reception of Bourdieu's work

There is, in looking at Bourdieu's engagements with education,[3] a significant challenge that we need to signal, as it bears relevance to the potential of Bourdieu's work and to the engagements with his work on education in different nation-states. In essence, the reception of Bourdieu in different education research traditions reveals a range of different national variations.[4] There is not one single univocal narrative that can be told about Bourdieu's influence, in part because of issues of the timing of translation of his work, but also because of the significance and reception of his specific arguments in national debates about education issues, and the question of how dominant scholars in each national education research field at the time of their emergence engaged with these arguments. Robbins (2004), for example, has written about the reception of Bourdieu's work in Britain in relation to the sociology of education, demonstrating the relationship between this reception and the chronology of the translation of Bourdieu's work into English and the significance of his reproduction account in this reception. There are also questions of the specific disciplinary paths through which Bourdieu's theories have been adapted and influential in education research, and the flows of intellectuals between nation-states whose work references Bourdieu's.

We note, for example, that in Australian education research the initial links between Bourdieu's work and that of Australian education researchers follow people such as one of Bourdieu's translators, Richard Teese, whose works on Bourdieu first appeared in *Melbourne Studies* (Teese 1980), and the writing of Richard Bates, an Australian scholar linking Bourdieu's theories to education administration (Bates 1980).[5] Yet the subsequent pick up of Bourdieu's ideas in education appeared somewhat curtailed through the reception of dominant Australian sociologists such as Connell, whose then position on education in Australia (argued with colleagues), though theoretically similar, was marked by a sharp refusal of Bourdieu's central arguments about the mechanisms of reproduction through education, and her view that Bourdieu and Passeron presented a static model of education (Connell et al. 1982). This view was presented in *Making the Difference* (Connell et al. 1982), but also in Connell's broader critique of reproduction theory (Connell 1983), where she argued that a focus on practice, as opposed to structure, leads to an emphasis on change, rather than structural reproduction. In recounting the uptake of Bourdieu in Australian sociology, Woodward and Emmison (2009) talk about this opposition in stark terms: '[t]here appeared to be no place in Connell's *oeuvre* on class for Bourdieu' (p. 4).[6]

In contrast, the initial engagement with Bourdieu's work in England can be traced to a conference of the British Sociological Association in Durham. At this conference a range of concerns were raised about reproduction and how the 'taken-for-granteds' of pedagogy and curriculum helped reproduce the class structure, class codes and class relations through schooling. Discussions at this BSA conference led to collaboration on an edited book, *Knowledge and Control* (Young 1971), which illustrated a broad engagement with and alignment between Bourdieu and English-speaking scholars such as Basil Bernstein and Michael Young. This book heralded what was to become referred to as the *new sociology of education*. The authors in this book were soon to become dominant scholars within an emerging research concentration bringing together different critical, philosophical and sociological traditions to bear on education. Through this book Bourdieu's writing on education was to become central to scholarship and research on education in the United Kingdom. Bourdieu and Bourdieu and Passeron's work also aligned with the reproduction theories that were heavily influenced by Marxist and neo-Marxist scholarship (Bowles and Gintis 1976). Bourdieu's (1977, published in French in 1970) book with Passeron, *Reproduction in Education, Society and Culture*, was central to the take-up of his work in the sociology of education. It may appear a little odd in a book devoted to education theory to raise two small historical vignettes related to the international circulation of ideas, and in this case, Bourdieu's ideas. However, it is in the links between these two aspects of Bourdieu's work that his theories hold relevance for particular and located scholars positioned in different national fields.

Theoretical and generative resources: Bourdieu's *thinking tools*

Alongside theoretical understandings of specific social cases, Bourdieu developed a set of what Wacquant (1989) described as 'thinking tools'. Each of these tools was adapted from other scholarship, from philosophy, sociology and anthropology, but reworked to have a specific location and purpose in Bourdieu's work. We separate these theoretical resources from Bourdieu's theorisation of specific empirical cases to illustrate the development of a cumulative framework of specific tools to understand the social. Hence, while some scholars may disagree with specific theorisations of social cases offered in Bourdieu's work, the thinking tools themselves may have some utility in broader applications to research. The extensibility of this framework was tested in a variety of different research projects, and over the course of Bourdieu's writing there were shifts in the emphasis and use of these tools to suit specific research purposes. These tools serve multiple purposes and help to create a break with the pre-conceived objects of the social world,[7] and to create a distancing that allowed the examination of specific kinds of relationships that are often overlooked.

While we have previously suggested that these tools form a 'theoretical triad' (Rawolle and Lingard 2008), here we group two conceptual couplet from Bourdieu's *thinking tools*, namely habitus/practice and forms of capital/social fields. These are grouped primarily for theoretical congruence and the reasonableness of their combination. We arrange these families largely according to their chronological emergence in Bourdieu's work, as the specific couplets discussed are supplemented by subsequent thinking tools, rather than being completely replaced.

Theory of practice: practice and habitus

The first couplet important to Bourdieu as a way of breaking with common-sense views of activity was that of *practice* and *habitus*. These two concepts were developed as part of a project of developing a coherent yet open theory of practice, exemplified in two major works, *Outline of a Theory of Practice* (Bourdieu 1977) and *Logic of Practice* (Bourdieu 1990), both based on anthropological research in Algeria. The broad theory of practice was developed as a way to understand a number of specific anthropological research interests in Algeria (Bourdieu 1977). Bourdieu refused to approach research in France in ways that completely differed from his research in Algeria and this led to the gradual adaptation of his (broadly) anthropological theory to sociological studies in later works (Bourdieu 1984). Consequently, *practice/habitus* is an important couplet in Bourdieu's work, in that it signifies one of the fundamental conceptual breaks that led to a distinctive approach to sociology, noting an ontological complicity between the two.

Marked by a sharp refusal to offer a definition of practice,[8] Bourdieu's account of practice was characterised by attentiveness to the logic, flow and contest of practical activities and their connections in time. Practice was, in many respects, the core element of social life that required explanation, and it was in the process and carrying out of practice that other aspects of social life, such as the exclusions and exclusivities, classifications and struggles, were located. Within practice, Bourdieu saw the patterned development and flow of social energy, associated with patterns of meaning, and in their carrying out, a reinforcement of selections of those meanings. The other part of this couplet, *habitus*, was a collection of the sets of dispositions that allowed individual agents and groups of agents to engage with and make meaningful contributions to practice. Elsewhere we have described this as a kind of socio-genetic relationship: that *habitus* is required as a prior condition for producing practice, and for consuming practice. However, the contribution to practice is dependent on other things in the environment, as well as considerations of strategy and tactics.

The concept of *habitus* was borrowed by Bourdieu from philosophical thought that can be traced to Aristotle. However, Bourdieu's conceptualisation of *habitus* was an original contribution, which he defended against multiple charges.[9] Perhaps the most urgent task that Bourdieu saw for the development and application of *habitus* in both his earliest and late works lay in a reconciliation of two separated features of social science: that of explanations in sociology and economics. In a posthumously published book on the construction of a housing market, *The Social Structures of the Economy* (Bourdieu 2005b), this application was located specifically as an alternative account to the abstractions of *homo economicus*, the human being as rational utility maximiser. There Bourdieu argued for a specifically considered economic *habitus*, stating that:

> [i]nsofar as he or she is endowed with a habitus, the social agent is *a collective individual or a collective individuated by the fact of embodying objective structures*. The individual, the subjective, is social and collective. The *habitus* is socialised subjectivity, a historical transcendental, whose schemes of perception and appreciation (systems of appreciation, tastes, etc.) are the

product of collective and individual history. Reason (or rationality) is 'bounded' not only, as Herbert Simon believes, because the human mind is generically bounded . . . but because it is socially structured and determined, and, as a consequence, limited.

(Bourdieu 2005b, 211)

Habitus then is the basis for apprehending practice, for noticing differences and being aware of the subtleties of practice, through an alignment borne of collective experiences and histories that are carried in the body. *Habitus* also provides the basis for mis-matches between practice moves and the flow of practice in a field, where collective individuals have moved or been taken out of the collective and individual histories that provided an innate feel for the flow and logic of practice, a 'feel for the game'. The symbolic violence of such mis-matches between the habitus of collective individuals and changes in objective conditions was also the focus of one of the first contributions that Bourdieu made from his research in Algeria, in the sustained focus on the imposition of a market economy on traditional agricultural workers (Bourdieu 1958/1962, 2004b). Such an explanation could also be tested in relation to the effects of rapid education policy changes.

Bourdieu's approach to field theory: forms of capital, social fields

As intimated in the discussion of the practice/habitus couplet, for Bourdieu the major locations in which practice is produced in capitalist societies are different social fields. Bourdieu thought of the social arrangement as consisting of multiple fields with varying degrees of autonomy (more or less autonomous or heteronomous) from an overarching field of power (and in his later work *Masculine Domination* (Bourdieu 2001) an overarching field of gender). In some ways, in this social conception Bourdieu was working across Marxist and Weberian approaches. When Bourdieu returned to France and continued research, an additional conceptual couplet was added as a way to explain different kinds of social arrangements. This couplet drew on the concept of field, borrowed primarily through the application of relations between elements evident in field theory in physics (although versions of the concept of social fields can be found in the much earlier and unconnected work of Kurt Lewin (1939): see Martin 2003 and Rawolle 2007 for discussion). For Bourdieu, social fields are spaces of competition, in which there are inequities in access to the stakes (capitals) of that competition, and the form in which this competition is carried out is through practice.[10] As a non-substantialist concept, social fields comprise an organisation of social forces, with the producers of these field forces being individual agents and collections of agents, located in the relations between these agents. It is through the movement and practice of agents that such fields continue and change. What is crucial to field analysis is locating specific properties that allow the description of relations between agents, and the locating of groups of agents relative to one another. This is the relationality central to Bourdieu's social theorising.

In order to understand the structuring of social fields, and the stakes around which fields were oriented, Bourdieu developed a multi-dimensional view of capital, which provided a variety of different forms of capital with which to discuss the stakes of competition within fields, and differences between various kinds of fields. There were two overlapping ways that Bourdieu theorised capital. On the one hand, Bourdieu argued that each distinct field provides a unique form of capital located within the field, and that practice was largely oriented as a kind of competition for this unique form of capital. Hence, Bourdieu would argue for scientific capital (2004d), educational capital (Bourdieu 2005b), and journalistic capital (1998), as ways to point to the specific forms located in particular corresponding fields that were irreducible to the stakes of other fields.

Such field-specific capital was accumulated through an investment in the field, and its distinctive forms of practice, with some agents being more successful in their strategies of accumulation and understanding of the rules of the games associated with these practices. On the other hand, Bourdieu (1986) would argue that these kinds of field-specific capital could be analysed into a number of elementary forms, which were described as social capital, cultural capital, economic capital and symbolic capital.[11] Each field-specific capital could then be described according to its composition of a ratio of social, cultural, economic and symbolic capital. Hence, as these forms of capital were a kind of trans-substantiated bundle of social energy, there were elementary and compound forms of this energy with the potential to be converted to economic capital. These different forms of capital could be converted by specifically located agents under specific circumstances, and with different exchange rates, dependent on the relations between the relevant social fields and the gatekeepers and dominant agents located within each field (Bourdieu 1984). Though the language used in relation to this couplet held a specific heritage from the physical sciences and from economics, Bourdieu's was not a mechanistic account of the social world.

An unfinished project: a general theory of fields

Bourdieu's successive studies of different kinds of social fields raised a broader question about how different fields relate. In short, this raised the possibility of a general theory of fields that would help to understand the patterns of relations between fields, movements of fields relative to one another, points of overlap or disconnect between fields, or whether parts of social space exist within which field-like relations are not present. While there has been some exploration of this incomplete theory of fields elsewhere (Couldry 2003a, 2003b; Kauppi 2002; Lingard et al. 2005; Rawolle 2005), at this point we will emphasise some of the kinds of linkages that Bourdieu raised about this meta-theorising of fields. This general theory of fields was explicitly discussed in one major location ('Some properties of fields', in Bourdieu 1993), and discussed intermittently in other locations, as a way to understand the effects of specific fields on other fields, the relations between fields or the emergence of fields. The first aspect of interest in this general theory of fields explored by Bourdieu related to a question: what quasi-taxonomic differences could be stated about different fields? While there were a number of different divisions offered, one key division expressed was between fields associated primarily with different kinds of social production and those fields associated primarily with different kinds of social consumption. One of the later points of exploration of Bourdieu related to a systematic understanding of ways in which specific fields, such as journalism and the economic field, have come to threaten the autonomy and logic of practice of different fields. In this point of exploration, Bourdieu directly dealt with processes such as globalisation and mediatisation, processes in which some fields gradually come to influence the patterns and functioning of other fields, and the principles of hierarchisation of these fields. In this process, these affected fields become less autonomous and more heteronomous in character.

The incompleteness of this general theory of fields presents a number of points for further exploration for researchers. Questions remain about how to understand the time-frames over which field-like relations develop and continue, and ways in which practice leads to the accumulation of different kinds of capital (see Rawolle's (2005) account of temporary social fields), or ways to group and connect different kinds of effects between fields. Thus, homologies between fields present one kind of explanation, but there may be other kinds of effects that deserve further attention (see Lingard and Rawolle 2004, and Rawolle and Lingard 2008 for a conceptual and empirical elaboration of 'cross-field effects'). Such effects may be based, for example, on the connections or interactions between practices, or the products of practice, such as policy texts or performance on specific indicators (Rawolle 2010). Such effects may also relate to the kinds of autonomy available within a field, and how positions of domination within a field are established (see Maton 2005 in relation to higher education). Bourdieu's inchoate outlines of global fields also present an opportunity for further development and exploration (see Lingard and Rawolle 2010, 2011; Lingard et al. 2005; Marginson 2010). Fields in Bourdieu's work refer to social relations, not necessarily geographic and spatial ones. This is productive for consideration of fields and globalisation. We have written about an 'emergent global education policy field', for example, which has effects (cross-field effects) in national education policy fields and how these effects to some extent are borne by the habitus of international and national policy makers (Lingard and Rawolle 2010, 2011). This brings us to the major point we would want to make about Bourdieu and educational research. His thinking tools that we have considered briefly here are generative ones, which can be reflexively utilised to research various topics in education. We turn in the next section to consider the necessary research habitus, according to Bourdieu, for utilising his work in education.

Methodological approaches and researcher stances: beyond epistemological innocence

[H]ow artificial the ordinary oppositions between theory and research, between quantitative and qualitative methods, between statistical recording and ethnographic observation, between the grasping of structures and the construction of individuals . . . These alternatives have no function other than to provide a justification for the vacuous and resounding abstractions of theoreticism and for the falsely rigorous observations of positivism, or, as the divisions between economists, anthropologists, historians and sociologists, to legitimise the limits of *competency*: that is to say that they function in the manner of *social censorship*, liable to forbid us to grasp a truth which resides precisely in the relations between realms of practice arbitrarily separated.

(Bourdieu and de Saint Martin 1978, 7, in
Bourdieu and Wacquant 1992, 27–28)

In this section, we will look at Bourdieu's contribution to methodology in the social sciences. The quotation above well encapsulates the challenges Bourdieu offers in respect of methodology in terms of many of the arid binaries, both theoretical and methodological, that surround and legitimate research practice and theorising in the social sciences. We are thinking in particular of the now old divisions between quantitative and qualitative approaches and note Bourdieu's use of both; this usage is determined by appropriateness to research topic. Bourdieu's eclectic, but principled, approach to methodology has made a significant contribution to the social sciences, particularly in respect of what we might see as necessary researcher disposition or habitus. We will outline the core elements of Bourdieu's contribution here.

Bourdieu (1990) has referred to his research methodology as 'fieldwork in philosophy', while Jenkins (2002), in his quite critical account of Bourdieu's contribution to sociology and social science methodology, describes Bourdieu's work as 'experiments in epistemology'. Indeed, Jenkins (p. 46) argues that one of Bourdieu's greatest contributions to sociology is 'that he never lost sight of the practicality of epistemological issues (or of their importance)': issues, as he puts it, that are concerned with how we know something (the evidence or data associated with that knowing), how we are able to say we 'know' something and the status of our claims (p. 46). This methodology has useful application in educational research, particularly in the sociology of education and in what has been referred to as 'policy sociology' in education.

What Bourdieu has argued for in his accounts of research and data collection and analysis is the application of his thinking tools (habitus and practice, fields and capitals) to the researcher and researcher's location in both the academic field and the research field. Indeed, he argued that this reflexive positioning was absolutely necessary, noting that many intellectuals and particularly positivist social scientists most often denied or neglected this reality. Such a self or socio-analysis will ensure a better social science. He thus sees the necessity of vigilant reflexivity in the research process, but also regards this vigilance as being central to an appropriate research habitus within the social sciences for producing good research and theory. This is what connotative descriptors such as research as 'fieldwork in philosophy', 'experiments in epistemology' and 'epistemological reflexivity' are trying to capture in relation to Bourdieu's contribution to theory and methodology. This is an important contribution, supporting a reflexive researcher disposition, but in the cause of better social science, not as a reflection of an epistemological anarchy of a relativist 'anything goes'. We also note here Bourdieu's use of quantitative data, but not within a positivist framework, as well as his use of qualitative data, also not within a positivist framework.

Bourdieu argues the necessity of reflexivity of the researcher in recognition of this dual reality, mirroring Durkheim's conception of 'social facts' in social science as both social constructions, but also having an empirical reality. This recognition, of the 'constructedness' of social science generally and in research necessitates, according to Bourdieu et al. (1999, 608), a rejection of 'epistemological innocence'. We think that this rejection of epistemological innocence is central to understanding Bourdieu's approach and contribution to research methodology. Here Bourdieu observes,

> The positivist dream of an epistemological state of perfect innocence papers over the fact that the crucial difference is not between a science that effects a construction and one that does not, but between a science that does this without knowing it and one that, being aware of work of construction, strives to discover and master as completely as possible the nature of its inevitable acts of construction and the equally inevitable effects those acts produce.
>
> (p. 608)

Bourdieu (2004d) reflects on this rejection of epistemological innocence further in his *Science of Science and Reflexivity*. Here he notes,

> Casting an ironic gaze on the social world, a gaze which unveils, unmasks, brings to light what is hidden, it cannot avoid casting this gaze on itself – with the intention not of destroying sociology but rather of serving it, using the sociology of sociology in order to make a better sociology.
>
> (p. 4)

This means that reflexivity is central to good social science research and to researcher habitus. We have to be aware of our own positioning in relation to data collection: we like the concept of 'positionality' (our word, not Bourdieu's) and the need to continually recognise and acknowledge our role in data collection as a way towards better social science.[12] It is such matters that Bourdieu argues must be reflected upon and laid bare in the conduct of good social science research. Yet others have attempted to extend the concept of positionality in research as a necessary component part of researcher habitus or disposition. Rizvi and Lingard (2010) in doing policy sociology on education in the context of globalisation argue that policy analysis needs to consider the location of the researcher in relation to the focus of analysis, explicate the theoretical and political stance adopted, and reflect upon the significance of the spatial location of the researcher to the analysis. Bourdieu's addition to such considerations of researcher positionality was to stress the need as well to locate oneself reflexively as researcher within the academic field.

It is important to note here that Bourdieu wrote about the need to reject epistemological innocence in a methodological reflection on research interviews conducted for the study of the impact of neo-liberal politics on the lives of 'ordinary' French people, *The Weight of the World: Social Suffering in Contemporary Society* (Bourdieu et al. 1999). In that reflection on methodology he has some interesting things to say about conducting research interviews, a most common mode of data collection. Thus he notes, as he says at the risk of shocking both the 'rigorous methodologist' and the 'inspired hermeneutic scholar', that 'the interview can be considered a sort of *spiritual exercise* that, through *forgetfulness of self*, aims at a true *conversion of the way we look* at other people in the ordinary circumstances of life' (p. 614; emphasis original). He continues:

> The welcoming disposition, which leads one to make the respondent's problems one's own, the capacity to take that person and understand them just as they are in their distinctive necessity, is a sort of *intellectual love:* a gaze that consents to necessity in the manner of the 'intellectual love of god', that is, of the natural order, which Spinoza held to be the supreme form of knowledge.
>
> (p. 614; emphasis original)

This observation indicates something of the centrality in Bourdieu's work of thinking about data collection in the field well beyond technical issues, utilising an ever present epistemic reflexivity.

Another important aspect of Bourdieu on methodology is his rejection of a dichotomy between theory and data, between theory and methodology; instead, he recognises the necessary relationship between the two and the impact that each has on the other, recognising an ontological complicity here. In keeping all theory open to empirical challenge, he is rejecting the doxa associated with certain accounts of the empirical and of the theoretical. As Wacquant (1992, 35) notes, 'Bourdieu maintains that every act of research is simultaneously empirical (it confronts the world of observable phenomena) and theoretical (it necessarily engages hypotheses about the underlying structure of relations that observations are designed to capture).' In our words, we see Bourdieu emphasising the epistemological issues associated with both and the need for alignment across the onto-epistemologies of both theory and methodology. Furthermore, we can see talk of his concepts, dealt with earlier in this chapter, as 'thinking tools' also grasping this provisionality of concepts and theory. In focusing on the ongoing imbrications of theory and data, we might see Bourdieu's approach as 'abductive', simultaneously applying both deductive (theory to data) and inductive (data to theory) approaches to analysis.

For Bourdieu, reflexivity is also central to the dissemination of research. The rejection of epistemological innocence and acknowledgement that all research is simultaneously empirical and theoretical, as well as practical, demands, Bourdieu suggests, an openness and vulnerability, indeed honesty, in the presentation of our research in both oral and written genres. In talking about handing down the trade of doing social science research, Bourdieu says this about research presentations:

> A research presentation is in every respect the very opposite of an exhibition, of a *show* in which you seek to show off and to impress others. It is a discourse in which you *expose yourself*, you take risks . . . The more you expose yourself, the greater your chances of benefiting from the discussion and the more constructive and good-willed, I am sure, the criticisms and advice you will receive.
>
> (Bourdieu and Wacquant 1992, 219; emphasis original)

As Bourdieu (1992, 219) noted, 'Homo academicus relishes the finished', but this should not disavow us of the reality of the practical and mundane elements of conducting research, the pragmatic decisions that need to be made about definitions of social objects and their operationalisation, what data to collect, who to interview, the cul-de-sacs and practicalities of data collection, and so on. Yet while these are pragmatic choices, at the same time 'the most "empirical" technical choices cannot be disentangled from the most "theoretical" choices' (p. 225).

Bourdieu is also eclectic in respect of theoretical and methodological traditions to frame our research, but principled not anarchistic in this eclecticism. Thus he observes:

> The long and short of it is, social research is something much too serious and too difficult for us to allow ourselves to mistake scientific *rigidity*, which is the nemesis of intelligence and invention, for scientific *rigour*, and thus to deprive ourselves of this or that resource available in the full panoply of intellectual traditions of our discipline and of the sister disciplines of anthropology, economics, history, etc.
>
> (Bourdieu 1992, 227; emphasis original)

He takes a similar stance in respect of quantitative and qualitative methodologies, using one or the other or both, depending on the object of the research. This is the point we made earlier about the need to align the onto-epistemologies of theory and methodology and with the focus of research. Bourdieu's choices of statistical methods to use in research reflect his relational account (this asserts the primacy of relations between things, rather than things in and of themselves) of the social and commitment to field analysis to ensure such alignment.

Grenfell (2008, 219–227) has outlined what he sees as the methodological principles deriving from Bourdieu's work. We will consider these briefly here, but note at the outset that these principles should not be seen as stages in a process, rather these principles continually interact in the conduct of research working with a Bourdieusian approach to methodology. The three principles are, first, the deconstruction of the research object, challenging everyday, taken-for-granted construction of the research topic. In many ways, this is akin to the distinction some in the social sciences have made between the 'making' and 'taking' of research problems; Bourdieu operationalises a 'making' of research problems and of concepts in the social world approach. What Bourdieu is suggesting is the necessity to deconstruct the prefigured. This deconstruction focuses on 'unthought categories of thought which delimit the thinkable and predetermine the thought' (Bourdieu 1982/1994, 187). The second element of Bourdieu's methodological principles, according to Grenfell, entails a 'three-level approach to study the field of the object of research' (2008, 220). This principle requires analysis of the position of the field being studied in relation to the overarching field of power, the mapping of the positioning of agents within the field and an analysis of the habitus and dispositions of these agents. The third and final principle is that of reflexivity to challenge what Bourdieu saw as three possible aspects of bias or distortion in social science research. The first potential form of bias derives from the positioning of the researcher in the social space, the second from the doxa or orthodoxies of the field and the researcher's positioning within it, and third from the fact that researchers actually have the time to do such research, outside the necessity of other actions in the world (p. 226).

In Bourdieu's earlier work that gave more emphasis to the autonomy of fields, academic work and research were seen to be operating and functioning within different fields with different logics of practice from that of politics. In his late work, however, when he became more directly political in the context of what he saw as the damaging consequences of the dominance of neo-liberal approaches and a performative representation of globalisation, Bourdieu reflected on the role of the intellectual in the public sphere. His posthumously published *Political Interventions: Social Science and Political Action* (2008) contains many of Bourdieu's political interventions across his career. In his reflections on the social science/political interventions relationship, he went beyond Sartre's conception of the 'total intellectual' who had something to say on everything, beyond the 'organic intellectual' of Gramsci serving the political interests of a class or other grouping, beyond the 'specific intellectual' of Foucault, where there were more micro-political engagements with social movements to what he referred to as a 'collective intellectual'. The use of 'collective' here was a way of recognising the collective aspects of the development of theory and the conduct of research, as with the way habitus attempted to capture the cultural, historical, structural embodied in the individual, so the collective intellectual recognised the impact and contribution of the academic field and colleagues to the production of knowledge. The idea of the 'collective intellectual' was also to grasp the need for an 'interdisciplinary and international' strategy in association with progressive social movements, particularly in the context of neo-liberal globalisation (Bourdieu 2004a, 387). In this context, Bourdieu argued the necessity of academics becoming collective intellectuals functioning *in* the field of politics, as well as in their academic fields. However, importantly, this did not mean they functioned *as* politicians. Here he was seeking to overcome a tension, a dichotomy between scholarship (and its logics of practice) and political commitment (and its logics of practice). He put it this way:

> The object was to overcome the opposition, particularly strong in English-speaking countries, between scholarship and commitment and restore with full force the French tradition of the intellectual, in other words the person who intervenes in the world of politics but without thereby becoming a politician, with the competence and authority associated with their membership of the world of science or literature, as well as in the name of the values inscribed in the exercise of their profession, as values of truth and disinterest.
>
> (Bourdieu 2008, 387)

So for Bourdieu, scholarship and commitment go together, but in terms of the researcher participating in political struggles, he argued, 'the most valuable contribution a researcher can make to the political struggles is to work, with all the weapons that science offers at the moment in question, to produce and promote the truth' (Bourdieu 2010, 271). Related, Bourdieu was also very critical of those academics who had become 'media stars' as a step in the dissemination of their work; these, he argued, most often had less academic capitals in the academic field than those academics who eschewed media participation. Indeed, these media academics only had capitals in the journalist field and as such their 'science' was distorted through the logics of practice of the journalistic field, which emphasised 'structural amnesia' and the necessity for things to be ever new. Both these logics of practice sit in stark contrast to the disposition or habitus of the good social science researcher, who acknowledges his or her positioning in the academic field and the collective contributions to their research habitus. The mediatisation of academic work most often ensures the antithesis of what Bourdieu meant by the necessity of the political commitment of the scholar, researcher and intellectual. Such mediatisation has also distorted or shaped politics and education policy making, with policies now resorting to aphorism with greater emphasis on the discursive representation of policy than its actual implementation into practice (Lingard and Rawolle 2004).

Conclusion

In this chapter, we have attempted to depict and characterise the central contributions of the work of Bourdieu, including outlining his generative thinking tools of practice and habitus, capitals and fields, as well as his work on education and reproduction, and his contribution more generally to considerations of methodology in the social sciences and the necessity of rejecting epistemological innocence and for being ever reflexive. In our own work we have found these thinking tools, his educational research and theorising, and his account of the features of the elements of a suitable researcher habitus to be very helpful. His insistence on the practicality of good research practice we have also found to be energising. Bourdieu assists us in managing the theoretical, political and methodological conundrums that confront those doing research in education framed as social science. His insistence on research and scholarship with commitment is attractive to us, as is his account of how researchers can be political without succumbing to the distorting logics of practice of the field of politics and the field of journalism. Drawing on Bourdieu, we also acknowledge here the ontological complicity between theory and the empirical, between structure and agency. It is the generative open-endedness of his work across those domains which we find most productive. His contributions to the social sciences generally and educational research more specifically must not function as straitjackets, but rather be enabling, generative, productive and open to ongoing empirical challenges and to present and immanent social change. Herein lies the worth and contribution of Bourdieu's extensive *oeuvre*.

Notes

1 For good introductions to Bourdieu's life and contributions to the social sciences, see Lane (2000), Webb et al. (2002), Grenfell (2004, 2008), Reed-Danahay (2005).
2 Bourdieu and colleagues directly include C. Wright Mills in an account of referent points for sociological work in Bourdieu et al.'s (1968/1991) *The Craft of Sociology: Epistemological Preliminaries.*
3 The collection *Political Interventions: Social Science and Political Action* (Bourdieu 2008) provides specific instances of Bourdieu's direct interventions into education policy (see part 2 and part 6).
4 This point mirrors a range of papers focused on the international circulation of Bourdieu's ideas in sociological work, which consider both the global reception and the individual national case studies that illustrate the way in which the global picture obscures the rather more difficult path of Bourdieusian ideas within specific national sociological traditions. See Santoro (2009) for an overview of these contributions.
5 These examples are used for illustrative purposes to highlight how movement of ideas was congruent with movement and location of scholars.
6 For overviews of these debates see Teese (1982) and see Kenway (1983) for an overarching critique.
7 In a sense, Bourdieu saw pre-conceived concepts taken directly from the social world without careful examination as an 'epistemological obstacle' to social

science, in that their social history and strategic use, signifying social position within specific fields, tended to be obscured (e.g., the use of the words 'choice', or 'quality' in education). The idea of an epistemological obstacle can be traced to Gaston Bachelard, a French philosopher of science.

8 Elsewhere we have borrowed from Warde's work to argue that

> when Bourdieu talks of practice, he indicates three interconnected associations:
>
> * practice is the carrying out of an activity, for example, running a policy review . . .
> * practice is the nominalisation of a process, or the formal naming of an activity that gives it social organisation, points of harmonisation and boundaries, such as the naming and instituting of specific policy reviews.
> * practice is differentiated from theories about practice, and is circumscribed by shorter cycles of time that give it structure, limits and meaning.
>   (Rawolle and Lingard 2008, 730)

Rawolle (2010) argues for the inclusion of a fourth association in the products of practice such as policy texts. For a further exploration of Bourdieu's account of practice in education research, see the special number of *Critical Studies in Education*, 2010, 51, 1 and Heimans (2011).

9 For Bourdieu 'Habitus provides the connection between agents and practices through "systems of dispositions", which are bodily incorporations of social history. Habitus provides predispositions towards and capacities for practice for agents, which are transposable to different contexts' (1990, 116).

10 As Rawolle (2005, 708) argues:

> Formally, Bourdieu (1993) suggested a number of properties . . . they:
>
> * are structured spaces of positions;
> * have general laws or logics that guide interactions and the stakes towards which practices are oriented;
> * contain social struggles for the stakes and the forms of capital valued and conversion rates between different forms of capital;
> * require a socialized body endowed with a habitus . . . that orients the dispositions of agents to the stakes, and so to the continuation of that social field;
> * are structured by a state of power relations at a given point in time;
> * produce distinctive patterns of strategies adopted by different agents relative to their own position and trajectory; [and]
> * function analogous to a game.

11 For clear definitions of each of these forms of capital see Bourdieu (1986).

12 Others, of course, have written about similar concepts. For example, in *Orientalism*, Said (2003, 20) speaks of '*strategic location*', which encapsulates the author's positioning in a text and of '*strategic formation*' to refer to the relationship between a particular text and others in the field. Said also spoke of the need to 'world' texts, that is, understand texts in context.

References

Bates, R. 1980. Educational administration, the sociology of science, and the management of knowledge. *Educational Administration Quarterly* 16, 2: 1–20.

Bourdieu, P. 1958/1962. *The Algerians.* Boston: Beacon Press.

Bourdieu, P. 1977. *Outline of a theory of practice.* Cambridge: Cambridge University Press.

Bourdieu, P. 1982/1994. A lecture on the lecture. In *Other words: Essays toward a reflexive sociology*, 177–198. Cambridge: Polity Press, and Stanford, CA: Stanford University Press.

Bourdieu, P. 1984. *Distinction.* Cambridge, MA: Harvard University Press.

Bourdieu, P. 1986. The forms of capital. In *Handbook of theory and research for the sociology of education*, ed. J. Richardson, 46–58. Westport, CT: Greenwood.

Bourdieu, P. 1989/1996. *The state nobility: Elite schools in the field of power.* Cambridge: Polity Press.

Bourdieu, P. 1990. *The logic of practice.* Stanford, CA: Stanford University Press.

Bourdieu, P. with L. J. D. Wacquant. 1992. *An invitation to reflexive sociology.* Chicago: Chicago University Press.

Bourdieu, P. 1993. *Sociology in question.* London: Sage.

Bourdieu, P. 1998. *On television and journalism.* London: Pluto Press.

Bourdieu, P. 2001. *Masculine domination.* Cambridge: Polity Press.

Bourdieu, P. 2003. *Firing back: Against the tyranny of the market.* London: Verso.

Bourdieu, P. 2004a. *Sketch for self-analysis.* Cambridge: Polity Press.

Bourdieu, P. 2004b. Introduction. In *The suffering of the immigrant*, ed. A. Sayad, 1–6. Cambridge: Polity Press.

Bourdieu, P. 2004c. From the King's house to the reason of state: A model of the genesis of the bureaucratic field. *Constellations* 11: 16–36.

Bourdieu, P. 2004d. *Science of science and reflexivity.* Chicago: University of Chicago Press.

Bourdieu, P. 2005a. The political field, the social science field, and the journalistic field. In *Bourdieu and the journalistic field*, ed. R. Benson and E. Neveu, 29–47. Cambridge, UK, and Malden, MA: Polity Press.

Bourdieu, P. 2005b. *The social structures of the economy.* Cambridge: Polity Press.

Bourdieu, P. 2008. *Political interventions: Social science and political action.* Cambridge: Polity Press.

Bourdieu, P. 2010. A sociologist in the world. In *Sociology is a martial art: Political writings by Pierre Bourdieu*, ed. G. Sapiro, 261–278. New York: The New Press.

Bourdieu, P. and J. C. Passeron. 1964/1979. *The inheritors: French students and their relation to culture.* Chicago: University of Chicago Press.

Bourdieu, P. and J. C. Passeron. 1970/1977. *Reproduction in education, society and culture.* London: Sage.

Bourdieu, P. and L. Wacquant. 1992. *An introduction to reflexive sociology.* Chicago: University of Chicago Press.

Bourdieu, P., J.-C. Chamberedon and J.-C. Passeron. 1968/1991. *The craft of sociology: Epistemological preliminaries.* Berlin: Walter DeGruyter & Co.

Bourdieu, P., A. Accardo, G. Balazs, S. Beaud, F. Bonvin, L. Bourdieu et al. 1999. *The weight of the world: Social suffering in contemporary society.* Cambridge: Polity Press.

Bowles, S. and H. Gintis. 1976. *Schooling in capitalist America.* New York: Routledge.

Brubacker, R. 1993. Social theory as habitus. In *Bourdieu: Critical perspectives*, ed. C. Calhoun, E. LiPuma and M. Postone, 212–234. Cambridge: Polity Press.

Connell, R. W. 1983. *Which way is up? Essays on class, sex and culture.* Sydney: Allen & Unwin.

Connell, R. W., D. J. Ashenden, S. Kessler and G. W. Dowsett. 1982. *Making the difference: Schools, families and social divisions.* Sydney: Allen & Unwin.

Couldry, N. 2003a. Media meta-capital: Extending the range of Bourdieu's field theory. *Theory and Society* 32: 653–677.

Couldry, N. 2003b. *Media, symbolic power and the limits of Bourdieu's field theory.* London: MEDIA@ LSE Electronic Working Papers.

Giddens, A. 1993. *New rules of sociological method* (2nd edition). Stanford, CA: Stanford University Press.

Grenfell, M. 2004. *Pierre Bourdieu: Agent provocateur.* London: Continuum.

Grenfell, M. 2008. Postscript: Methodological principles. In *Bourdieu: Key concepts*, ed. M. Grenfell, 219–227. Stocksfield: Acumen.

Heimans, S. 2011. Coming to matter in practice: Enacting education policy. *Discourse: Studies in the Cultural Politics of Education* 33, 2: 313–326.

Jenkins, R. 2002. *Pierre Bourdieu* (2nd edition). London: Routledge.

Kauppi, N. 2002. *Elements for a structural constructivist theory of politics and of European integration.* Centre for European Studies Working Paper Series 104, Minda de Gunzburg Center for European Studies Harvard University. Available at: www.people.fas.harvard.edu/~ces/publications/docs/pdfs/Kauppi104.pdf.

Kenway, J. 1983. Marking a difference to whom and to what? *Australian Journal of Cultural Studies* 1, 2: 212–221.

Lane, J. 2000. *Pierre Bourdieu: A critical introduction.* London: Pluto Press.

Lewin, K. 1939. Field theory and experiment in social psychology: Concepts and methods. *The American Journal of Sociology* 44: 868–896.

Lingard, B. and S. Rawolle. 2004. Mediatizing educational policy: The journalistic field, science policy, and cross-field effects. *Journal of Education Policy* 19, 3: 361–380.

Lingard, B. and S. Rawolle. 2010. Globalization and the rescaling of education politics and policy: Implications for comparative education. In *New thinking in comparative education: Honouring R. Cowen*, ed. M. Larsen, 33–52. Rotterdam, The Netherlands: Sense Publishers.

Lingard, B. and S. Rawolle. 2011. New scalar politics: Implications for education policy. *Comparative Education* 47, 4: 489–502.

Lingard, B., S. Rawolle and S. Taylor. 2005. Globalizing policy sociology in education: Working with Bourdieu. *Journal of Education Policy* 20, 6: 759–777.

Marginson, S. 2010. Global field and global imagining: Bourdieu and worldwide higher education. *British Journal of Sociology of Education* 29, 3: 303–315.

Martin, J. L. 2003. What is field theory? *American Journal of Sociology* 109: 1–49.

Maton, K. 2005. A question of autonomy: Bourdieu's field approach and higher education policy. *Journal of Education Policy* 20: 687–704.

Rawolle, S. 2005. Cross-field effects and temporary social fields: A case study of the mediatization of recent Australian knowledge economy policies. *Journal of Education Policy* 20, 6: 705–724.

Rawolle, S. 2007. *When the knowledge economy became the chance to change: Mediatization, cross-field effects and temporary social fields.* Unpublished PhD thesis, University of Queensland, Australia.

Rawolle, S. 2010. Practice chains of production and consumption: Mediatized practices across social fields. *Discourse: Studies in the cultural politics of education* 31, 1: 121–135.

Rawolle, S. and B. Lingard 2008. The sociology of Pierre Bourdieu and researching education policy. *Journal of Education Policy* 23, 6: 729–741.

Reed-Danahay, D. 2005. *Locating Bourdieu*. Bloomington: Indiana University Press.

Rizvi, F. and B. Lingard. 2010. *Globalizing education policy*. London: Routledge.

Robbins, D. 2004. The transcultural transferability of Bourdieu's sociology of education. *British Journal of Sociology of Education* 25, 4: 415–430.

Said, E. W. 2003. *Orientalism*. London: Penguin Books.

Santoro, M. 2009. Putting Bourdieu in the global field: Introduction to the Symposium. *Sociologica* 2–3: 1–31.

Teese, R. 1980. The contribution of Bourdieu and Passeron to the science of educational inequality. Melbourne working papers 1980. Melbourne: Melbourne University Press, 1–31.

Teese, R. 1982. Review of *Making the difference*. *Thesis II*, 5–6: 328–331.

Wacquant, L. 1989. Towards a reflexive sociology: A workshop with Pierre Bourdieu. *Sociological Theory* 7: 26–63.

Wacquant, L. 1992. Toward a social paxeology: The structure and logic of bourdieu's sociology. In *An invitation to reflexive sociology*, ed. P. Bourdieu and L. Wacquant, 1–59. Chicago: University of Chicago Press.

Wacquant, L. 1993. Bourdieu in America: Notes on the transatlantic importation of social theory. In *Bourdieu: Critical perspectives*, ed. C. Calhoun, E. LiPuma and M. Postone, 235–263. Cambridge: Polity Press.

Webb, J., T. Schirato and G. Danaher. 2002. *Understanding Bourdieu*. London: Sage.

Woodward, I. and M. Emmison. 2009. The intellectual reception of Bourdieu in Australian social science and humanities. *Sociologica* 2–3: 1–121.

Young, M. F. D. ed. 1971. *Knowledge and control: New directions for the sociology of education*. London: Collier Macmillan.

Chapter 9

Research in the new Christian Academies

Perspectives from Bourdieu

Elizabeth Green

Introduction

I first encountered Bourdieu on an MA Education degree course. When I enrolled for the degree, I was a secondary school teacher in England and my intention was to get an edge in the promotions game and not to get hooked on research, although that is ultimately what happened. Unwittingly, in that decision I was enacting one of Bourdieu's critical concepts: cultural capital. Education conferred on me a distinction or a material advantage; the MA opened the door to an Oxford DPhil and the rest as they say 'is history'. In fact Bourdieu (1986) would say that the whole of the social world is 'accumulated history' (p. 46). This means that there is no way out of the cultural assumptions and habits which we have inherited and which we will reproduce in the ways in which we interact with society. This chapter will argue that Bourdieu's theory of education, reproduction and distinction is a powerful tool for the analysis of education, particularly in faith-based settings, which is the context in which I work.

Bourdieu's writings are complex; first encounters with his work are stretching and sometimes off putting for new researchers. The first work by Bourdieu which I read was *The Forms of Capital* re-printed in A. H. Halsey et al.'s (2001) edited collection called *Education, Culture, Economy and Society*. I was drawn to Bourdieu's analysis of the social world and won over by his determination not to reduce it to a series of mechanical interactions between people, groups and social structures.

> The social world is accumulated history, and if it is not to be reduced to a discontinued series of instantaneous mechanical equilibria between agents, who are treated as interchangeable particles, one must reintroduce into it the notion of capital and with it, accumulation and all its effects.
>
> (Bourdieu 1986, 46)

This quotation illustrates why it is sometimes necessary to persevere with Bourdieu. I did not on first reading understand everything in *The Forms of Capital* but I got a sense of the scale of Bourdieu's contribution to the theory and practice of sociology and of his commitment to critical and systematic empirical research.

The second section of this chapter will explore the nature of that contribution in the context of Bourdieu's own history by introducing him as an academic and sketching in the trajectory of his research. I will introduce four key concepts which underpin Bourdieu's work: field, habitus, symbolic violence and cultural capital. Bourdieu remains a controversial figure and the section will conclude with a brief summary of some of the main criticisms of his theoretical work.

In order to get a handle on Bourdieu, I find it helpful to read empirical research which applies his concepts to education. My MA tutors introduced me to the work of Grace (1978, 2002) who applies Bourdieu's concepts to urban education and to Catholic education. I read avidly the work of Ball (2003) and Reay (1998) who draw on Bourdieu to analyse education reform and school choice in relation to class and to gender. This experience has led me to conclude that one of the most effective ways to introduce Bourdieu's theory and method to a new audience is through a case study of research. In UK sociology of education research, Bourdieu has chiefly been applied to the study of social class. My work broadens this to study the impact of religious faith in education. In the third section of this chapter, I present a case study from my own research carried out in English Academies sponsored by a Christian foundation. This will illustrate what Bourdieu's work offers to education researchers. The chapter will conclude that the loose definitions, the evolution of concepts and their application make Bourdieu's social theory a very adaptable tool for analysing contemporary religious culture and the impact of faith-based education.

Bourdieu and his concepts

In *Sketch for a Self Analysis*, Bourdieu (2007) wrote that 'to understand is first to understand the field with which and against which one has been formed' (p. 4). The aim of this section is to introduce some of the primary concepts in Bourdieu's work set against the backdrop of Bourdieu's own formative experiences and early career history. *Sketch for a Self Analysis* was born out of the final lecture which Bourdieu gave at the Collège de France. Bourdieu was adamant that the text was not an auto-biography but rather an attempt to analyse himself 'from the point of view of sociology' (p. 1). By analysing himself as the sociological object Bourdieu was putting into practice what is arguably one of his most important legacies for research: the exercise of reflexivity.

Throughout his work Bourdieu consistently challenged the assumption that the production of academic knowledge was a neutral activity. Bourdieu insisted that researchers needed to submit themselves to the same rigorous critique that they would apply to the object of their research. This would include reflecting on things such as their own history and academic formation and require a kind of 'double-distancing' which Bourdieu termed 'objectification of objectification' (Jenkins 2002, xvi). Objectification of objectification requires two steps. Most of us will be familiar with the first step and it represents stepping back or distancing ourselves from the object of our research. For example, when researching classroom interaction, many researchers would initially assume a position of distance so that they can observe and analyse the interaction. Bourdieu calls that 'objectifying' and advocates that the researcher needs to go further than this and reflect on the nature of the distance they have created. The second step is to put under the same reflective microscope the relationship that the researcher has to the researched when they are carrying out fieldwork. In the case of our example, this would mean 'objectifying' the relationship that the researcher has to the class and to the classroom interaction. Bourdieu was an active empirical researcher himself, he essentially provides the researcher with a toolkit of concepts to support their reflexive analysis of the social world. These concepts are both theoretical and analytical but they are also allied closely to the practice of research; in other words, they are also methodological. My argument is that these concepts are highly practical and of direct relevance to the daily practice of fieldwork; thus it is worth persisting through Bourdieu's dense and at times verbose articulation of how they work. I am going to use the history of Bourdieu's own academic formation to introduce the following key concepts: habitus, field, symbolic violence and cultural capital.

Bourdieu was born in 1930; he grew up in Béarn, a rural village in south-eastern France. His grandfather had been a peasant sharecropper, but his mother came from a wealthier peasant family and his father was a minor civil servant. Bourdieu describes himself as separated from his classmates at primary school because of his father's white collar education and separated from his peers at the boarding school he subsequently attended because of his rural accent and provincial ways. One of the things that characterises Bourdieu's early education is a feeling of not belonging and an awareness that his relationship with his peer group did not match the lofty ideals proclaimed in the rhetoric of the classroom. He described this acute awareness of social difference as 'a terrible education in social realism' (Bourdieu 2007, 91). When Bourdieu died in 2002, he held the high honour of a Chair at the Collège de France and was a famous public intellectual. There may well be an element of mythologising in the story of the peasant boy made good but as Bourdieu reflects on his early experiences in *Sketch for Self Analysis*, he illustrates how attitudes, assumptions and dispositions are unconsciously formed; in this he is offering an explanation of what habitus is and how it can be applied in research.

The concept of habitus dates back to the time of Aristotle, it was a moral concept associated with virtue ethics. This is the belief that good or virtuous dispositions can be acquired which will form moral character and regulate our actions through good practice or 'habit'. Bourdieu uses habitus to refer to the deeply rooted assumptions, not explicitly reflected upon but held almost subconsciously, which we all inherit. These assumptions regulate both individual and collective action in the social world. Bourdieu (2007) wrote that his history and cultural formation in Béarn shaped his habitus, giving him 'a marked taste for disputation' (p. 89). Robbins (2000) writes that Bourdieu first applied the concept in relation to dancing when in 1962 he published an account of peasant life in Béarn. Bourdieu described the country dances held in the village as being 'occasions of a clash of civilisation' between rural and urban habitus (p. 28). Bourdieu was also trying to get away from the separation of mind and body, or of theory and practice, in his understanding of the social world. For Bourdieu habitus is not something which happens just in the mind but is physical, for example, in the dancing; it is not something which people consciously reflect on but nor is it simply mechanical, and nor was Bourdieu saying that habitus is identical for all people. Bourdieu took seriously the fact that society comprises people, classes and groups who occupy positions relative to each other and to society as a whole. This way of conceptualising society is called structuralism. Structuralism was very popular when Bourdieu took up his academic posts in the late 1950s. After Bourdieu had graduated and taught for a year in a provincial school, he was conscripted into the army and served two years in Algeria (1956–58). His fieldwork during the time of revolution and agricultural crisis in Algeria was to prove formative. He produced a structuralist analysis of the culture of the Kabyle, the largest cultural and linguistic community in Algeria (Bourdieu 1979). Bourdieu's study of this group led him to reject one of structuralism's key assumptions, which is that different societies adopt intrinsically different functions – this is referred to as functionalism. Bourdieu found that *within* the Kabyle people constructed differences and took up different positions and roles regulated by the habitus. Later in his work he accounted for the nature and impact of position taking using the concepts of symbolic violence and cultural capital. We will consider these concepts after first picking up the thread of Bourdieu's history in order to get a handle on his concept of field.

In 1960, Bourdieu returned to France to take up a position as assistant at the Faculty of Arts at the University of Paris. The dominant intellectual discipline of the Paris Academe had been philosophy. Bourdieu was well acquainted with the legacy of Jean-Paul Sartre whose existentialism he rejected. Jenkins (2002) writes that Bourdieu believed there was more to the social life 'than the subjective consciousness' of the individuals 'who move within it and produce it' (p. 17). Bourdieu argued that there was a real or objective social world beyond the interaction and self-awareness of individuals. Field is a concept used to define the dimensions of this social space. So, for example, when Bourdieu joined the Faculty of Arts, the field of philosophy was being threatened by the rise in popularity of the field of social sciences. This also helps to illustrate Bourdieu's argument that habitus can only operate 'in relation to the social field' (p. 82). Bourdieu believed that different groups compete for recognition or cultural validation within a social field and thus it is always an arena of struggle and competition. Bourdieu experienced this struggle first-hand. In 1968, the same year in which he founded his research centre, the Centre de Sociologie Européenne, there were violent student protests in Paris. Bourdieu (2007) interpreted the student movement as a reaction to the threat that the rise of the social sciences represented to the traditional dominance of philosophy. The late 1960s marked the beginning of a prolific period of research and publications,

Bourdieu turning education itself into the object of his sociological analysis. By investigating the habitus of students (see Bourdieu and Passeron 1979, *The Inheritors*) and exploring where power lay within the structure of the university field, he called into question its apparent meritocratic values and the dominance of particular disciplines. Bourdieu concluded that education is one of the key ways in which social reproduction takes place.

It is primarily within the field of education that Bourdieu developed his theory of social reproduction. The key text which sets out this theory is *Reproduction in Education, Society and Culture*, first published by Bourdieu and Passeron in 1970. *Reproduction*, as I will refer to it for short, is probably one of the best known and well used of Bourdieu's texts in sociology of education. Its arguments underpin the work done on school choice, class and gender that I mentioned in the introduction to this chapter. Unfortunately, it is also one of the least accessible texts in terms of language and construction partly because Bourdieu presents his theory as a series of propositions and glosses. This is a stylistic device in which a proposition is a statement proposing a definition or thesis and a gloss provides further explanation or description for clarity. A central concept in *Reproduction* is symbolic violence. This refers to the way in which culture is imposed upon people or groups and is experienced by society as legitimate, but Bourdieu argued that it conceals the power relationships which make it possible.

> 0. Every power to exert symbolic violence, i.e. every power which manages to impose meanings and to impose them as legitimate by concealing the power relations which are the basis of its force, adds its own specifically symbolic force to those power relations.
>
> (Bourdieu and Passerson 1977, 4)

Symbolic violence is often exercised via social structures such as education or religion. The concept of symbolic violence can be used to track the exercise of power and explore how particular cultural practices – for example, passing an examination or submitting a thesis – are recognised and legitimated to validate and preserve control in the social field. As a form of protest, Bourdieu refused to submit a thesis when he graduated from the École normale supérieure in Paris. If you share the habitus of the dominant cultural elite, so in Bourdieu's context if you are a philosopher and a sophisticated Parisian intellectual, you will inherit and reproduce a set of cultural assumptions and expectations which will preserve the existing social order and the dominance of Parisian intellectuals. Similarly, if you are a rural peasant from Béarn, your cultural assumptions and expectations stem from a cultural habitus, one which is not recognised in the elite French university, but which reproduces the cultural practices of rural life in south-eastern France. Whilst one or two bright exceptions might become French public intellectuals, the exercise of symbolic violence means that one cannot do so without participating and, therefore, reproducing the cultural practices of the dominant social group. There are clearly some problems with this theory, not least the very real criticism to which Bourdieu's work is often subjected that this is a deterministic view of culture which does not take into account individual action or agency. Criticisms of Bourdieu's concepts will be discussed at the end of this section; there is one more key concept to explore first, that of cultural capital.

Bourdieu posited his concept of cultural capital directly against the philosopher Kant's notion that the pursuit of the aesthetic is pure and somehow morally neutral, or at least disinterested (Jenkins 2002). The title of Bourdieu's (1984) publication, *Distinction: A Social Critique of the Judgement of Taste*, is a direct reference to Kant, who published *Critique of Judgement* in 1790. Bourdieu (1984) challenged the notion that 'culture' had an intrinsic value and that the appreciation and the quest for culture was thus untainted by such base extrinsic rewards as economic value. With the concept of cultural capital, Bourdieu extended the meaning of 'capital' beyond its typical use in economic exchange theory where it primarily denotes monetary profit (Moore 2004). Bourdieu argued that the acquisition of cultural capital primarily through the social institution of education can confer distinction upon an individual and therefore material advantage (Bourdieu and Passeron 1977, proposition 3.1.3., 35). In his introduction to the first edition of *Distinction*, Bourdieu (1984) writes that sociology endeavours to understand how culture and cultural tastes are produced. He argues, however, that cultural practices such as the appreciation of fine art or music, cannot be fully understood unless they are situated back into the wider context of social relationships, particularly class, and then analysed. Jenkins (2002) writes that Bourdieu is applying reflexivity here; the double distancing or 'objectification of objectification' which insists that we reflect both on culture as a product and on our definition of culture as a process. Bourdieu is reminding us to ask this question: what has produced the classifications which we use to define art or music etc. as 'culture'? He argues strongly in *Distinction* that all cultural practices are linked to educational level and social origin; in other words, cultural taste functions as 'a marker of class' (Bourdieu 1984, xxv).

There are a series of critiques of Bourdieu's work not least of which is that he fell short of the overarching grand sociological theory he sought to produce. As a public intellectual in his later career, Bourdieu extended his 'objectification of objectification' to comment on French politics, society and culture. His critics point out that he never really dealt with the question of what makes the sociological perspective authoritative in its account of the social world as opposed to the philosophical and structuralist perspectives which Bourdieu sought to refute. Indeed, Bourdieu's theory remained heavily influenced by structuralism as he sought a more 'scientific' account of socialisation and social reproduction. This leads us to perhaps the major criticism of Bourdieu's work, which is that his theory is essentially deterministic. Critics argue that Bourdieu's assertion that there is 'no way out of the game of culture' suggests 'a self perpetuating and mechanical model of society' (Jenkins 2002, 118). Bourdieu pays little attention to the capacity of individuals to act in the world; this is referred to in philosophy and sociology as agency. Connell (1983) argues that Bourdieu does not really explain what habitus is or how it interacts with agency and that he is vague about how institutions work. She also argues that Bourdieu's theory doesn't account for the way institutions and social systems change, especially over a period of time. Despite these significant flaws, many of Bourdieu's critics do accept that his theoretical work has made a significant contribution to our understanding of the social world and has equipped research with 'a way of talking about what living in the world is really like' (Connell 1983, 153).

Applying Bourdieu's concepts to research

In this section of the chapter I intend to illustrate how I applied Bourdieu's concepts of field, habitus, symbolic violence and cultural capital to my own research in an Academy sponsored by a Christian foundation. As I indicated in my introduction, one of the ways to get a handle on Bourdieu's social theory is to see it applied in practice. I begin by setting the scene and contextualising the 'field' of the new academies as well as briefly summarising my research questions and methodology. Next I take Bourdieu's concepts in turn, demonstrating how they were applied and giving examples of what kinds of things they revealed in my data. I have found that Bourdieu's concepts provide a helpful framework in which to analyse the impact of religion on school culture. This is important because, as Grace (2004) has argued, religion, as opposed to class, race and gender, is often left out when researchers in the West analyse education.

The Academies policy

To set the scene it is important to outline the history of the policy before I explain why I conceptualise Academies as a field within my own research. Academies are 'publicly-funded independent schools' (DfE 2012). At the time of writing, there were 1,635 Academies open in England. Under the coalition government their number has increased dramatically because primary schools as well as secondary schools have been actively encouraged to convert to Academy status (these are referred to as 'converter Academies'). Academies were originally a central part of the New Labour government's education policy. The initiative extended a Conservative government policy of the 1980s, which had established City Technology Colleges (CTCs) in areas of urban deprivation. My research was carried out in a CTC and two Academies sponsored by a Christian Foundation who have been a provider throughout all the various iterations of the policy. CTCs and Academies have greater freedom to set their own curriculum, pay and conditions because they are free from local education authority control. Under New Labour, the Academies had to have a sponsor, which were drawn from business, private philanthropists, Christian churches and Christian charitable foundations. About a quarter of the first wave of Academies had a Christian sponsor (these are referred to as 'sponsored Academies').[1] The Church of England remains the biggest provider of Academies; they run 45 sponsored and 109 convertor Academies (The Church of England 2012). The following Christian Charitable Foundations are responsible for 39 Academies between them: Oasis Community Learning (OCL) 14 Academies, the United Learning Trust and the Emmanuel Schools Foundation (ULT and ESF) 19 Academies and Grace Academies six Academies (OCL 2012; Grace Academy 2012; and ULT 2012).

Methodology

Framing questions is a key technique in my research methodology and analysis. I have modelled this approach on Grace's (2002) work in Catholic education. Grace conceptualised Catholic education as a field and framed a set of questions using Bourdieu's concepts to trace the nature and impact of power and cultural assumptions in the field; this is a form of reflexivity. The practice of research always starts with a question and mine was: how does the Christian ethos of the sponsor show itself in the social and academic experiences of the students and staff? Bourdieu argued that most research accounts are remote; separate to what is really going on in the social world. He therefore saw his familiarity with the rural settings in which he carried out his early work as an aid to reflexivity because he was not positioned entirely outside the field. I too am familiar with my research setting. Although I had no prior association with the CTC or Academies where I did my fieldwork, I attended an independent Christian school up until the age of 16 and I taught history in Church of England and Roman Catholic secondary schools before commencing my research. As with Bourdieu's early fieldwork, my study was an ethnography. Ethnography is a form of research method closely associated with anthropology. It is essentially a study of culture in which the researcher is a participant in the social world asking questions with a view to explaining it to the outsider and clarifying it for the insider (Green 2009a). I spent six months at my research site carrying out ethnographic observations of formal and informal settings, conducting a series of in-depth interviews with a purposive sample of 18 members of staff in key roles and 30 Year 10 (15 and 16 years old) students and doing documentary analysis. I was typically on site five days a week from 8am to 5pm and I also attended after-school events and meetings during the evenings and weekends. I am very thankful to the sponsors for providing me with entirely open access to the site.

Field

In my research, I conceptualise the Academies sector as a field. Bourdieu's use of field denotes a site of competing interests where there is struggle for recognition. I applied the concept to Academies for two main reasons. First, at policy level the creation and expansion of the Academies has generated fierce debate. The existence of Academies outside local authority provision initiates a set of questions about equity, funding and competition in relation to existing state provision in common schools (for a more in-depth discussion of this see Gorard 2005). The sponsorship of Academies by businesses, philanthropists and religious organisations sets up a second set of questions about the ideologies and/or religious beliefs gaining influence within the education system as a whole (for a more in-depth discussion of this see Ball 2007). I applied the concept of field in my research as a way to keep me mindful of the wider context in which Academies are located. Reflecting back on this enabled me to relate my data to the ongoing emergence of Academies as the new 'norm' in institutional provision. When I began my fieldwork in 2007, Academies were still fairly new, now they are arguably a mainstay of provision. Education in the United Kingdom is in the midst of transition. Bourdieu's concept of field helps researchers to reflect on the nature of the model for education that is emerging as dominant in the social world. Bourdieu prompts us to ask what kind of knowledge is valued in the field, what groups hold power in the system and what do they assume education is for? This leads to the second reason I applied the concept of field in my research. I wanted to focus in particular on the impact of a Christian sponsor competing for recognition in the field. The types of questions I reflected on included: was the sponsor a powerful influence, what kind of knowledge did they value and what did they believe about the purpose of education?

Habitus

The CTC and Academies in which I carried out my research were non-denominational and it was not necessary to be a Christian either to work there or attend as a student. Unlike many church-sponsored Academies, no places were reserved for the children of Christian families. Nevertheless I did find that the sponsors and the senior staff shared a set of religious beliefs and assumptions which I conceptualised in my research as a habitus. A key finding of the research was that the habitus was embedded in institutional structures such as the order of the school day, assemblies and tutor times. I concluded that the habitus did regulate certain aspects of cultural practice. The sponsors and members of the senior team attended the same local churches and often met to pray and study the Bible together during their leisure time. The exceptions to this were three members of senior staff at the Academies recruited from predecessor schools who did not identify as Christians. In theological terms, the shared religious beliefs are best described as reformed or conservative Protestant Christian. Evidence from interviews with the sponsors and senior staff, analysis of policy documents and observation of meetings and assemblies conducted by senior staff demonstrated a highly unified and regulated Christian discourse (Green 2012). My research found that this was characterised by a high view of the authority of the Bible, a belief in the physical death and resurrection of Jesus, personal conversion, an emphasis on personal morality and an imperative to teach and proclaim the 'gospel' or good news about Jesus in the world (Green 2012).

Habitus was a central tool in my analysis because it enabled me to explore the extent to which the sponsor and senior team's habitus influenced practice in the

Academy even though Christian beliefs were not universally shared by the rest of the staff and students. In his essay 'Genesis and structure of the religious field', Bourdieu (1971) conceptualised religion as a field within the social world; he argued that religious habitus imposes particular practices and meanings which regulate the structures of society. He had observed this in his earlier fieldwork and he wrote about the significance of Islam for Algerian culture and of Puritanism for European culture in his first book, *Sociologie de l'Algerie* (1958). The problem with Bourdieu's account of religious habitus is that he seems unwilling to allow that it might contribute anything good and he does not really acknowledge that spiritual and/or mystical encounters are widespread in human experience (Rey 2007). This is another example of Bourdieu's tendency towards determinism. Cannell (2006) has argued that religion should be taken seriously as a cultural fact; she believes that it is often marginalised in ethnographic accounts as if the religious experience of others can always be explained away by other structures such as politics or the economy. Bourdieu did, however, criticise religious scholars for not paying enough attention to the ways in which religious assumptions and practice are physically embodied in the social world (Rey 2007). I believe this is why sociologists and students of religion persist in using his concepts. They offer a set of tools which are flexible enough to probe the complex relationship between institutional structures, religious practices and individual agency. This is where legitimate questions about the nature and impact of religious faith and experiences are located. I wanted to take seriously the religious beliefs of my research participants; I also wanted to acknowledge that they were not held by everybody in the institution and to be realistic about where power and influence lay. To that end I will provide a brief example of one way in which the religious habitus impacted organisational structure, in this case the physical ordering of the school day (this is discussed in more depth elsewhere, see Green 2009b). This example will lead into a discussion of the concept of symbolic violence and its application in my research.

In the CTC and Academies, every day began with an act of collective worship, either in the form of an assembly or during tutor time, which was known as tutor prayers. Such occasions were deliberately formal. Quiet movement around the building, an emphasis on correct uniform and high standards of conduct and behaviour were all features for which the Foundation has received both praise and criticism (see Green 2009a). The CTC and Academies were deliberately modelled on a traditional educational pedagogy such as one might associate with post-war grammar school education in England. The approach is also driven by the habitus of the sponsors whose objective in their 2005 Mission Statement is to provide a 'Christian religious education with a daily Christian Assembly and the teaching of biblical values and morality'. The sponsors fear that society is becoming increasingly more secularised and that, as a consequence, a sense of public morality and familiarity with the Bible's teaching may be lost. Students attended three assemblies a week and two tutor prayer sessions. I found that assemblies and tutor prayers were key motifs in school life for the religious habitus and its expression in corporate identity. Themes for assemblies and tutor prayers were all planned on a rolling cycle to provide students with an overview of the Bible's narrative. This would encompass what conservative Protestants regard as the key 'turning points' of the narrative, namely, the stories of creation, fall, Old Testament history, the incarnation, death and resurrection of Jesus (Carson 2008, 44). There was less emphasis on teaching about corporate holiness or social justice as one might find within Catholic theology for example. Worship was structured around the written word of the Bible rather than around meditation or reflection which are practices one might associate with other Christian or alternate faith traditions. During assemblies and in tutor time, students kept silent as a passage from the Bible was read. In the assemblies, an explanation of the passage was given in the form of an address or short sermon and a Christian hymn would be sung. During tutor prayers, students were given comprehension questions about the passage to discuss. Students had all been given a copy of the Bible which they were expected to have with them as part of their basic school equipment. Bibles were bound in corporate colours identical to the students' uniform and stored in classrooms on specially constructed shelving. The impact of these routines and practices on staff and students will be considered in the next sections as I reflect on Bourdieu's concepts of symbolic violence and cultural capital. For the moment this example serves as an illustration of how belief in the authority of the Bible impacted the physical ordering of the school day. I argued in my research that the formal presentation of 'Christian ethos' within the CTC and Academies rested upon a particular biblical interpretation which could be conceptualised as the religious habitus of the sponsors and senior staff. This habitus ensured that biblical teaching and the presentation of Christian ethos in the institutions stemmed from a consistent framework which staff and students primarily encountered as forms of 'symbolic violence'.

Symbolic violence

One of the key findings of the study was that teaching the Bible was a high-status activity. Only those who shared the religious habitus of the sponsors taught the Bible in RE and in assemblies. These staff members were therefore much more visible in the formal or public life of the CTC and Academies. This placed them in a symbolically powerful relationship to the Bible because they were seen as the spokesmen and women authorised to interpret the text; they embodied the Christian ethos of the school and as such they regulated it. Bourdieu (1992) described symbolic violence as 'the power to constitute the given by stating it' (p. 147). In *Language and Symbolic Power*, Bourdieu uses the Catholic Church in France as an example of how sacred rites, routines and practices carried out by the clergy could regulate assumptions in society. In his example, the clergy embodied in their practice a message about what kind of relationships between groups in society were legitimate and what kind of behaviours were approved and which were not. In so doing, Bourdieu argued that the clergy imposed and preserved their own status and hierarchy which he described as a form of symbolic violence. I used the concept of symbolic violence in my research to delineate which groups were powerful in the CTC and Academies. I found that a kind of theological hierarchy had emerged within staff culture. The hierarchy ranged from those who shared the religious habitus at the top, through those who identified as Christians but were members of other church denominations, down to those of other faiths and those who identified with no religious faith at the bottom of the hierarchy. There were, therefore, a whole range of voices absent from the formal occasions and structures that I had identified as 'key motifs' for the religious habitus and its expression in corporate identity.

The theological hierarchy is well illustrated through the tutor prayer system. Most members of the teaching staff were form tutors and thus required to deliver tutor prayers whether or not they identified as Christians, so this example very effectively demonstrates two key elements of symbolic violence. First, it demonstrates how an authorised interpretation of biblical text was secured, and second, it demonstrates a gap between the perceived effectiveness of those staff members who shared the religious habitus compared to those who did not. A tutor prayers booklet had been prepared by a senior teacher and was used by all the tutor groups at the CTC and Academies. The booklet specified the Bible reading for the day, together with some comprehension-style questions and provided background context for the passage to prompt tutors who were not familiar with the Bible. Tutors who did not identify as Christians lacked confidence in taking tutor prayers. One form tutor said to me that it was like having to teach history at advanced level when your specialism was in languages (Interview Transcript, 2 May 2007). Another said that she sometimes felt under additional pressure to push a particular moral or theological perspective which she may not personally agree with such as a conservative view of marriage (Interview Transcript, 3 May 2007). This contrasted with my observations of the tutors who shared the religious habitus. Having prior knowledge of the Bible and an experience of its teaching in their churches meant that these tutors were far more familiar with the biblical content included in the tutor prayer programme and how to situate and teach Bible passages. The students also gave me the impression that, even if they ultimately considered tutor prayers to be boring and irrelevant, it was the Christian tutors who did them 'correctly'. One of the conclusions of the research was that being able to teach the Bible together with possessing a good level of biblical literacy functioned as a form of cultural capital. The concept of cultural capital helped me to answer two key questions. First, what were the assumptions and practices legitimated through symbolic violence, and second, how effectively did they shape student culture?

Cultural capital

Applying the concept of cultural capital to my data helped to account for one of the most significant findings of the research. I found that the religious habitus of the sponsors did have an impact upon student culture but that it was limited and I found that the values and assumptions of the habitus had been re-appropriated by the students in ways that were quite different from the sponsors' intentions. Bourdieu's concept of habitus encompasses the idea that assumptions can be appropriated and re-appropriated, hence old beliefs can persist and continue to have currency, or cultural capital, in alternate settings where you might not expect them to be widely shared (Robbins 2000). Students did value being knowledgeable about religion and they were biblically literate; these were forms of cultural capital. Being able to discuss, affirm or refute biblical claims was seen by them as one of the marks of being a good and successful student; but within student culture this was not dependent on sharing the religious habitus of the sponsors. As Julie, aged 15, explained it to me:

> I think some people who are atheists just say they don't believe but they don't know what they don't believe . . . I know what I don't believe.
>
> (Interview Transcript, 29 March 2007)

Julie is rehearsing here one of the key assumptions of the sponsors' habitus which is that the students should be presented with the Bible's narrative so that they can decide for themselves whether or not its claims about Jesus are true. This assumption had been re-enforced for students by their daily encounter with Bible teaching in an approved format regulated through symbolic violence. I argued in my research that in weighing up the claims of the Bible and deciding whether to accept or, as in most cases, reject them students were doing precisely what was being asked of them. I found in my research that, with the exception of RE, the religious habitus of the sponsors had no discernible impact on the curriculum or on teaching and learning. The students only encountered the Bible and the religious habitus of the sponsors in tightly regulated spaces in the life of the CTC and Academies. I concluded that this served to re-enforce the commonly held view that religion was not really relevant to the rest of their lives. This stands in opposition to the sponsors' desire to counter the marginalisation of religion in an increasingly secular society. This finding also highlights an important point which Bourdieu's social theory does not address fully. It suggests that the habitus of the dominant cultural group does not by definition render other groups in the culture passive and without agency.

Conclusion

Bourdieu's concepts are applied extensively in UK education research often to analyse the impact of class on social reproduction. I have argued in this chapter that a significant legacy of Bourdieu's work is his development of a set of conceptual tools capable of integrating theory and analysis with methodology. By setting the development of Bourdieu's social theory against the backdrop of his biography I have exemplified another significant contribution of Bourdieu's work which is reflexivity. Bourdieu challenges us to take account of the relationship of the researcher to the researched and to the social world. I have argued that his tools equip the researcher with practical ways in which to do this. In my research I apply Bourdieu's concepts of habitus, field, symbolic violence and cultural capital to the study of religion in the new Christian Academies. Within this chapter I have used the examples from my research to do two things. First, I have illustrated a way of applying Bourdieu's theory in a real research setting. Reading how other researchers make use of Bourdieu's conceptual tools is a helpful way for new researchers to access Bourdieu's writings. Second, I have illustrated how current research is broadening the traditional application of Bourdieu's social theory beyond the study of class, in this case to the analysis of religion. The flexibility of such concepts and their application make Bourdieu's social theory a very adaptable tool for analysing contemporary culture and the impact of habitus on education. New researchers should be encouraged to take on the vigorous debate that surrounds Bourdieu's work and make his tools for analysis their own.

Note

1 In April 2011, 53 of 203 Academies open had a Christian sponsor: non-denominational Christian (31), Church of England (19), Catholic (2), Church of England/Catholic (1) (Source: DfE 2011).

References

Ball, S. J. 2003. *Class strategies and the education market: The middle classes and social advantage*. London: Routledge.

Ball, S. J. 2007. *Education plc: Understanding private sector participation in public sector education*. London: Routledge.

Bourdieu, P. 1958. *Sociologie de l'Algerie*. Paris: Presses Universitaires de France.

Bourdieu, P. 1971. Genèse et structure du champ religieux. *Revue française de sociologie* XII, 3: 295–334.

Bourdieu, P. 1979. *Algeria 1960*. Cambridge: Cambridge University Press.

Bourdieu, P. 1984. *Distinction: A social critique of the judgement of taste*. London: Routledge Kegan Paul.

Bourdieu, P. 1986. The forms of capital. Reproduced in *Education: Culture, economy and society* (2001), ed. A. H. Halsey, H. Lauder, P. Brown and A. Stuart Wells, 46–58. Oxford: Oxford University Press.

Bourdieu, P. 1992. *Language & symbolic power*. Cambridge: Polity Press.

Bourdieu, P. 2007. *Sketch for a self analysis*. Cambridge: Polity Press.

Bourdieu, P. and J. C. Passeron. 1970. *La reproduction. Éléments pour une théorie du système d'enseignement*. Paris: Éditions de Minuit.

Bourdieu, P. and J. C. Passeron. 1977. *Reproduction in education, society and culture*. London: Sage.

Bourdieu, P. and J. C. Passeron. 1979. *The inheritors: French students and their relation to culture*. Chicago: University of Chicago Press.

Cannell, F. ed. 2006. *The anthropology of Christianity*. London: Duke University Press.

Carson, D. 2008. *Christ and culture revisited*. Nottingham: Apollos.

Connell, R. W. 1983. *Which way is up?* Sydney: George Allen & Unwin.

DfE. 2011. *Statistical first release: Schools, pupils, and their characteristics*. Available at: www.education.gov.uk/rsgateway/DB/SFR/s001012/index.shtml (accessed 21 November 2011).

DfE. 2012. *About academies*. Available at: www.education.gov.uk/schools/leadership/typesofschools/academies/b0061252/about-academies (accessed 11 April 2012).

Gorard, S. 2005. Academies as the 'future of schooling': Is this an evidence-based policy? *Journal of Education Policy* 3, 20: 369–377.

Grace Academy. 2012. *Grace Academy Specialist Business & Enterprise Academy*. Available at: www.graceacademy.org.uk/ (accessed 17 April 2012).

Grace, G. 1978 *Teachers, ideology and control: A study in urban education*. London: Routledge and Kegan Paul.

Grace, G. 2002. *Catholic schools: Missions, markets and morality*. London: RoutledgeFalmer.

Grace, G. 2004. Making connections for future directions: Taking religion seriously in the sociology of education. *International Studies in Sociology of Education* 14, 1: 47–56.

Green, E. H. 2009a. *An ethnographic study of a city technology college with a bible-based ethos*. Unpublished DPhil Thesis. University of Oxford.

Green, E. H. 2009b. Speaking in parables: The responses of students to a bible-based ethos in a Christian city technology college. *Cambridge Journal of Education* 39, 4: 443–56.

Green, E. H. 2012. Analysing religion and education in Christian academies. *British Journal of Sociology of Education* 1–17 iFirst article. Available at: http://dx.doi.org/10.1080/01425692.2012.659456 (accessed 11 April 2012).

Halsey, A. H., H. Lauder, P. Brown and A. Stuart Wells. 2001. *Education: Culture, economy and society*. Oxford: Oxford University Press.

Jenkins, R. 2002. *Pierre Bourdieu*. Revised edition. London: Routledge.

Moore, R. 2004. Cultural capital: Objective probability and the cultural arbitrary. *British Journal of Sociology of Education* 25, 4: 445–456.

OCL. 2012. *Our Academies*. Available at: www.oasiscommunitylearning.org/academies/ (accessed 17 April 2012).

Reay, D. 1998. *Class work: Mothers' involvement in children's schooling*. London: University College Press.

Rey, T. 2007. *Bourdieu on religion: Imposing faith and legitimacy*. London: Equinox Publishing.

Robbins, D. 2000. *Bourdieu and culture*. London: Sage.

The Church of England. 2012. *Church schools and academies*. Available at: www.churchofengland.org/education/church-schools-academies.aspx (accessed 11 April 2012).

ULT. 2012. *ULT & ESF Academies*. Available at: www.ucst.org.uk/academies/view/23 (accessed 17 April 2012).

Chapter 10

Bourdieu applied

Exploring perceived parental influence on adolescent students' educational choices for studies in higher education

Irene Kleanthous

Introduction

Bourdieu's theoretical framework has become prominent for exploring differences between social groups and parenting practices in various educational settings. This chapter draws on some interview data from six family case studies in Cyprus and reflects on the use of Bourdieu's theory to explore adolescent students' perceptions of parental influence on their educational choices for future studies in higher education (HE).

The role of familial capital (economic, social and cultural) was investigated and it became evident in the data that familial capital mediates parental influence. Students benefit from private tutorials (economic capital), visit their parents' workplace (social capital) and accumulate educational credentials for entering higher education (cultural capital). Nevertheless, adolescent students 'deny' their parents' influence on their educational choices in their interviews and stress their autonomous decision making for future studies in HE.

The mobilisation of familial capital from middle-class parents to enhance their children's educational choices is well documented in the literature. Nevertheless, this chapter questions whether capital is adequate as a theoretical tool to theorise parental influence on students' educational choices. It is argued that parental influence on students' educational choices for future studies in HE may be a form of 'symbolic violence' after Bourdieu (1980), which students and their parents 'misrecognise' because parental influence is largely unconscious (Bourdieu 1996). This new theoretical conceptualisation of parental influence is discussed in this chapter along with some current debates in the literature about familial habitus (Reay 2010) and familial doxa (Atkinson 2011).

Background

The concepts of habitus and cultural capital, suggested by Bourdieu and Passeron (1990), have become prominent for investigating and understanding inequalities between social groups and for understanding parents' practices and their involvement in various educational contexts (Levine-Rasky 2009). Brooks (2003) argues that various studies of educational choice have outlined what have been called the 'class strategies of middle-class parents: attempts to achieve a class fit between the habitus of home and institution' (p. 86). Brooks also notes considerable differences in the extent to which families were involved in the decision-making process and in their knowledge about HE, generally, and the relative status of institutions and subjects, more specifically.

By the same token, Reay et al. (2001) argue that there are class inequalities involved in making decisions about higher education. According to Reay et al. the inequalities arise from lack of information and general perplexity and confusion about post-compulsory education among working-class families. They note that 'while more working-class and minority students are entering university, for the most part they are entering different universities to their middle-class counterparts' (p. 858). The role of parents as holders of crucial information on the educational system, what Bourdieu refers to as 'informational capital' (Bourdieu and Wacquant 1992), might explain the differences noted between different social groups.

Interestingly, Lareau and Weininger (2004) provide a review of the literature on cultural capital and refer to its different operationalisations by various researchers. For example, they cite McDonough who used the concept of parental cultural capital in a qualitative study of influences on students' college choices:

> For McDonough cultural capital comprises the 'first-hand' knowledge that parents have of the college admission process, particularly knowledge that they do not get from schools (e.g. detailed understanding of the significance of SAT scores, the possibility of raising SAT scores through tutoring . . . as well as the initiative to secure private tutors).
>
> (p. 121)

This informational capital that parents possess on the educational system has arguably been accumulated through parents' interaction with the educational system. Reay (1998a) pointed out that parents' engagement with their children's primary school differed in ways attributable to differences in habitus and the different kinds of capital held by the family. In a study on parental involvement in primary schools in Cyprus, Symeou (2007) argues that families' knowledge of the educational system and their ability to work it to the advantage of their children varies according to social class and also within classes. Professional–managerial families seem more able to mobilise goods, status and social connections in order to advance their children's education. However, working-class families are usually intimidated by the educational system and feel neither competent to criticise the school nor capable to help their children with their school homework. 'Therefore, working-class parents tend to blame themselves or their children for school problems and to find the school difficult to challenge, whereas upper-class and middle-class parents are more apt to blame the school and to challenge it, and to buy educational services from outside experts if necessary' (p. 475).

A qualitative study by Green and Vryonides (2005) regarding the educational choices of modern Greek-Cypriot parents points out that parents consider it to be their duty to provide children with as much support for education as possible, expecting better life opportunities for them than themselves, and perceived costs being outweighed by expectations of the future benefits of educational achievement. Nevertheless, they argue that social capital is an important factor affecting educational choice-making practices. The main finding of their study was that families from lower social classes lack effective social capital and set low aspirations for their children's education: 'For some parents the lack of social capital seems to entail making compromises on the level of education that their children might aim for' (p. 336).

This chapter discusses some data from a recent study (Kleanthous 2012) which explored perceived parental influence amongst adolescent students in Cyprus who were about to make their choices for future studies in higher education. The analysis and interpretation of the data relied heavily on Bourdieu's theoretical framework. In particular, I utilised his concepts of habitus, and economic, social and cultural capital to explore parental influence on students' dispositions towards studying in HE. I conceptualised students' dispositions to study in HE as part of their habitus and I sought to explore how these dispositions might have been inculcated by their family. Bourdieu's notion of 'symbolic violence' was also used to suggest how students misrecognise their parents' influence on their dispositions and their decision making for studies in HE. Bourdieu defines symbolic violence as 'the violence which is exercised upon a social agent with his or her complicity . . . I call *misrecognition* the fact of recognizing a violence which is wielded precisely inasmuch as one does not perceive it as such' (Bourdieu and Wacquant 1992, 167–168). These theoretical tools, 'symbolic violence' and 'misrecognition', were used to interpret the 'denial' of parental influence by adolescent students and some of their parents.

An overview of Bourdieu's theoretical framework

Bourdieu and Wacquant (1992) argue that class habitus is 'the structural affinity of habituses belonging to the same class, capable of generating practices that are convergent and objectively orchestrated outside of any collective 'intention' or 'consciousness' (p. 125). They also argue that 'habitus is the product of a particular economic condition, defined by the possession of the minimum economic and cultural capital necessary actually to perceive and seize the "potential opportunities" formally offered to all' (p. 124). So it could be argued that in the educational field, seizing the 'potential opportunities' for studies in higher education relies on students' habitus and arguably middle-class students are pre-disposed to pursue studies in HE. Bourdieu and Passeron (1990) outline how middle-class students' habitus is inculcated by their family and their parents' social class and how their middle-class habitus aligns with the educational system:

> the disposition which middle-class students or middle-rank teachers, and a
> fortiori, students whose fathers are middle rank teachers, manifest toward
> education – e.g. cultural willingness or esteem for hard work – cannot be
> understood unless the system of scholastic values is brought into relation

with the middle class ethos, the principle of the value the middle classes set on scholastic values.

(p. 192)

Apart from habitus, another important element of Bourdieu's theory is capital in its various forms (economic, social and cultural). Bourdieu (1986) calls capital those resources whose distributions define the social structure and whose deployment figures centrally in the reproduction of that structure. Such resources are not just economic, but also social and cultural. Economic capital consists of financial stock and income and may be institutionalised in forms of inheritance. Social capital includes social networks and identities of individuals as members of social groups, which provide 'connections' as assets. Cultural capital consists of a large number of types of cultural knowledge and possessions including educational credentials and informational capital. Bourdieu (1998) elaborates on intergenerational transmission of informational capital:

> It is difficult to anticipate fluctuations on the stock exchange of scholastic value, and those who have the benefit, through family, parents, brothers, sisters, acquaintances, and so on, of information about the formation circuits and their actual or potential differential profit can make better educational investments and earn maximum returns on their cultural capital.
>
> (p. 25)

Bourdieu's theory of social reproduction posits that the acquisition of cultural capital and consequent educational success depends on the cultural capital passed down by the family, which in turn is largely dependent on social class. Bourdieu and Passeron (1990) argue that middle-class students' habitus aligns with the requirements of the educational system because they have acquired more cultural capital from their families than their working-class counterparts. Moreover, they argue that middle-class students are 'equipped with the linguistic and cultural capital and the capacity to invest it profitably, which the system presupposes and consecrates without ever expressly demanding it and without methodically transmitting it' (p. 99). Bourdieu (1973) writes:

> The educational system demands of everyone alike that they have what it does not give. This consists mainly of linguistic and cultural competence and that relationship of familiarity with culture which can only be produced by family upbringing when it transmits the dominant culture.
>
> (p. 80)

Bourdieu on family and symbolic violence

Bourdieu (1996) argues that family 'functions, in habitus, as a classificatory scheme and a principle of the constructions of the social world' (p. 21). Bourdieu also considers belonging to a 'normal family' a privilege, and this is one of the major conditions of the accumulation and transmission of economic and cultural capital:

> The family plays a decisive role in the maintenance of the social order, through social as well as biological reproduction, i.e. reproduction of the structure of the social space and social conditions. It is one of the key sites of the accumulation of capital in its different forms and its transmission between the generations.
>
> (p. 23)

The mobilisation of capital from middle-class parents to enhance their children's educational choices is well documented in the literature (e.g., Reay 1998a, 1998b; Symeou 2007). Nevertheless, this chapter questions whether Bourdieu's theoretical tool of capital is adequate to theorise parental influence. I now turn to discuss Bourdieu's view on the family and how parental influence can be conceptualised as a form of symbolic violence. According to Bourdieu (1980) symbolic violence is at the heart of every social relation and it is present in a gift exchange economy:

> debts and gifts, the overtly economic obligations imposed by the usurer, or the moral obligations and emotional attachments created and maintained by the generous gift, in short, overt violence or symbolic violence, censored, euphemised, that is misrecognizable, recognized violence.
>
> (p. 126)

It is suggested in this chapter that parental influence might be a form of 'symbolic violence' and the denial of parental influence – whether by students or their parents – serves as a 'misrecognition'. This argument is exemplified with some data indicating how parents invest time and money in their children's education and how this creates a 'debt' for their children. Moreover, it is argued that parents have more power in the family field because of the capital they possess and this asymmetry of power relations enables 'symbolic violence' to be exerted on their children. Bourdieu (1998) argues that family tends to function as a field, 'with its physical, economic and, above all, symbolic power relations (linked, for example, to the volume and structure of the capital possessed by each member) and its struggles to hold on to and transform these power relations' (p. 69). This study adopted Bourdieu's view that family functions as a field which inculcates students' habitus and discusses later in this chapter some alternative conceptualisations of parental influence as familial habitus (Reay 1998b, 2010) and familial doxa (Atkinson 2011).

Methodology

In this chapter I draw on six in-depth interviews that I conducted with adolescent students who were attending public upper secondary schools (lyceums) in Cyprus at the end of the process of completing the university entrance application form. The six case study students were accessed from a larger sample of 563 students who completed a survey for the same study (Kleanthous 2012); each student provided me with their parents' contact details and hence I was able to contact their parents on the phone. Students were interviewed twice over a period of one year in order to explore their perceptions of parental influence on their choices for future studies in HE and additional interviews were conducted with one of the parents of each student. Students' perceptions were then triangulated against their parents' interviews; this provided a basis for grounding the interpretation of students' 'misrecognition' of parental influence and enabled me to explore how parental influence is mediated by familial capital.

The parents' educational level and occupation varies across the sample but these six family case studies are considered to be middle-class families in the Greek-Cypriot cultural context. Although most of the parents were not university degree holders, apart from one parent who was a secondary school teacher, they all have a middle-class status because of their occupation as most of them are public servants (see Table 10.1). It should be noted that in the Greek-Cypriot cultural context parents' occupation is often used as an indicator of a family's socio-economic status rather than the educational level of the parents.[1] In this sample of parents, only one father had studied at university (i.e. Socrates)[2] but all six families are considered to be middle-class families because most parents have a 'middle-class status' occupation apart from one mother who is a cleaner (i.e. Georgia).

Findings from students' interviews on familial capital

The data indicated that students 'misrecognise' their parents' influence on their dispositions for future studies in HE. The majority of students who participated in this study claim 'It's my choice' and deny their parents' influence on their

Table 10.1 Demographic information on students' parents

Name	Gender	HE qualification	Occupation
Andreas	Male	No	Semi-government position
Maria	Female	No	Private employee (medical visitor)
Helen	Female	No	Public servant (Ministry of Public Constructions)
Socrates	Male	Yes (Master's)	Secondary school teacher (Physical Education)
Georgia	Female	No	Cleaner
Monica	Female	No	Public servant (Ministry of Employment)

dispositions and decision making; nevertheless they assert that they draw on their parents' capital before they make their choices for future studies in HE. They often benefit from expensive private tutorials (economic capital) and may access their parents' workplace or work colleagues' expertise before making their career choice (social capital). Most of them are positively disposed towards studying at university and are preparing for university admission by acquiring educational credentials, for example General Certificates of Education (cultural capital). I argue that these are instances of the economic, social and cultural capital of the family utilised for enhancing students' education. For the rest of this chapter, I will draw on the six case studies of students and their parents' interviews to illustrate my findings regarding this.

With regards to finances, some students are thinking about studying abroad, thus drawing significantly on the *economic capital* of the family:

> CHRIS: I think if I want to go to England they will help me financially. Or if I go to Greece, they won't tell me to stay in Cyprus because of finances. I think they will let me do what I want.
> CHRISTINA: They let me free if I want to go abroad, they will support me there is no problem. This helps me because I don't have to think that I might 'overcharge' them financially. They let me free.

Notably, when they were uncertain about their choices for future studies, students turned to their parents' *social capital* and networks such as colleagues from work, or members of the extended family for advice.

> INTERVIEWER: Who said that it is good to combine Law with Chartered Accountancy?
> CHRISTINA: Lots of people from my mum's work. And two cousins of mine who are both working as Chartered Accountants. They heard at the office that it's very 'strong'.

Interestingly, most students seem to accumulate *cultural capital* by attending private tutorials in order to obtain educational credentials which will give them access to HE. This is what Bourdieu (1986) calls 'conversions between capitals': buying educational credentials is one way of investing familial economic capital which then converts to cultural capital. Access to university was the most common reason given by students for accumulating educational credentials such as GCE:

> CHRIS: It depends, if I didn't have the GCE I would do something else. Either go to England for a year and then get in the university or . . .
> INTERVIEWER: You mean for a foundation year?
> CHRIS: Yeah if I didn't have the GCE. But now I can get into any British university.

Although most of these students are the first from their family background to go to university, they seem to have adequate *informational capital* and have chosen elite universities for their studies. One of the students elaborates on his choice of university by referring to the league tables indicating he has a good 'feel for the game' as Bourdieu (1980) calls it:

> CHRIS: Yeah I saw a few. I will put Imperial first and then some lower [ranking] universities. I think Imperial is the first.
> INTERVIEWER: Imperial? Yeah it's one of the best universities in the UK.
> CHRIS: I think it's the third, but in these courses it is the first.

Denial of parental influence from adolescent students

Bourdieu's (1980) notion of symbolic violence was used to discuss the 'misrecognition' of parental influence in students' interviews and a glimpse of the data is provided here. I argue that parental influence can be conceptualised as a form of 'symbolic violence' that parents exert on their children (Kleanthous 2012). For example, parents pay for their children's private tutorials to try to improve their grades and their children feel their consequent debt and a moral obligation to try harder at school and pursue studies in HE. Arguably, parental influence is thus a: 'gentle invisible form of violence, which is never recognized as such, and is not so much undergone as chosen' (Bourdieu 1977, 192). I argue that in the family field parents possess more power and capital than their children, thus parents can exert symbolic violence on their children by investing familial capital for their education; familial capital then becomes a 'gift' their children need to return in a gift-exchange economy (Bourdieu 1980) by pursuing studies in HE.

Bourdieu (1980) also argues that symbolic violence creates a bond between persons and 'masks the asymmetry of the relationship *by symbolically denying it*' (p. 127, my emphasis), thus symbolic violence is misrecognised. As I examined the data, it became clear that these adolescent students 'denied' their parents' influence on their educational choices for future studies in HE. Here I provide some quotes from three students who shared the view that they are not influenced by their parents regarding their decision making for future studies in HE.

> CHRIS: She [my mum] *lets me choose* on my own but she will tell me her opinion. Or I might tell her about my choices and she will say yeah that's good.
> INTERVIEWER: Did she try to encourage you, or guide you towards a certain direction?
> CHRIS: No, no. I took my own initiative so she didn't.

> INTERVIEWER: Do you think that your parents have high expectations of you to study at university?
> CATHERINE: Oh yes they do. They want me to go to university. But it is always what I want. I feel that *they let me choose*.

INTERVIEWER: Do they [your parents] agree with your choices?
CHRISTINA: Yes they agree, *they gave me the freedom* to decide what I want.

This discourse was common across the whole dataset and all students implied that their parents are the ones with more power in the family field who 'let' their children make their own choices. A point I illustrate with examples from fieldwork is that parental influence is unconscious for adolescent students and even their parents, because it relies on the asymmetry of power relations in the family field. Bourdieu (1998) argues that intergenerational relations are driven by 'the logic of debt':

> But in order for intergenerational exchanges to continue despite everything, the logic of debt as recognition must also intervene and a feeling of obligation or gratitude must be constituted. Relations between generations are one of the sites par excellence of the transfiguration of the recognition of debt into recognition, filial devotion, love.
>
> (p. 109)

Thus parents 'give' students 'freedom of choice' by making familial capital available to them and indeed students articulated in their interviews that they draw on familial capital before they make their choices for HE, although they denied parental influence on their decision making. I argue that symbolic violence in the family field is mediated by familial capital which in a gift-exchange economy makes the students feel indebted to their parents.

Misrecognition of parental influence from parents

Although parental influence on students' dispositions towards studying in HE seemed mainly unconscious for the students, their parents appear to be more aware of their parenting practices and the utilisation of their economic, social and cultural capital for the enhancement of their children's education. They explicitly refer to financial support for their children's future studies in HE (economic capital), asking people they know (social capital) about certain courses and providing cultural goods to their children drawing on their own cultural capital. Most parents refer quite explicitly to the utilisation of the economic capital of the family for financially supporting their children's studies:

HELEN: I told him he can go anywhere he wants. Chris was a bit sceptical about England because of the cost but I told him don't think about it. For me either you go to England or Greece it's the same [cost].

Some parents also seemed to draw on their 'connections', their social capital as Bourdieu (1986) calls it, to help their children make up their mind for future studies in HE. Their social capital consists of either members of the extended family, or professional career advisors. A father who did not have the informational capital to advise his daughter about her school subjects turned to professional career advisors for his daughter:

> ANDREAS: Sure. What we did was, the teachers we knew who advise about choosing subjects . . .
> INTERVIEWER: Career advisors?
> ANDREAS: Yeah career advisors, we talked to a lady we knew. We didn't talk to her, we took Christina to this lady and they talked about some questions she had. And at school, she talked to the career advisor at school about some questions she had. So it's her decision.

Another father's account draws a picture of a parent who transmitted his cultural capital to his daughter by buying cultural goods such as books. This was an incident where the mobilisation of familial capital might have influenced the decision making of the student for studies in HE.

> INTERVIEWER: Her specific choice of studies in Archaeology, is that something you agree with?
> SOCRATES: I do agree with this although I know in terms of finding a job she might face some difficulties. Because I also like Archaeology, and you can see here because I also like Archaeology I don't influence her in a negative way. On the contrary I am positive about it.
> INTERVIEWER: Right. Is that a dream she had from a very young age, becoming an archaeologist? Is that something she used to say to you earlier on or did she just decide?
> SOCRATES: Yes, yes way back. And from the tendency that I could see, when she was in primary school *I used to buy Archaeology books for her.*

However, the parents also 'misrecognised' their influence on their children's final decision making about future studies in HE, claiming that it was the student's 'autonomous' decision:

> INTERVIEWER: How come he has decided to study Civil Engineering? Whose idea was it?
> HELEN: His own. It wasn't . . .
> INTERVIEWER: He likes it?
> HELEN: Yeah he likes it, because Chris is inclined towards mathematics a lot, he likes these subjects rather than theoretical subjects. He just told us, and we said there is no problem, he can follow any studies he wants.

A number of parents shared the view that they 'plant the idea' of studying at university in their children's head. Arguably, this reflects the inculcation of students' habitus in the family field which predisposes them to go to university:

INTERVIEWER: You had these expectations since they were young?

MONICA: Yes, since they were babies. I *put this in their head*, they have to study. It's final, it's final they have to study. Even if she becomes a hairdresser or works at a beauty treatment salon she has to study at university.

One of the case studies illustrates how she 'planted this idea' in her children's head.

INTERVIEWER: I guess you wanted him to study at university?

HELEN: Definitely.

INTERVIEWER: Did you tell him that when he was younger?

HELEN: From a very young age (laughs). . . . I believe that every parent wants if possible to see his kid educated, with a good job. *I 'plant' this to my kids* from an early age. And because we are many here, one was influenced by the other.

INTERVIEWER: Many cousins?

HELEN: Yeah when my sister's kids went to university, they [my kids] were influenced. They would say I will study too, why shouldn't I study as well? And then his brother studied, for example Chris, he will say my brother studied why shouldn't I study as well? They are influenced. I believe it's the environment you live in, the family.

A strong family tradition is therefore evident in the data, that of going to university is 'what people like us do'. These two quotes exemplify how 'symbolic violence' is exerted by parents on their children, by convincing their children of the value of studying at university. A widely shared theme in parents' interviews, and one I return to later in this chapter, is the unconscious beliefs that family members share and the inculcation of students' habitus in the family field in a way that predisposes students to study in HE. Whether these shared unconscious beliefs could be conceptualised as familial habitus (Reay 1998b, 2010) or familial doxa (Atkinson 2011) is discussed in the next section.

Discussion of findings on parental influence

This study attempted to understand perceived parental influence on HE choice by drawing on six case studies of students and their parents engaged in the choice process. Bourdieu's theoretical tools were deployed in order to understand the practice of HE decision making amongst these adolescent students. Bourdieu's tools of economic, social and cultural capital, symbolic violence and misrecognition were used as theoretical tools to analyse the data. I found that parental influence is subtle and often 'denied' by students and their parents but students 'admit' drawing on their parents' capital to make their choices for future studies in HE, thus I argue that familial capital mediates parental influence.

The 'denial' of parental influence and its unconscious effect on students' habitus led me to conceptualise parental influence as 'symbolic violence' which is 'misrecognised'. Bourdieu (1980) argues that symbolic violence is at the heart of every social relationship. Arguably, if symbolic violence is at the heart of every social relation, it must be present in intergenerational relations as well. In his writings, Bourdieu (1998) clarifies that 'symbolic violence is the transfiguration of relations of domination and submission into affective relations . . . which can extend to affection or love, as can be seen particularly well in relations between generations' (p. 102). According to Bourdieu (1998), 'they are relations of symbolic violence which can only be established with the complicity of those who suffer from it, like intradomestic relations. The dominated collaborate in their own exploitation through affection or admiration' (p. 111). Thus 'symbolic violence' could describe the affective relationship between parents and their children, but it is not, by all means, a consciously violent exertion of power. Bourdieu and Wacquant (1992) argue that 'symbolic violence accomplishes itself through an act of cognition and of misrecognition that lies beyond – or beneath – the controls of consciousness and will' (p. 172).

The interview data presented here suggest that there is denial of parental influence from adolescent students regarding their choices for studies in HE; however, their parents argue they 'plant the idea of studying in HE' in their children's head. Thus, I argue that students' educational choices for future studies in HE are not wholly independent choices as they assert, because they arise from a habitus inculcated by their family as a result of the pedagogic work of the family (Bourdieu and Passeron 1990). Taken for granted, students do not need to articulate their parents' influence on their educational choices to study at HE because going to university is what 'people like us do'. Reay (2010) also highlights how within middle-class families going to university is simply 'what people like us do', and is often too obvious to articulate.

There is currently a debate in the literature as to whether shared beliefs and dispositions amongst family members could be conceptualised as 'familial habitus' (Reay 2010) or 'familial doxa' (Atkinson 2011). Reay (2010) stresses that Bourdieu sees habitus as a product of early childhood experience and in particular socialisation within the family: 'Such a view provides the genesis for a conceptualisation of familial habitus' (p. 76). Furthermore, she points out that familial habitus – the deeply ingrained system of perspectives, experiences and predispositions family members share (Reay 1998b) – helps us to make better sense of gendered and intra-class as well as inter-class differences in both secondary school and HE choice practices. Reay (2010) argues that an important aspect of familial habitus is the complicated compilation of values, attitudes and knowledge base that families possess in relation to the field of education: 'It is profoundly influenced by the educational experiences of parents' (p. 77).

On the contrary, Atkinson (2011) criticises Reay's notion of 'familial habitus' and argues that we should call these shared beliefs amongst family members 'familial doxa'. Atkinson (2011) claims the family 'shapes the tacit perceptions of the possible and verbalised projections of those implicated in it, and as it is inevitably shaped by the available (pooled) capital stocks and the consecutive trajectories of the generations . . . we should call these beliefs the family-specific doxa' (p. 340). For example, attendance at university (especially Oxbridge) is the effect of 'doxic expectations generated by a constructed family history' (p. 341). In this chapter I adopt the view that family is a field that inculcates students' habitus after Bourdieu (1998); the asymmetry of power relations and distribution of capital in the family field enables parents to exert symbolic violence on their children. This argument adds to the current debate in the literature about 'familial habitus' (Reay 2010) and 'familial doxa' (Atkinson 2011) a new theoretical conceptualisation of parental influence as the exercise of symbolic violence from parents on their children in the family field.

Reflection on the use of Bourdieu's theory in educational research

The aim of this chapter is to reflect on the use of Bourdieu's theoretical framework for understanding and theorising students' perceptions of parental influence on their educational choices for future studies in HE. It also questions whether Bourdieu's conceptual tool of capital is adequate as an analytic tool in educational research. This study highlighted how familial capital in its different forms is used in various ways by middle-class families to enhance their children's educational choices. A common pattern in the data was utilising the economic capital of the family for buying private tutorials, cultural goods and overseas studies. The enactment of social capital of the family was mediated by visits to the parents' workplace for seeking crucial information. As far as parents' cultural capital is concerned, most parents in the sample had not been to university themselves, but they had high aspirations for their children to study at university, thus their offsprings' habitus was inculcated in a way that predisposed students for studies in HE. But is this an in-depth analysis and interpretation of the data or is capital just a descriptive tool? How can sociological knowledge be challenged and Bourdieu's framework be developed and extended if capital is dominating in educational research projects about parental influence?

I argue that symbolic violence as a theoretical tool can help us investigate power relations in the family field, and in conjunction with familial capital it can help us understand how parental influence operates in adolescence. Beyond exploring symbolic violence's analytic potential, this chapter attempts to make connections between 'familial habitus' (Reay 2010) as a conceptual tool and 'familial doxa' (Atkinson 2011) for contributing to new theorisations of parental influence. If we go back to the original writings of Bourdieu, and some of his classic books such as the *Logic of Practice* (1980) and *Practical Reason* (1998), we can see that there is no reference to either of these terms, which researchers working within a Bourdieusian framework have coined. Bourdieu has never used the term 'familial habitus' or 'familial doxa' in his writings; on the contrary he writes about the family as a field (Bourdieu 1998) which inculcates students' habitus as part of the pedagogic work of the family (Bourdieu and Passeron 1990).

This is not to say that we cannot extend Bourdieu's theoretical framework and develop it, but any new conceptual terms researchers coin should be consistent and coherent with Bourdieu's theory. I argue that symbolic violence (Bourdieu 1980) can help us theorise how parents inculcate students' habitus in the family field, even when adolescent students misrecognise their parents' influence and 'deny' it in their interviews, because parental influence is largely unconscious and this is consistent with Bourdieu's view on the family (Bourdieu 1996).

The concept of symbolic violence comes with theoretical scepticism and methodological challenges. One major concern is how can we theorise unconscious phenomena and publish our findings without strong empirical data supporting our argument. The concept of symbolic violence provides a helpful lens through which to view power relations in the family field and especially in adolescence, when students are in the threshold of adulthood and 'deny' their parents' influence to assert their autonomy and identity. I found that symbolic violence is extremely useful as a conceptual tool, as long as we ensure that our empirical data lead the analysis rather than imposing the conceptual framework on the empirical data. Undoubtedly, it is hard to theorise unconscious phenomena such as parental influence in adolescence and it is even more difficult to convince the research community of the usefulness of this theorisation without strong empirical evidence.

Since symbolic violence cannot be directly observed in empirical research and has to be understood interpretively, much of this section is devoted to the resistance this idea received from reviewers. Although for the wider study (Kleanthous 2012) both quantitative and qualitative data were collected, in this chapter I presented only some of the qualitative data. The quantitative data of the study showed that parental influence was not statistically significant for predicting students' dispositions towards studying mathematically demanding courses in HE. A paper that reported the statistical analysis of the quantitative data and the use of symbolic violence to interpret the non-statistically significant effect of parental influence as 'misrecognition' received strong critique from reviewers before it was accepted for publication (Kleanthous and Williams, in press). Although the mathematics education research community has embraced Bourdieu's theoretical framework in recent years (e.g., Zevenbergen 2005; Williams 2012), it is still difficult for this research community to accept theorisations of unconscious phenomena without statistical evidence.

Apparently, the concepts of 'symbolic violence' and 'misrecognition' are still received with scepticism from other researchers working within a Bourdieusian framework, but what I tried to demonstrate in this chapter is how crucial these theoretical tools are for understanding 'unspoken' parental influence and that they are consistent with Bourdieu's original writings.

Conclusion

In *Distinction*, Bourdieu (1984, 101) maps out a formula for his theoretical framework (Habitus x Capital) + Field = Practice. With this algebraic representation of his theory he highlights the importance of the interaction between these theoretical concepts. The habitus is structured by engagement in practice with the field but at the same time it is thereby structuring the field. This reciprocal relationship should always be taken into consideration as 'the theoretical concepts of his theory cannot be isolated from one another' (Lareau and Weininger 2004, 127). Bourdieu and Wacquant (1992) argue that 'such notions as habitus, field, and capital can be defined, but only within the theoretical system they constitute, not in isolation' (p. 96). This formula is a way of reminding researchers of the interrelation between Bourdieu's theoretical tools and a call for using all his tools when analysing data in any educational research project. Although symbolic violence does not appear in this equation, it is very central to Bourdieu's theory, thus it is legitimate to use it to theorise parental influence but only in relation to the rest of his theoretical toolkit. We need to put symbolic violence next to habitus, practice and capital in relation to a field in order to understand its potential as an analytic tool.

Notes

1 In order to measure the socio-economic status (SES) of the family for the quantitative aspect of this study, I used a scale of occupations which is the standardised scale used in Cyprus for measuring SES by the government and the Pedagogical Institute (Ministry of Education). There is no equivalent allowance such as free school meals (FSM) or education maintenance allowance (EMA) in the Greek-Cypriot educational system as a proxy indicator of SES.
2 All names are pseudonyms.

References

Atkinson, W. 2011. From sociological fictions to social fictions: Some Bourdieusian reflections on the concepts of 'institutional habitus' and 'family habitus'. *British Journal of Sociology of Education* 32, 3: 331–347.

Bourdieu, P. 1973. Cultural reproduction and social reproduction. In *Knowledge, education and cultural change: Papers in the sociology of education*, ed. R. Brown, 71–112. London: Tavistock.

Bourdieu, P. 1977. *Outline of a theory of practice*. Cambridge: Cambridge University Press.

Bourdieu, P. 1980. *The logic of practice*. Stanford, CA: Stanford University Press.

Bourdieu, P. 1984. *Distinction: A social critique of the judgment of taste*. Cambridge, MA: Harvard University Press.

Bourdieu, P. 1986. The forms of capital. In *Handbook of theory and research for the sociology of education*, ed. J. C. Richardson, 241–258. New York: Greenwood Press.

Bourdieu, P. 1996. On the family as a realised category. *Theory, Culture and Society* 13, 3: 19–26.

Bourdieu, P. 1998. *Practical reason: On the theory of action*. Cambridge: Polity Press.

Bourdieu, P. and J. C. Passeron. 1990. *Reproduction in education, society and culture* (2nd edn). London: Sage.

Bourdieu, P. and L. Wacquant. 1992. *An invitation to reflexive sociology.* Cambridge: Polity Press.

Brooks, R. 2003. Young people's higher education choices: The role of family and friends. *British Journal of Sociology of Education* 24, 3: 283–297.

Green, A. and M. Vryonides. 2005. Ideological tensions in the educational choice practices of modern Greek Cypriot parents: The role of social capital. *British Journal of Sociology of Education* 26, 6: 327–342.

Kleanthous, I. 2012. *Perceived parental influence on adolescent students' mathematical dispositions: A Bourdieusian perspective.* Unpublished PhD dissertation, University of Manchester.

Kleanthous, I. and J. Williams. 2013. Perceived parental influence and students' dispositions to study mathematically-demanding courses in Higher Education. *Research in Mathematics Education* 15, 1: 50–69.

Lareau, A. and E. B. Weininger. 2004. Cultural capital in education research: A critical assessment. In *After Bourdieu*, ed. D. L. Swartz and V. L. Zolberg, 105–144. Dordrecht: Kluwer.

Levine-Rasky, C. 2009. Dynamics of parent involvement at a multicultural school. *British Journal of Sociology of Education* 30, 3: 331–344.

Reay, D. 1998a. Cultural reproduction: Mothers' involvement in their children's primary schooling. In *Bourdieu and education: Acts of practical theory*, ed. M. Grenfell and D. James, 55–71. London: Falmer Press.

Reay, D. 1998b. 'Always knowing' and 'never being sure': Familial and institutional habituses and higher education choice. *Journal of Education Policy* 13, 4: 519–529.

Reay, D. 2010. From the theory of practice to the practice of theory: Working with Bourdieu in research in higher education choice. In *Cultural analysis and Bourdieu's legacy: Settling accounts and developing alternatives*, ed. E. Silva and A. Warde, 75–86. London: Routledge.

Reay, D., J. Davies, M. David and S. Ball. 2001. Choices of degree or degrees of choice? Class, 'race' and the higher education choice process. *Sociology* 35, 4: 855–874.

Symeou, L. 2007. Cultural capital and family involvement in children's education: Tales from two primary schools in Cyprus. *British Journal of Sociology of Education* 28, 4: 473–487.

Williams, J. S. 2012. Use and exchange value in mathematics education: Contemporary CHAT meets Bourdieu's sociology. *Educational Studies in Mathematics* 80, 1: 57–72.

Zevenbergen, R. 2005. The construction of a mathematical habitus: Implications of ability grouping in the middle years. *Journal of Curriculum Studies* 37, 5: 607–619.

Part V

Derrida

Chapter 11

Derrida and educational research

An introduction

Jones Irwin

Introduction

The reception of Jacques Derrida's work (Irwin 2010a) in the discipline of the philosophy of education and, more generally, in the field of educational research has become increasingly positive in recent years. Theorists such as Michael Peters (2004b) and Peter Trifonas (2000) have argued persuasively and influentially that accusations of nihilism or textualism (Lather 2004) against deconstruction do not hold up and that his philosophical work has much to say concerning issues of 'power, violence and domination' (p. 4), in a way not dissimilar to the work of critical theory. At the same time, the main representatives of the latter ideology in educational theory and research, the school of Critical Pedagogy, often express significant suspicion of the emancipatory potential of deconstruction and warn against its employment in educational theory and research (McLaren 1994; Giroux 2000).

In this chapter, I will explore the reasons for these tensions in the reading of the relationship between deconstruction and education. At the forefront of this analysis will be the question of the respective affinities and disaffinities between deconstruction and critical theory most especially, or what we might refer to more generally as the legacy of Marxist thinking in education (Balibar 2007). In exploring this affinity and disaffinity, I will delineate the relevance of Derrida and deconstruction for issues in educational research and especially for the current crises in the institution of the university per se (Irwin 2010b). The latter crisis in the university sector very clearly frames the issue of the future of educational research, both specifically in philosophy of education and more generally across educational studies. But we can also trace the influence of deconstruction on education across the full gamut of research areas, including programme evaluation (Stronach and MacLure 1997), emancipatory ethnographic research (Lather 2004), curricular reform (O'Cadiz et al. 1998) and practitioner-oriented research in early years and maths education (Brown and Jones 2001). Nonetheless, the primary influence of Derrida's work to date remains within the philosophy of education and related disciplines of education (Blake et al. 2003), in pedagogy (Trifonas 2000) and in specialised applications of the latter such as feminist post-structuralist educational interventions (St Pierre and Willow 2000; Lather 2004). My main focus in this chapter will thus be on the latter rather than the former.

The changing education context vis-à-vis postmodernism

The relationship between later twentieth-century French philosophical thinking and the ideology of Marxism has often been a fraught one. Slavoj Žižek (Žižek 1994), for example, has recounted how, in former Yugoslavia, any attempt to explicate French thinking at an academic level had to justify the latter's relation to the orthodox state ideology of Marx.[1] We can trace a similar movement in the disciplines of education. While philosophy of education developed initially through an Anglo-American analytical lens, grounded in a rather strict conceptualism (Blake et al. 2003), by the 1990s the discipline had broadened to accommodate the insights of critical theory and Marxism and a more socio-political interpretation of education (Blake and Masschelein 2003). A key figure here in the transition between a more analytical view of education and a more politicised conception was the Brazilian philosopher Paulo Freire (Freire 1996; Irwin 2012). Indeed, many of the theorists associated with the Critical Pedagogy movement take their cue from the work of Freire (Giroux 2000).

In this initial evolution of the discipline, philosophy of education demonstrated a clear suspicion of postmodernist thought (McLaren 1994) as at least apolitical and as, at worst, politically pernicious. However, there has been a gradual weakening of this anti-postmodernist reading in pedagogy and, more and more, at least some aspects of postmodern thinking have become influential both in the philosophy of education and in the wider realm of the discourse on educational research per se (Blake et al. 2003; Peters and Wilson 2003). Even in this renewed liberal context, however, it is perhaps Derrida's work which has been the most resisted within educational research and theory, whereas his contemporaries such as Lyotard, Deleuze and Badiou have become paradigm figures (Irwin 2010b). A powerful example of how postmodernist thinking has only been accepted on the terms of a more neo-Marxist approach to education is McLaren's distinction between what he terms 'resistance' and 'ludic' postmodernism (McLaren 1994). The first concept refers to a kind of postmodernist thinking, most especially for McLaren, identifiable with the work of Michel Foucault and postmodern feminism, which works to debunk hegemonic assumptions of the West. Thus, this approach to postmodern thinking is congruent with a more emancipatory approach to education. However, what McLaren terms a 'ludic' postmodernism is a more loose or 'nihilist' version of postmodernism which eschews the emancipatory potential of the former and which is thus unassimilable to any emancipatory pegadogy. Derrida's work is especially associated with this latter strain (McLaren 1994; Derrida 1977). Thus, while we might say that postmodernism has become increasingly influential in educational research (Peters and Wilson

2003), the relationship specifically between deconstruction and educational research remains complex and rather more fraught (Trifonas 2000; Lather 2004).

Having said this, there are theorists who work very much against this view of deconstruction. The most notable examples are Michael Peters (Peters and Wilson 2003) and Peter Trifonas (Trifonas 2000). Both of these writers have been keen to point to the importance of Derrida's work for education, while not underplaying the tension which exists, for example, between deconstruction and, more explicitly, emancipatory projects such as Critical Pedagogy or neo-Marxism more generally (Giroux 2000). The significance of Derrida's work for education has also been enhanced by the publication in English in more recent years of several important collections of essays on education by Derrida. Many of these essays date from the early 1970s, showing the continuity of the educational problematic in Derrida's *oeuvre*, but the translation of these texts has brought this rather neglected aspect of his thinking to a much larger public (Derrida 2002). In so doing, it has given the lie to those who would see Derrida's work as simply anti-materialist (Lather 2004) and as being detached from political–educational or institutional questions. Derrida's early work with GREPH in France (focusing on the teaching of philosophy in French schools), for example, demonstrates his interest in, and commitment to, philosophy as a teaching discipline outside the university sector and with children (Derrida 2002). By the same token, his important and leading role in the development of the College of Philosophy in France in the 1980s (alongside Lyotard, amongst others) demonstrates his role in 'applying deconstruction' (Lather 2004) to educational and political contexts (Trifonas 2004b). We can also see in this a development of the 1968 spirit, from the creation of the university at Vincennes onwards (a project which several key postmodernist thinkers were involved in, from Lyotard to Badiou) (Irwin 2010b).

Deconstruction and education

We can thus recognise the crucial importance of deconstruction as a philosophy for education and pedagogy, while also pointing to certain reservations which have been expressed in some quarters concerning its more radical implications (McLaren 1994; Giroux 2000). But, in clarifying this relevance, we are left with the more important question of the exact detail of this legacy. In what way can we understand the key implications of deconstruction for education research? One approach to this problematic is to argue that it is the very tensions which deconstruction generates in relation to education paradigms of research which constitutes its strength as a relatively new perspective in this area. In this section, I will explore some of these relevant tensions. I will employ a significant essay by Patti Lather (Lather 2004), in one of the most important collections of essays on deconstruction and education, to focus on some of the issues (Peters and Trifonas 2004). What makes Lather's essay so helpful, in this context, is that she precisely seeks to do justice to both the conceptual and the theoretical innovations of Derrida's work while also developing the potential of the latter in the area of educational praxis and empirical research. Significantly, Lather's work develops out of an original Marxist context of ideology and she thus also thematises the complexity of the relationship between Derrida's philosophy and this latter tradition (Balibar 2007).

In their respective Introduction (Trifonas 2004a) and Preface (Peters 2004a) to the collection of essays (Peters and Trifonas 2004), Trifonas and Peters contextualise their renewed reading of Derrida's work and its acute relevance for current educational debates in theory and empirical research. The balanced emphasis on both the latter elements is significant in relation to what is often perceived as an overly theoretical emphasis in Derrida's work. This tendency in education studies to be suspicious of certain theoretical emphases is the consequence of a move away from theory which, for example, Nigel Blake has examined in a British context of pedagogy (Blake et al. 2003). For Blake, in the 1990s in education, the ideology of 'progressivism' (Darling and Nordenbo 2003) became a target for those wishing to indict the supposed decline of traditional educational standards, this targeting itself finding its original source in the Thatcherite ideology of the 1980s. The philosophy of education and its cognate disciplines came to be accused of an excessive liberalism and their theoretical aspects were regarded as a significant part of the problem, leading them to be viewed as out of touch with education and schooling on the ground. This obscurantist and confused set of ideas, essentially the basis of the New Right in political terms, ushered in a whole new culture of anti-theoreticism in education, culminating in the development of the contemporary culture of managerialism and performativity which became hegemonic in the late 1990s (Blake et al. 2003). Paradoxically, however, as Blake is already elaborating in 2003, this repression of theory in education was to lead to a subsequent re-emergence of theory or what Blake calls a 'renewal of theory' by the early twenty-first century.[2] It is in the latter context that we can best understand the reinvocation of Derrida and deconstruction by Trifonas and Peters (Peters and Trifonas 2004).

As Trifonas elaborates in his Introduction to the volume of essays, 'the essays collected here take the premise that Derrida is indeed a most profound thinker of matters educational' (Trifonas 2004a, 1). Trifonas and Peters cite the opposition to deconstruction which comes not simply from within Marxist or analytical educational circles but from even within the postmodernist discourse itself. Here, they cite the vehement criticisms of Derrida by Foucault, who was in fact one of Derrida's original teachers of philosophy in Paris, at the école normale supérieure: 'Foucault suggested that deconstruction is nothing but the elaborate expression of a new didactic, a new pedagogy of the text' (p. 1). Against this view, they cite their own positive interpretation of the relevance of Derrida to pedagogy: 'Rather what deconstruction is seeking to do is to point to the undecidability [of the institution] at the expense of the metaphysical grounding of its architectonics' (p. 1). This concept of undecidability will become central to the analysis of the importance of deconstruction and Derrida, specifically for educational discourse. Unlike the clarity of the critical theory discourse of education which has been accused by some critics of a certain 'positivism' (Blake and Masschelein 2003), precisely because of its lack of undecidability (its excessive certainties), what is paradigmatic about deconstruction is the very instability of meaning it induces. Here, Trifonas and Peters invoke another central concept of Derrida's, that of 'aporia' or rather here, more specifically, they refer to the 'tensions of its aporias' (Trifonas 2004a, 1). In a similar vein, they also point to the need to eschew finalised solutions or completed understandings; 'and there is no need to enact the last word on this topic' (p. 1). In this context, Trifonas also refers significantly to both the 'ethics' and the 'politics' of deconstruction or the 'ethics of deconstruction' as it applies to what he terms the 'politics of education'. The latter problematic, in more recent times, connects directly to the issue of the status of the university, the politics of the university as it has come under siege from what has been referred to by some commentators as a new 'managerialism' in education (Blake et al. 2003).

Applying Derrida to educational research

In her essay 'Applied Derrida: (Mis)reading the work of mourning in educational research' (Lather 2004), Patti Lather seeks to provide a more specific focus to this analysis of deconstruction and its relation to education. Most significantly for our purposes, she is especially concerned with the issue of the relation between deconstruction and educational research. As Lather notes, '[my] primary interest is the uses of deconstruction in thinking about the improvement of educational policy and practice through research by way of a focus on reinscribing praxis under conditions of postmodernity' (p. 3). Clearly, for Lather, as for Trifonas and Peters, deconstruction has something to say of worth not simply in an intra-philosophical sense or theoretically, but also to the context of educational research and policy. Here, Lather points to the possibility that taking on board the nuances and insights of Derrida might or should lead to an 'improvement' in this sector of analysis. She also invokes the Marxist term of *praxis*, the reciprocity of theory and practice, and her reading of this notion can be supplemented by the subtle reading of Marx, which Étienne Balibar gives in his *The Philosophy of Marx* (2007).

In thus invoking the relationship between deconstruction and Marxism, Lather is also aware, however, that not all Marxists or neo-Marxists see deconstruction in such positive terms. Citing the important example of Peter McLaren (McLaren 1994), Lather points to his suspicions of Derrida's work which he interprets as being on the wrong side of his opposition between 'resistance postmodernism' and 'ludic postmodernism' (McLaren 1994). For McLaren, there is a real danger in employing deconstruction as a method in education, as the wrong kind of post-modernist turn, bringing about the 'decline of class politics and textualism' (Lather 2004, 4). Lather, herself coming from a neo-Marxist background, is not unaware of these criticisms of Derrida's work but, while acknowledging these dangers vis-à-vis the relation between Marxism and deconstruction, she points to a rather different approach as possible in this context. Unlike those theorists who read the implications of Derrida's work as diminishing political and ethical significance, Lather rather reads the situation in reverse. There are new 'relational structures' created by Derrida's work which point towards open ethical and political possibilities. This is due to what she terms the 'speculative force of Derrida's work': 'the speculative force of this excess works towards establishing new relational structures with a "greater emphasis on ethics and its relationship to the political"' (quoting Spivak in Lather 2004, 4). Here, in invoking Spivak's (1993) work, she also points to the impact that Derrida's work has had on a subversive political, and especially feminist, tradition of thinking. That notwithstanding the fact that Derrida has constantly warned against a simple emancipatory logic: 'one needs another language besides that of political liberation' (Derrida in Kearney 1984, 122). As Lather observes, 'Derrida is clear that we "cannot not be" heirs of Marx's break with myth, religion and nationalism as ways to think the world and our place in it' (Lather 2004, 5). This she counts as Derrida's 'turn or return to Marx'.

Specific implications of deconstruction for education research

In such a context, we can start to map what might be the specific implications of deconstruction for education research. Lather thematises the most significant implication of deconstruction for education research in terms of the need to overcome a certain scientism, which remains endemic in educational studies: 'It is tempting to revert to the quick and narrow scientism of the past. But the game has changed' (Lather 2004, 7). For Lather, the impact of Derrida's work on educational research should be seen as especially important in the current context. Whereas scientism opts for a narrow kind of calculability and reductionism, deconstruction allows the researcher in education to look at complexity and contingency, 'without predictability' (p. 7). This, for Lather, is not anti-scientific; quite the contrary. It rather can be seen as enhancing our idea and practice of scientific understanding in educational research: 'Accounting for the complexity and contingency "without predictability" is what now shapes our conversations and expands our idea of science as cultural practice and practice of culture' (p. 7).

Lather thus extends and develops her argument for this more nuanced and developed understanding of pedagogy, enhanced by the advantages a more deconstructive methodology brings: 'My argument is that cutting-edge educational research will be produced out of and because of the paradoxes of projects that develop a better language to describe a more complicated understanding of what knowledge means and does this by reinscribing the idealised natural science model' (p. 7). *We can thus hold onto a scientific model while avoiding scientism*; this is very much in keeping with Derrida's claim that it is a complete misunderstanding to think of deconstruction as wholly capricious. Rather it invokes a deconstructive (scientific) rigor and logic, which is very strict in its own right.

How does this logic work? Lather is keen to explicate the key differences between this deconstructive approach and the critical theory approach which is often confused with it. In the first case, Lather cites the key difference between a deconstructive and critical theory approach as one of a contrast between an emphasis on the principle of 'complicity' and the principle of 'unveiling' (the former associated with deconstruction, the latter with critical theory). 'Deconstruction; its interest is in complicit practices and excessive differences rather than unveiling structures and illuminating the forces and relations of production; deconstruction works against the critical righteousness of ideology critique' (p. 6). This righteousness leads to a 'propaganda' which seeks to posit what is termed a 'correct consciousness' (p. 6). Again, what we have here encompassed is the whole complex history of the Marxist concept of ideology, as it relates to the notion of false consciousness and the related concept of the masses (Balibar 2007; Irwin 2012). It is clear that this rereading of ideology and false consciousness has significant implications for educational research, as it eschews any patronising reading of research subjects.[3]

Crucially for educational research, there are also implications for the concept of subjectivity or the subject. Lather puts this matter cogently concerning a deconstruction of the subject, perhaps Derrida's most significant contribution to this whole debate: 'in reading the subject, modes of investment are no longer based on traditional notions of categorical thinking such as false consciousness, on the one hand, or the more idealised model of intentional agency of reason or will' (Lather 2004, 7). The stable model of the individual or subject, so often the centre of educational research analysis, is thus undone by a fundamental instability: 'Indeterminacy and paradox become conditions of affirmative power by undoing finalities and mapping new possibilities of playing out relations between identity and difference, margins and centres' (p. 7).

What Lather does here is especially important for our purposes in the measure to which she eschews the tendency to keep the discussion at a purely intra-theoretical level. Rather she seeks to 'apply deconstruction', as it were, to explore the very real possibilities for empirical research attendant on these new theoretical and philosophical innovations of Derrida's work. Her own work, in collaboration, has recently focused on stories of women living with HIV and she wants to exemplify the deconstructive method precisely in this context of empirical testimony: 'tell the stories of women living with HIV to ask hard questions about necessary complicities, inadequate categories dispersing rather than capturing meanings and producing bafflements rather than solutions' (Lather 2004, 7). This relates once again to Spivak's (1993) work, a key interlocutor in the debate concerning the status of the subaltern in education or politics. What this also debunks is the notion of some kind of self-sufficient or complete ontology, of, for example, the realist or Thomistic kind; as what Spivak calls a 'practical academic', I will draw on this work not so much to give flesh and blood to abstractions, as to evoke what Derrida terms a '"ghost effect" of spectral movement where ontology can only be a conjuration, a more demanding ontology of an other logic calling for other concepts' (Lather 2004, 7). Crucially, ontology is not disavowed here but rather resituated and reinscribed in a more complex and nuanced context.

Again, it is clear that, for Lather, there is no ultimate disjunction between a true Marxist philosophy of education and deconstruction. Rather, Derrida here extends the Marxist paradigm in education and we can make reference, in this context, to Balibar's somewhat revisionistic account of Marxist thought (Balibar 2007). Employing Balibar's subtle rereading of Marx, we can argue that Marx's conception of praxis undoes the dualism between theory and practice. Instead, we get a loop effect or a proper dialectical relationship between theory and practice and theory must not be understood as contemplative in this regard. Theory rather is infused with a practical understanding. This also constitutes a significant redefinition of philosophy itself as a praxis; 'Marx put together a practice of material transformation that brought theory and practice together in a relationship of reciprocity, with a theorising quite other to contemplation, "proposing to philosophy that it view itself in the mirror of practice"' (Balibar 2007, p. 41). Philosophy must thus reinvent itself, and such a reinvention can generate a much more integrated relation between philosophy and educational practice.

The teaching of philosophy and the issue of the university

We can see the practical implications of this reinvention of philosophical endeavour after deconstruction also in the pedagogical work of Egéa-Kuehne (Egéa-Kuehne 2004), Trifonas (Trifonas 2004b), Peters (Peters 2004b) and Garrison (Garrison 2004). In each case, these thinkers and educational practitioners apply Derrida's insights (like Lather) to situations of educational complexity in the contemporary era.

In her essay 'The teaching of philosophy: Renewed rights and responsibilities' (Egéa-Kuehne 2004), Denise Egéa-Kuehne begins by citing Derrida's renewed call with regard to the importance of philosophy in contemporary education and politics. This also relates to Derrida's later work, where there is a far more explicit engagement with the issue of pedagogy and education: 'never has philosophy appeared to me as vitally indispensable as today' (Derrida 2002, 134). This is a debate which, in France, has raged throughout the twentieth century in institutional philosophy and especially with regard to both the teaching of philosophy in schools and the status of the university itself, especially with regard to the issue of the philosophical foundations of the university system and third-level education. As Egéa-Kuehne makes clear, there is a strong continuity in Derrida's work in education, as he has been arguing since the 1970s for the foregrounding of philosophy in education: '[Derrida] agreed with Canguilhem's statement that "the defense of the teaching of philosophy would require a critical philosophy of teaching"' (Egéa-Kuehne 2004, 21). Thus, for Derrida, the link between pedagogy and philosophy is intrinsic rather than merely extrinsic. Derrida is also quoted reinforcing the centrality of this notion of education to his work, early to late: 'the question of teaching runs through all my work and all my politico-institutional engagements whether they concern schools and the university or media' (quoted in Egéa-Kuehne 2004, 21). Egéa-Kuehne's essay draws on the renewed significance of this relation between education and institutional politics which, of course, has become even more acute in recent times, with mass student demonstrations, for example in the UK.

Trifonas develops this thematic in his own essay in the volume, entitled 'The ethics of science and/as research: Deconstruction and the orientations of a new academic responsibility' (Trifonas 2004b, 31). Here, Trifonas focuses on some Derridean texts with an explicitly pedagogical thematic (Derrida 2002). Derrida here elaborates the whole philosophy behind the College of Philosophy: '"the principle of reason" – I am defining the necessity for a new way of educating students that will prepare them to undertake new analyses in order to evaluate these ends and choose, when possible, among them all' (Derrida, quoted in Trifonas 2004b, 35). As Trifonas makes clear, less than a year after the above comment, the *Collège International de Philosophie* (CIPH) would open its doors to students and scholars (during January of 1984) providing perhaps a much anticipated answer to the suggestion of a rethinking of the institution of 'higher' education. Derrida was to be its first acting director, followed by Jean-François Lyotard and others, in a succession of one-year appointments.

Thus, while Derrida's understanding of the university looks back to the original Kantian model, it also deconstructs that model relentlessly and critiques its limitations and restrictiveness. Thus, Trifonas links what he terms the 'meta-logic' of deconstruction (2004b, 39) with the praxis of a new understanding of institutional education. On Trifonas' terms, this can be described as follows:

> the meta-logic of deconstruction defines the site of the struggle for a new academic responsibility. To effectuate a change in the thinking of the being of the university and the academic responsibility of our roles in it as researchers and intellectuals; to avoid reproducing the classical architectonic of the Kantian institution (grounded in the principle of reason), thereby entrenching its effects still further.
>
> (p. 39)

Deconstruction and pedagogy

In his essay, 'Derrida, pedagogy and the calculation of the subject' (Peters 2004b), Michael Peters reinforces much of what we have seen Trifonas and Lather argue for in terms of the importance of deconstruction for pedagogy and education. Peters makes this point in a more general way but perhaps even more vehemently, against those accusations of textualism and nihilism we quoted earlier:

> The relation of both Derrida and deconstruction to pedagogy is as clear as it is fundamental; Derridean philosophy offers an active interpretation, resistance and reevaluation of humanist pedagogy, of forms of pedagogy based on the

sovereign subject – which is to say, the predominant forms of pedagogy existing today that structure our pedagogical institutions, theories and practices.

(p. 61)

The subtlety of the phrasing is crucial to see here; Derrida offers not a destruction of the subject but a *re-evaluation*, perhaps we can say a reconstruction or certainly a 'resituation', as Derrida uses the term elsewhere.

In a final essay in this collection worthy of note, Jim Garrison takes up the fascinating problematic of the relation between deconstruction and pragmatism and most especially the complex relation between Derrida and the educational work of John Dewey (Garrison 2004). What is also at stake here is the aforementioned question of the status of progressivism as an educational ideology. As Garrison makes clear, Dewey's own philosophy itself is subject to the contingency which Derrida so well elaborates: 'Still every construction is contingent in a Darwinian universe; hence, every construction is subject to deconstruction and reconstruction' (p. 104). So, according to Garrison, Dewey's philosophy also contains a deconstructive component. From a pedagogical perspective, we might argue that this leaves the possibility of a greater rapprochement between progressivism, pragmatism and deconstruction in education. Often in educational research, these theoretical paradigms are seen as mutually exclusive and conflictual.

Some conclusions

In conclusion, we can say that there are certain key concepts in our analysis of deconstruction which provide a matrix for the analysis of deconstruction and education. Most notably, they are 'the subject' or subjectivity, reflection and the notion of praxis itself. Lather (2004) refers to contemporary theory as post-enlightenment and there is a clear rereading of the notion of philosophy here, as we have noted especially in relation to Marx and specifically the interpretation invoked by Balibar (2007). In this context, Lather sees herself as being faithful exactly to Derrida's own word, especially in his later work and revisions of the meta-level reading of deconstruction as a radicalisation of Marx: 'I have echoed Derrida's claim that deconstruction only ever made sense to him as a radicalisation of Marx' (Lather 2004, 13). At the beginning of this chapter, we mentioned the tensions which exist between the theories of deconstruction and critical theory in education. However, we have seen how Derrida's later work particularly holds out the potential for a rapprochement in this regard, with significant implications for educational research. By the same token, we can perhaps employ the suspicions of McLaren (McLaren 1994), amongst others, in a constructive way to avoid a simple identification of these two philosophies which make such a significant contribution to contemporary educational research. We can avoid unnecessary conflict, while maintaining distinctiveness.

The final distinction which Lather wishes to employ and to ground her conclusion is between what she terms 'lovely knowledge' and 'difficult knowledge'.

The one is simply reinforcing of what we already know, the latter constitutes, so to speak, a genuinely searching and provocative epistemology; 'the distinction between lovely knowledge and difficult knowledge; the former reinforces what we want from what we find and the latter is knowledge that induces breakdowns in representing experience' (Lather 2004, 13). These *breakdowns* are paradigmatic for the effect of deconstruction on the whole field of philosophy of education and educational research per se. To invoke another term used by Lather, they induce 'bafflements' and yet what is interesting is that the term or concept of 'knowledge' is never eschewed. Rather, it is held on to and defended as a difficult rather than as a lovely knowledge, the latter understood as a kind of pseudo-philosophising, which merely masks its real intention as an apologetics for the status quo:

> Here, accepting loss becomes the very force of learning and what one loves when lovely knowledge is lost is the promise of thinking and otherwise; such thinking is within and against enlightenment categories of voice, identity, agency and experience so troubled by incommensurability. . . in the case of Derrida's 'difficult knowledge', my argument has been that there is plenty of future for Derrida in educational research.
>
> (p. 14)

This incommensurability and uncertainty, then, which undermines agency and subjectivity understood metaphysically, is precisely what has made deconstruction such a subtle and sought after 'methodology' in recent educational research. More and more, educational researchers are eager and brave enough to seek out the 'difficult knowledge', which Lather describes. Whether it be the kind of revolutionary curricular reform undertaken in Brazil by Paulo Freire (O'Cadiz et al. 1998), feminist poststructuralist educational interventions (St Pierre and Willow 2000) or, as we have seen in detail, innovative work in pedagogy and the politics of education (Trifonas 2000), it is clear that Derrida and deconstruction have only just begun to register their full and most powerful impact on educational research and practice.

Notes

1 Žižek initially had his Master's thesis rejected in Slovenia until he added a chapter which argued for the affinities between French 'structuralism' (broadly understood) and Marx. On this point see Žižek (1994).
2 What this analysis, alongside that of Lather's, also allows us to do is to unpack some of the misunderstandings which were attendant on the aforementioned critique of progressivist education in the 1980s and 1990s. The debate concerning the contested understanding of progressivism (Darling and Nordenbo 2003) is at the heart of the question of how we understand the educational enterprise itself as well as the vision we might have for educational research (Irwin 2012).
3 Certainly, not the least complicating factor in this regard is the fact that many neo-Marxists, from Gramsci (1988) onwards if not before, have complicated and rejected the false consciousness picture. Thus, the deconstructive version of

ideology is not necessarily at odds with more refined conceptions of ideology in the Marxist tradition. Indeed, another more recent evolution of this debate concerns a more psychoanalytical or specifically Lacanian reading of ideology, whether through the work of Alain Badiou or Jacques Rancière or paradigmatically in Slavoj Žižek's seminal *The Sublime Object of Ideology*, later developed in Žižek (1994).

References

Balibar, E. 2007. *The philosophy of Marx*. London: Verso.

Blake, N. and J. Masschelein. 2003. Critical theory and critical pedagogy. In *The Blackwell guide to the philosophy of education*, ed. N. Blake, P. Smeyers, R. Smith and P. Standish, 38–57. Oxford: Blackwell.

Blake, N., P. Smeyers, R. Smith and P. Standish, eds. 2003. Introduction. In *The Blackwell guide to the philosophy of education*, ed. N. Blake, P. Smeyers, R. Smith and P. Standish, 1–18. Oxford: Blackwell.

Brown, T. and L. Jones. 2001. *Action research and postmodernism: Congruence and critique*. Buckingham: Open University Press.

Darling, J. and S. E. Nordenbo. 2003. Progressivism. In *The Blackwell guide to the philosophy of education*, ed. N. Blake, P. Smeyers, R. Smith and P. Standish, 288–308. Oxford: Blackwell.

Derrida, J. 1977. *Margins of philosophy*. Trans. Alan Bass. Chicago: Chicago University Press.

Derrida, J. 2002. *Who's afraid of philosophy?: Right to philosophy I*. Stanford: Stanford University Press.

Egéa-Kuehne, D. 2004. The teaching of philosophy: Renewed rights and responsibilities. In *Derrida, deconstruction and education: Ethics of pedagogy and research*, ed. M. Peters and P. Trifonas, 17–31. Oxford: Blackwell.

Freire, P. 1996. *Pedagogy of the oppressed*. London: Penguin.

Garrison, J. 2004. Dewey, Derrida and 'the double bind'. In *Derrida, deconstruction and education: Ethics of pedagogy and research*, ed. M. Peters and P. Trifonas, 95–109. Oxford: Blackwell.

Giroux, H. 2000. *Breaking in to the movies*. New York: Routledge.

Gramsci, A. 1988. *The Antonio Gramsci reader: Selected writings 1916–1935*. Ed. D. Forgacs. London: Lawrence and Wishart.

Irwin, J. 2010a. *Derrida and the writing of the body*. Aldershot: Ashgate.

Irwin, J. 2010b. Re-politicising education – Interpreting Jean-François Lyotard's May '68 texts and *The postmodern condition* in a contemporary educational context. In *Yearbook of the Irish Philosophical Society*, ed. C. McDonnell, 37–53. Maynooth: NUIM.

Irwin, J. 2012. *Paulo Freire's philosophy of education: Origins, development, impacts and legacies*. London: Bloomsbury.

Kearney, R. 1984. *Dialogues with contemporary continental thinkers*. Manchester: Manchester University Press.

Lather, P. 2004. Applied Derrida: (Mis)reading the work of mourning in educational research. In *Derrida, deconstruction and education: Ethics of pedagogy and research*, ed. M. Peters and P. Trifonas, 3–17. Oxford: Blackwell.

McLaren, P. 1994. Postmodernism and the death of politics: A Brazilian reprieve. In *Politics of liberation: Paths from Freire*, ed. P. McLaren and C. Lankshear, 93–215. London: Routledge

O'Cadiz, M., P. del Pilar, C. A. Torres and P. Lindquist. 1998. *Education and democracy: Paulo Freire, social movements and educational reform in Sao Paulo.* Oxford: Westview Press.

Peters, M. 2004a. Preface. In *Derrida, deconstruction and education: Ethics of pedagogy and research*, ed. M. Peters and P. Trifonas, viii–x. Oxford: Blackwell.

Peters, M. 2004b. Derrida, pedagogy and the calculation of the subject. In *Derrida, deconstruction and education: Ethics of pedagogy and research*, ed. M. Peters and P. Trifonas, 59–79. Oxford: Blackwell.

Peters, M. and P. Trifonas. 2004. *Derrida, deconstruction and education: Ethics of pedagogy and research.* Oxford: Blackwell.

Peters, M. and K. Wilson. 2003. Postmodernism/Post-structuralism. In *The Blackwell guide to the philosophy of education*, ed. N. Blake, P. Smeyers, R. Smith and P. Standish, 57–72. Oxford: Blackwell.

Spivak, G. 1993. *Outside in the teaching machine.* New York: Routledge.

St Pierre, B. and W. Willow, eds. 2000. *Working the ruins: Feminist poststructural practice and theory in education.* New York: Routledge.

Stronach, I. and M. MacLure. 1997. *Educational research undone: The postmodern embrace.* Buckingham: Open University Press.

Trifonas, P. 2000. *The ethics of writing: Derrida, deconstruction and pedagogy.* Oxford: Rowan and Littlefield.

Trifonas, P. 2004a. Introduction: Derrida and the philosophy of education. In *Derrida, deconstruction and education: Ethics of pedagogy and research*, ed. M. Peters and P. Trifonas, 1–3. Oxford: Blackwell.

Trifonas, P. 2004b. The ethics of science and/as research: Deconstruction and the orientations of a new academic responsibility. In *Derrida, deconstruction and education: Ethics of pedagogy and research*, ed. M. Peters and P. Trifonas, 31–43. Oxford: Blackwell.

Žižek, S. 1994. Introduction: The spectre of ideology. In *Mapping ideology*, ed. S. Žižek. London: Verso.

Chapter 12

'Derrida applied'

Derrida meets Dracula in the geography classroom

Christine Winter

Introduction

Derrida contends in his *Letter to a Japanese Friend* that 'deconstruction is not a method' (1988, 3). It is not a set of rules that can be instrumentally applied, neither is it an act or an operation. Instead, 'deconstruction takes place' (p. 4). In other words, things self-deconstruct or are opened up to deconstruction when they are read carefully. This contention presents an immediate challenge in the writing of this chapter when my designated purpose is to 'apply' theory in a research setting for an audience of educational researchers and advanced practitioners. Whilst expressing my apologies to Jacques Derrida and his followers as I write this chapter, at the same time, I note the need to interpret and engage with thinking about deconstruction in ways that allow for its dissemination, given the opportunities it accords for thinking differently about educational and curriculum matters. In order to pursue my purpose, I have divided the chapter into three sections. In the first section I provide my interpretation of deconstruction together with a brief account of the work of researchers who are concerned about 'applying' Derrida in education. As a link into the curriculum project itself, I explain the relevance of Derrida's ideas to the curriculum problem under study. The focus in section two is the school-based research project and how Derrida's ideas were engaged in the development, teaching and evaluation of a curriculum unit for a class of students aged 12 to 13 in a state comprehensive school in the north of England. The project was not without its challenges and high points and these are recounted in the third section of the chapter.

Deconstruction

Deconstruction involves the close reading of texts of any kind in such a way as to demonstrate the three tenets of Derrida's work: first, that meanings of words are insecure and never fully under our control; second, that the metaphysics of presence implies the existence of an underpinning unity of knowledge that needs to be disrupted to expose its internal illogicalities as well as the source of its authorisation; and third, that deconstruction opens up a space for justice – a space in which the other (something new, productive and unforeseeable) emerges. The first tenet (the insecurity of word meanings) rests on two ideas: *différance* and deferral. Derrida argues against the proposal that the relationship between a word (sign or signifier) and its meaning (signified) is determined, concrete and stable. He proposes that an inscription or mark does not represent a thing or image, as if reflected in a mirror. Instead, the relationship between a word and its meaning is more diffuse and active, what he describes as 'the regulated play of differences' and 'the instituted trace' he calls *différance* (Derrida 1976, 62). The implication of this argument for the reading of texts suggests that word meanings escape accurate definition and conceptualisation because word meanings arise from differences to other words, allowing semantic slippage or deferral to occur, whereby meanings become parts of ever-emerging chains of signification:

> It is because of *différance* that the movement of signification is possible only if each so-called 'present' element, each element appearing on the scene of presence, is related to something other than itself, thereby keeping within itself the mark of the past element, and already letting itself be vitiated by the mark of its relation to the future element, this trace being related no less to what is called the future than to what is called the past, and constituting what is called the present by means of this very relation to what is not: what it absolutely is not, not even a past or a future as a modified present.
>
> (Derrida 1972, 13)

Exceeding the metaphysics of presence, the second tenet in Derrida's way of thinking suggests that the unity of knowledge seemingly underpinning arguments, concepts and frameworks of thinking is an illusion and needs to be prodded and questioned to expose its cracks and crevices, to expose who authorised it and why. A deconstructive reading achieves this, first, by considering what the author intends or means to say, and, second, by considering what is going on in terms of language and meaning behind the author's back. The former requires the reader to engage in critical depth with the author's ideas, background, context, presuppositions and purpose. This first re-productive reading provides access to the author's intended meaning within which an initial interpretation can occur. But a second, *productive* reading that *exceeds* the author's framework and parameters is required next: 'The possibility must be kept alive of reading otherwise, which means passing *through* the classical discipline, and never having abandoned or jettisoned it, to explore what it omits, forgets, excludes, expels, marginalises, dismisses, ignores, scorns, slights, takes too lightly, waves off, is just not serious enough about!' (Caputo 1997, 79). The latter approach opens onto a generative reading, a reading that transgresses the metaphysics of presence and looks through other frameworks, other parameters, other differential plays of the trace. Such reading is described as providing exteriority because it goes beyond the assumed authority of the text and opens up the text to other ways of thinking that were not encountered during the first re-productive reading.

The third tenet, that 'deconstruction is justice' (Derrida 1992, 15) is problematical in the light of the denial of self-present meaning as argued above. According to Derrida justice here serves as an enframing concept, in need of deconstructive attention. Allowing justice to self-deconstruct will reveal it as beyond definition. Nevertheless, although justice remains 'an experience of the impossible' (p. 15), it should never be neglected. It is an unquestionable 'responsibility without limits' (p. 19) in the sense of opening up a space for a more just and democratic future than the experience of the present. The responsibility for justice rests on the act of bringing fresh eyes to a problem, on drawing on a unique and responsible interpretation of the problem in order to reinstitute and reinvent what was and what could be (*democratie à venir*). In the context of this study, the relation between justice and the curriculum is located in the questioning of the performative school culture and of traditional versions of curriculum knowledge about a place, leading to an openness towards other ways of knowing.

The aporia of 'Derrida applied'

I return briefly to the quandary expressed at the start of this chapter. If deconstruction is not a method or a tool that can be applied (Derrida 1997, 9; Brannington et al. 1996, xix), then, as educators we are faced with a dilemma when we wish to think about deconstruction in pursuit of ethical practice in the school classroom. We are confronted with an impossible situation: an aporia. The aporia, according to Derrida, is 'the impossible or the impractical' (1993, 13), 'the non-passage' (p. 12). When paralysed, immobilised by our confrontation with the aporia, we look around for another way, a space for the other, something Derrida describes as the *arrivant*. In other words, to recap: deconstruction occurs whether we wish it to or not. It is automatic, non-applicable. It is not a programme that can be applied. Our role in education, is, then, to follow an-other way, in showing, disclosing, witnessing the event by revealing how the impossible is always and already the possible. Bennington describes our role as showing 'metaphysics in deconstruction' and in so doing, opening up a space for 'repeating metaphysics differently' (2000, 11). Our showing as teachers is an ethical experience because we are responsible for the future of the others in our care (Edgoose 2001, 131). It involves us in the disruption of the metaphysics of presence underpinning the knowledge and culture of our classroom practices that exclude the other (Biesta 2009a, 109; Blake et al. 1998, 38–39). It involves a responsibility for the engagement and engrossment of our students in their studies, a concern for and commitment to undecidability where fresh and free decisions can emerge and an openness to the arrival of the unforeseeable other, what Caputo describes as 'inventionalism' (1997, 42; see also Biesta 2009b, 395). Egéa-Kuehne draws attention to the affirmation of otherness and alterity available when educators disrupt the safety and comfort of assumedly well-established, transparent, neutral knowledge and the illusion of cultural homogeneity by facilitating the bringing out for students that which is overlooked: controversy, multiple voices, risk-taking, difference and the unknown (1996, 160; 2001, 203).

Addressing the first aporia encountered in the project and opening a space for 'repeating metaphysics differently' (Bennington 2000) requires some background information. The school subject of geography for 11 to 14 year olds (known as Key Stage 3 (KS3) in England) experienced a tough time during the first decade of the twenty-first century. The current geography curriculum bears a legacy from the first Geography National Curriculum of 1991 of out-dated subject knowledge (Rawling 2001). A steep decline in school-based curriculum development, a reliance on non-specialist teachers and on textbook teaching in some schools did not aid its recovery. In addition, the severing of links between university and school geography cut off access to the input of fresh and innovative thinking. Competition with other school subjects and the arrival of skills-based competency curricula in early 2000, in which Humanities subjects such as geography, history and religious education were 'integrated', did little to enhance the status of the discrete subject. In 2005, Ofsted stated 'in many schools geography lacks rigour and fails to motivate young people' (pp. 8–9). In 2008, the same organisation reported school geography as 'boring' and 'lacking relevance', 'heavy in content' and 'driven by textbooks' (para. 49, 23). Given this situation, any self-respecting geography educator who, believing that the word geo-graphy (meaning 'writing the earth') carries responsibilities to investigate and improve the means available to students and teachers of writing/righting the earth, is motivated to act. I argued in 2009 (Winter 2009) that the concepts underpinning the knowledge and language used in school geography curriculum policy traps meaning in certain ways that prevent other ways of knowing from emerging. Armchair theorising like this has its place, but some form of showing, disclosing, witnessing this argument *inside* the geography classroom was called for and took effect in the form of a commitment to attempt to revitalise school geographical knowledge through the development and teaching of a new KS3 curriculum unit for a class of youngsters.

The school-based research project

The curriculum unit was developed and taught by two geography teachers (Sally and John) and myself between December 2008 and April 2009. The official policy context for the unit was the Geography National Curriculum (DCSF/QCA 2007, 100–109). The two teachers identified the need for a new unit focusing on the topic of coasts for Year 8 students, and we agreed that the overall scheme of work should be planned around an introduction to a stretch of coast in the UK; a study of the physical landscape of that coast and of a specific place located on the coast, followed by a field trip. There is insufficient space here to report full details of discussions within the team about decisions made and actions taken, although these were all recorded, transcribed and analysed as part of the research project. For the same reason, I will be unable to recount the process and results of the entire curriculum project; instead, I will concentrate on the one section for which I took the main responsibility. Needless to say, a key and obvious dimension of this process of showing metaphysics in deconstruction in the classroom involved negotiation and compromise on the part of the team; for example, in complying with Geography National Curriculum (GNC) requirements and school performativity pressures at the same time as reading these policy drivers differently, that is in accordance with the idea of *différance*. In respect to policy requirements, these comprised the following: an understanding of the physical and human characteristics of real places; developing 'geographical imaginations' of places; knowing where places are located; understanding the relationship between the physical and human worlds and developing cultural understanding and understanding of diversity. In respect to school performativity pressures, these will be discussed later. In respect to the third condition, of reading GNC requirements differently, the team sought to exceed the GNC requirements by bringing into being other knowledge about a place, not through the traditional conceptual gaze of the geographer, but through writing the earth differently (Winter 2009, 64). The area chosen for study was that of the north-east coast of Yorkshire, England, between Whitby and Spurn Head, because it is well known to families of students attending the research school, being a traditional, popular and accessible holiday destination. Our task was to engage productively with knowledge about Whitby through disclosure of metaphysics in deconstruction: disclosing an-other Whitby in a way that engaged our students by revealing something unexpected, inventive and unknown. The two teachers took the lead in developing a problem-solving activity about the problems of and solutions to coastal erosion in the southern part of the coast under study. I took the lead in a study of the coastal town of Whitby which offers a multitude of opportunities for disrupting the metaphysics of presence assumed to reside within traditional conceptualisations of place study in the discipline of geography. In the descriptions of the research enquiries to follow, the focus is on the planned lesson topics, activities and their rationales relating to the northern section of coast, specifically on the town of Whitby. This is followed by showing metaphysics in deconstruction with respect to data analysis, the performativity culture residing in the school and traditional conceptualisations of geographical knowledge held by the two project teachers. The chapter ends with an account of spaces for thinking otherwise created within the project and a reflection on the notion of 'Derrida applied'.

The curriculum unit: introduction

After a lesson introducing the coastal area under study, students worked in groups to construct their own questionnaires to find out what their families, friends and neighbours thought about the area under study. The process involved a move away from a reliance on an authoritative textbook perspective of the place, enframed through a traditional geographical lens to a more localised, multi-vocal and immediate view, from the perspectives of those who know it well and have experienced it first-hand. We wanted students and those responding to the questionnaires to be aware of the range of different ways of understanding this place and to participate actively in contributing to those understandings. Students collected their data, analysed it and devised presentation methods to disseminate the findings to a wide audience, including their respondents. The section of the curriculum unit focusing on the harbour town of Whitby consisted of four research enquiries. Each group of Year 8 students conducted one enquiry.

The research enquiries

1 Whitby Abbey

An important attraction for tourists visiting Whitby are the abbey ruins, owned and looked after by English Heritage. The abbey is located on the site of an Anglo-Saxon monastery dating from AD 657. The famous 199 steps lead from the town to the site of the abbey. The ruins of the abbey are visible from miles around in the daytime because of its strategic position high up on a headland overlooking Whitby Harbour. At dawn and dusk, the ruins are silhouetted against the sky, adding to the eerie atmosphere of the town. The abbey is important because of its contribution to the town's history and present-day tourist economy. It is interesting to geographers and historians because of its strategic location on a promontory jutting out into the North Sea, high above the surrounding land and because of the significant role the monastery community played in the history of Christianity (Barnwell et al. 2003; Bede 731/1999). The first curriculum activity used different sources (pictures in brochures, a painting by Turner and various kinds of maps) to encourage students to think about different ways to portray the location of Whitby Abbey. The second activity involved the analysis of a text about Whitby Abbey/Monastery in which the language used plays on the idea of the 'head'. The third activity involved students searching websites to find images of Whitby Abbey showing the importance of its location high above the town. In the second activity, students explored how the text plays with the word 'head' in different ways. Students were asked to identify as many words as possible in the text which bore some connection to the word 'head' and to underline them before making a list of the words and explaining the connection of each to the word 'head'. This example was provided from the text below: 'High-up – the head is high-up at the top of the body'.

> A Monastery was founded in 657 AD on the Headland in Whitby. It is located <u>high up</u> on the cliff-top of the Headland, overlooking Whitby harbour. This is now the site of the ruins of Whitby Abbey.

In the seventh century Whitby Monastery was an important religious place, at the head of the Christian Church. It was at the top level of religious learning. It was the place where important religious people visited and were buried. It was also a place where people saw holy visions and experienced miracles.

The Monastery was situated on a high cliff overlooking the harbour where boats and ships of all kinds arrived and departed. Some of the ships carried new discoveries, inventions and ideas from the European continent into Britain.

Whitby Monastery was an important nerve-centre of the region.

In 664 AD, the Monastery formed the focal point for an exciting event in the Christian Church called the Synod of Churches. This was where an argument was ended about two things:

1) the precise timing of Easter in the Christian calendar and
2) which hairstyle the monks should wear.

2 The Whitby jet set

Anyone walking along Whitby's main Church Street cannot fail to notice the number of shops selling jewellery made from Whitby jet. Jet is one of the world's oldest gems, a black shiny material formed in the Jurassic period from decaying monkey puzzle trees and is called a 'mineraloid'. It was mined in the Whitby area in the past and pieces of jet eroded from the cliffs can still be found on Whitby beaches. Today the sale of jet in Whitby shops contributes to Whitby's economy and jet forms an important part of Whitby's cultural heritage and life. A traditional approach to studying Whitby in school geography would treat the geological formation of the gemstone as an aspect of the physical geography of the place and the production and sale of the stone as economic or human geography. In this study, the boundaries between physical and human geography are collapsed into a web-based enquiry into the place of a gemstone in a particular place. The activity involved using contemporary websites about Whitby jet to research its geological formation, history and politics. The final activity consisted of a close and critical analysis of three Whitby jet websites as cultural texts in order to understand how website designs, colours, language, styles of lettering, graphics and media are used in different ways to achieve different purposes.

3 The 'explorer' Captain James Cook

The explorer Captain James Cook served his apprenticeship as a trainee seafarer in Whitby from 1747 to 1756, working on the 'coal cats', small flat-bottomed ships carrying coal from the north-east of England to London. A skilled cartographer, Cook was employed by the British Admiralty to map the world on three successful 'voyages of discovery' in 1768 (on the *Endeavour* – to look for the 'Great Southern Continent' (GSC), 1772 (on the *Resolution* – again to look for the GSC) and 1776 (on the *Resolution* and the *Discovery* – to find out if a North-West Passage existed). All three ships were built in Whitby. Cook died on the shore in Kealakekua Bay, Hawaii in 1779. A range of explanations about his death exist, including the disappointment of locals when they discovered that the Captain and his crew were mere mortals and not the gods they had supposed them to be (Villiers 1967) and local resistance to the 'invaders' when Cook and his crew threatened to take a local leader as ransom for the theft of one of his cutters. Williams (2008) describes the rise in popular interest about 'How did Captain Cook meet his death?', with various interpretations by authors such as Dawes (1968), Beaglehole (1979), Sahlins (1985, 1995) and Dening (1996). There is a statue of Cook on the West Cliff in Whitby, overlooking the harbour.

Studying Cook's voyages raises interesting political questions for geographers, which were covered in the curriculum unit. These included claims to British 'ownership' of coastal lands and their 're-naming' by Cook and his crew; the idea of 'discovery' of lands; the objectives of his voyages which were to secure trading destinations for British goods and manufacturers; to acquire land and raw materials and to 'discover' and classify 'new' natural species, including 'new' human societies and intercultural issues focusing on power relations between indigenous people, Cook and his crews.

4 Dracula

Bram Stoker thought of the idea of a story about vampires when he was on holiday in Whitby in 1890 and published the novel *Dracula* in 1897. The harbour port of Whitby figures strongly in several sections of the story – and two were selected for closer examination by the Year 8 students. The first extract was taken from the play *Dracula* adapted by David Calcutt (Stoker 1999, 40–41). It is the story of the arrival during a great storm of a Russian ship called the *Demeter* into Whitby harbour. The ship carried Count Dracula from his home in Transylvania to England. Dracula's arrival in England was a little unusual and is portrayed vividly in the script. The second extract was taken from the original novel. It describes how one of the novel's characters, Lucy, first met Count Dracula in St Mary's churchyard on the East Cliff overlooking the harbour. The students were asked to trace the route taken by Lucy as she sleep-walked from her lodgings on the West Cliff, to learn about the geography of the town using the novel, maps and photographs. The two extracts illustrate how the real place of Whitby can be thought about in a different way from how geographers usually think about real places, this time through fiction. Both extracts emphasise the mystery, suspense, thrill and chill that still remain around the harbour town. The Whitby tourist industry takes advantage of the Dracula connection in several ways: shops selling Goth clothing and artefacts, a twice-yearly Goth weekend which attracts visitors from around the world, the 'Dracula Experience' and regular guided ghost walks around the town 'in search of Dracula'. A significant shift in tone and subject matter will be experienced by the reader in the next section, as I debate about the nature of data and its analysis in the context of this deconstructive study.

Challenges and high points

Showing the metaphysics of data analysis

The school-based project described above was, on the one hand, a curriculum development project and, at the same time, it was an educational research project. The design of the project occurred with an eye on the importance of 'dissemination', 'impact' and 'publication' of educational research findings as valued currency for transaction within the contemporary era of performativity in the educational research community. Adopting a traditional research approach, I conducted a logical sequence of research stages, moving from research questions to literature and theory to methodology, methods, analysis and presentation of findings. I organised comprehensive, rigorous and systematic data collection and analysis during the project's duration. I made audio recordings of all the planning meetings held with the two project teachers. I interviewed each project teacher individually on two separate occasions and conducted four student focus group interviews with students who had studied each of the topics described above. I collected samples of student work throughout the project as well as recording lesson observations and keeping a research diary. It was not until the point when I began data coding, analysis and interpretation that I hit the second aporia of the project. It consisted of an obstacle to the showing of metaphysics in deconstruction with regard to the orthodoxy of analysis in educational research. I realised the danger that treating the 'data as given' reduces it to an inert raw material awaiting the application of procedure; that the tight framing of the project with certain instrumental goals and time frame in mind shapes the end result; that an assertive, logical analytical procedure applied to 'the data' serves as a one-way track to fast and efficient completion that can easily overlook the messiness and the ethical importance of the whole experience (Standish 2001, 498). Faced with the metaphysics of objectifying systematic analysis, the identification of recurring themes and anomalies and the measurement of their degree of correspondence with, or challenge to, the findings of previous studies, I took a walk:

> When you go for a walk you must let your thoughts flutter randomly, letting them have a go now here, now there. That is how to arrange one's housekeeping. Themata are the accidents that the week should deliver to you in abundance. But the more you see to it that the dividends are uncertain, the freer, better, richer they will become, and the more striking, surprising, penetrating.
>
> (Kierkegaard 1996, 454, cited in Standish 2001, 504)

Deconstructive reading of the interview transcriptions showed the metaphysics of presence lurking beneath the language of educational, school and subject policy discourses engaged with by project teachers. I identified two dominant themata or totalising discourses embedded within the 'data'. These emerged as challenges during the project to impede the unrolling of a more dangerously inventive approach. One is the performativity-driven culture of the school and the other is constraining versions of school geographical knowledge.

Showing the metaphysics of performativity culture

Ball (2007) describes performativity as 'a culture and mode of regulation' which 'ties the effort of management to the information systems of the market and customer choice-making and/or to the target and benchmark requirements of the state' (p. 27). The curriculum project began several months after the school received an Ofsted report which was not as favourable as expected, and the agreement of the school to work with the project was linked to the Ofsted report in the sense that the project was 'steered' to comply with Ofsted requirements to some degree, thus limiting the project's aim of undermining dominant totalising discourses to make way for the Derridean incoming of the other. The thrust of the report focused on the need to raise standards of attainment in the school through, among other things, increased challenge in lessons, improvements in students' learning skills and curriculum development in line with students' needs. A clear directive was given to improve the school's management and leadership capacity in order to achieve these and other goals. At the start of the project, Sally reported the headteacher's reference to the school as 'coasting' in a meeting. This term refers to schools which are 'underperforming', 'drifting', and 'content to muddle along without trying hard to improve' (Number 10, 2012). In the case of examination attainment in geography in this school at GCSE level 2007–09, results were consistently below the regional average for grades A*–A and grades A*–C.

Two further issues were evident as contributing to the school's willingness to participate in the project. The first was the decline, year-on-year, in the numbers of students opting to study geography at Key Stage 4 (KS4, GCSE) and the second was the increasing pressure to move from a curriculum in which the subjects of geography, history and religious studies were taught discretely to an integrated, competency-based Humanities curriculum. This was a change John and Sally determined to resist as they identified themselves as established subject specialists. Alongside teachers' aims to improve the teaching of geography in the school in a general sense, the aims of the strategies introduced in response to the Ofsted report were twofold: first, to improve examination attainment at KS4 by appropriate development of the curriculum at KS3 and second, to increase the attractiveness of geography to KS3 students in order to improve recruitment to the KS4 course. The project contributed to the achievement of these aims by presenting opportunities for integrating into the KS3 programme of study knowledge and activities that would prepare students to achieve at higher levels at KS4 and the addition of a field trip to the new KS3 curriculum unit which would attract students to continue their study of the subject beyond KS3. The metaphysics of performativity demonstrates, by its instrumentalism and emphasis on outcomes of improved examination grades and increased subject recruitment, the kinds of constraints that limit the scope for inventionalism and the incoming of the other. Another metaphysics was at work in the project to influence its possibilities – that relating to totalising concepts underpinning subject knowledge and teacher identities.

Showing the metaphysics of school geography knowledge

The second obstacle to the incoming of the other through the curriculum project was the conceptualisations of knowledge operating between Sally and John with regard to the subject of geography. Both teachers had a strong commitment to 'physical' geography and understood the geographical world through long-established scientistic ideas. Scientism or quasi-science assumes the ascendance of scientific objectivity in the form of concepts, principles and procedures and applies them to matters that lie outside the realm of science. Examples include the domination of school geography by universalising discourses that attempt to impose true order and control on the world through, for example, notions of physical and human geography as separate domains of knowledge; cause and effect and the existence of regular patterns and processes that exist 'out there' in the 'real world', awaiting identification, description and explanation as if they were objective truths (Cloke et al. 1991, 187). Examples in the project include references by teachers in the interviews and planning meetings to 'the interaction between people and the natural world', 'the way in which the physical features have, I suppose, led to economic activities' and 'an awful lot of the culture comes from the sea . . . so the culture and the sort of economic activity is inextricably linked'.

In the division of labour within the project, I took the lead in planning the section which focused on the historical, literary and cultural geography of Whitby, the harbour town located in the north of the stretch of coast under study. Sally and John developed the unit sections focusing on the interaction between the physical and human environments in the southern coastal region, together with planning the field trip. This allocation of tasks highlights our respective identities as 'human/cultural' and 'physical' geographers, keen to remain in the comfort zone of our knowledge, skills and experience within the subject domain. This idea of the teacher's subject identity and desire to remain in her/his comfort zone are illustrated through an example which arose during a planning meeting when we contemplated different activities associated with Whitby which might be developed. Two suggestions came up: Goths and whaling. John, whose undergraduate degree was in geology, said: 'I like the idea of the whaling more than the Goths, because I think I'd feel a bit out of my depth with the Goth thing to be honest. I don't think I'd know enough, because they'd [students] know quite a bit as well. I think . . . you know when you can see how much you're going to have to sit at home and go "right . . . how am I going to plan this lesson?"'

Opening a space . . .

A key limitation to collaborative curriculum development in the research school prior to the introduction of the project under examination here was the senior management responsibilities of geography teachers and the scattered location of their offices in the school building. The time demands of management and infrequency of serendipitous meetings in a common staff room reduced opportunities for discussion about the curriculum amongst geography teachers. Prior to the arrival of John, responsibility for developing the curriculum lay in the hands of Sally, as Head of Department. She worked alone and passed on new ideas to senior colleagues who made their own interpretations of these ideas and taught accordingly. This situation was exacerbated by the increasing use of ICT whereby each geography teacher developed and saved her/his own electronic resources, compared to the situation in more collaborative contexts where curriculum materials are held on and accessed via a shared drive.

The first space opened by the project was a space for collaboration. Its arrival was welcomed by John and Sally as an opportunity to participate in a different kind of curriculum planning based on cooperation and discussion. Sally described the project as 'extra work, but it's come from sort of discussion where we've talked about and been enthusiastic about a new direction we're going in. And I suppose the best measure of extra work is whether you look up and think "oh crikey I didn't realise it was that time"' (1.04.09, 13).[1] She believed there was strength in three people working together because of the generation of ideas: 'we bounced a lot of ideas around to start with' (ibid., 14), continuing: 'when there's three of you, we looked at, talked about, rejected some things introduced things that anyone of us would never have come up with, that we did have lots of good discussions about loads and loads of interesting and different ways of doing things. I think it was a learning experience for us all' (ibid., 14). John concurred: 'Well, the good thing is the sort of fact that we actually sit down and have time to think about it which is huge . . . and it's more than one person. Because sometimes you sit by yourself and you go: "I don't know. . ."' (23.02.09, 11).

The second space was one which was opened up for the students by the introduction of the study of places with which most were familiar in some ways, but not in those ways to which the project introduced them. Sally summed it up: 'we are taking kids where they know but are not familiar with and looking at something from a perspective that they normally wouldn't take. So they come away from it with a greater depth of knowledge and, hopefully enthusiasm, for something that is quite close to them but far away enough not to be too familiar' (01.04.09, 15). Third, the teachers themselves felt that they participated in the opening of a space for new geographical knowledge and understanding entering the curriculum through their rejection of pre-made, textbook-based resources about case study places and their preference for their own ideas and materials: 'The fact that everything is fresh and new and developed really from the ground-up is good . . . it is that creativity thing, because we do know our kids and we know how well they'll respond. And I think what we've designed and what we've presented plays to their strengths as well' (Sally 01.04.09, 15). This creativity was not without its risks, as all three of us engaged with the new knowledge and felt insecure about no longer relying on our well-established, well-practised knowledge and skills in teaching the subject.

The questionnaire activity at the start of the project opened up a fourth space not only for the students' voices to be heard, but for those of their parents, families, neighbours and friends. As John said: 'we just wanted to get what they [students] already knew about it rather than teaching them' (06.04.09, 4). Several parents remarked positively and curiously about the project at the parents' evening which took place towards the end of the project. A fifth space for the emergence of a new kind of geography was created out of the breakdown of the binary of physical and human geography. John, the geologist, said: 'I think it's made us think a little bit more about doing cultural stuff, which we didn't really touch on before, maybe in discussion but not to the same extent' (06.04.09, 3) and added later 'it's kind of quite varied and I like the fact that there's no real "just physical" [geography] lessons, it's a sort of mix all the way through' (23.04.09, 12). The final space was space for the incoming of the unknown, something that is noticeable by its absence in conventional geography lessons. The idea of the unknown is not so much that students do not know something before a lesson and consider this as unknown, before learning it during the lesson and then knowing after the lesson. It is more that, through the study of Dracula and Captain Cook's death, students encountered, in the first example, the unknown beyond the human form and the feelings of mystery, thrill and chill previously unknown in the geography classroom. In the second example, the cause of Cook's death remains an anathema today, and yet, unsurprisingly, is subject to a variety of perspectival explanations. Some mysteries are never solved.

Did the curriculum project open up a space for a more just and democratic future? In the first place, the project involved thinking other-wise about a place, in ways that were very different from those constrained by the protocols of conventional place studies in school geography. In bringing a fresh interpretation to place study, it opened spaces for knowing an-other side of Whitby, even opening up spaces for knowing the unknown associated with the town. This re-invented knowledge, knowledge of the other, transgressed place knowledge enframed within a disciplinary discourse to demonstrate a more just way of thinking. Second, elements of justice emerged through the research enquiries themselves; for example, through the study of the struggle for power between the Irish and the Roman churches that was resolved at the Synod at Whitby Monastery in AD 664, the politics of jet jewellery making and its wearing, Cook's 'discovery' of foreign lands for British imperialist gain and views about the novel *Dracula* from a feminist stance. Justice came closer through the project in a third way, that is, through revealing the constraining influences of totalising discourses of performativity and of those enframing the subject. The former influenced the project; for example, in the school's initial agreement to participate and also in the selection of activities and resources. The latter influenced the project in terms of the division of labour within the project and the inability of cultural and physical geographers to work in a truly collaborative fashion within time constraints.

'Deconstruction is not a method or some tool that you apply to something from the outside' (Derrida 1997, 9). Is Derrida's warrant for deconstruction a sufficient reason for *not* engaging his help in the process of classroom-based curriculum development? Perhaps it is a question of different kinds of texts. When showing the metaphysics in deconstruction in the classroom, the number, scale and complexity of things involved are far greater than when examining a single text. The politics and ethics of the educational system, of school culture, of school subject policy, of teacher professional identities, of relationships between the participants and their histories are only a few examples of the multiple texts that make showing the metaphysics in deconstruction of curriculum policy and practice in – and through – practice a very different undertaking from deconstructive reading of an education policy document.

Acknowledgements

I would like to thank Sally and John for their enthusiasm and commitment to the project, to their students and to school geography. Both teachers approved the interpretation of events presented in the chapter. Thanks also to my colleague Jane Ferretti for her valuable comments on an earlier draft.

Note

1 Sources for these quotes are from transcripts of interviews with the project teachers.

References

Ball, S. J. 2007. *Education plc: Understanding private sector participation in public sector education*. Oxford: Routledge.

Barnwell, P. S., L. A. S. Butler and C. J. Dunn. 2003. The confusion of conversion: Streanaeshalch, Strensall and Whitby and the Northumbrian Church. In *The cross goes north: Processes of conversion in Northern Europe AD 300–1300*, ed. M. Carver. York: York Medieval Press.

Beaglehole, J. C. 1979. *The death of Captain Cook* (2nd edn). Wellington, New Zealand: Alexander Turnbull Library.

Bede 731/1999. *The ecclesiastical history of the English people*. Oxford: Oxford University Press.

Bennington, G. 2000. *Interrupting Derrida*. London: Routledge.

Biesta, J. J. G. 2009a. Education after deconstruction. In *Derrida, deconstruction and the politics of pedagogy*, ed. M. A. Peters and G. Biesta, 97–113. New York: Peter Lang.

Biesta, J. J. G. 2009b. Witnessing deconstruction in education: Why quasi-transcendentalism matters. *Journal of Philosophy of Education* 43, 3: 391–404.

Blake, N., P. Smeyers, R. Smith and P. Standish. 1998. *Thinking again: Education after postmodernism*. London: Bergin and Garvey.

Brannington, J., R. Robbins and J. Wolfreys, eds. 1996. *Applying: To Derrida*. Basingstoke: Macmillan Press.

Caputo, J. ed. 1997. *Deconstruction in a nutshell*. New York: Fordham University Press.

Cloke, P., C. Philo and D. Sadler. 1991. *Approaching human geography: An introduction to contemporary theoretical debates*. London: Arnold.

Dawes, G. 1968. Kealakekua Bay revisited: A note on the death of Captain Cook. *Journal of Pacific History* 3: 21–23.

DCSF/QCA. 2007. The National Curriculum Statutory requirements for key stages 3 and 4. London: DCSF/QCA.

Dening, G. 1996. *Performances*. Chicago: University of Chicago Press.

Derrida, J. 1972. Différance. In *Margins of philosophy*, trans. A. Bass, 1–17. Chicago: University of Chicago Press.

Derrida, J. 1976. *Of grammatology*, trans. G. C. Spivak. Baltimore: Johns Hopkins University.

Derrida, J. 1988. Letter to a Japanese friend. Trans. D. Wood and A. Benjamin. In *Derrida and différance*, ed. D. Wood and R. Bernasconi, 1–5. Evanston, IL: Northwest University Press.

Derrida, J. 1992. Force of law: The 'mystical foundation of authority'. In *Deconstruction and the possibility of justice*, ed. D. Cornell, M. Rosenfeld and D. G. Carlson, 4–67. London: Routledge.

Derrida, J. 1993. Finis. In *Aporias*, trans. T. Dutoit, 1–43. Stanford: Stanford University Press.

Derrida, J. 1997. The Villanova Roundtable: A conversation with Jacques Derrida. In *Deconstruction in a nutshell*, ed. J. Caputo, 3–28. New York: Fordham University Press.

Edgoose, J. 2001. Just decide! Derrida and the ethical aporias of education. In *Derrida and education*, ed. J. J. G. Biesta and D. Egéa-Kuehne, 119–133. Oxford: Routledge.

Egéa-Kuehne, D. 1996. Neutrality in education and Derrida's call for 'double duty'. In *Philosophy of Education 1996*, ed. F. Margonis, 154–163. Urbana: Philosophy of Education Society.

Egéa-Kuehne, D. 2001. Derrida's ethics of affirmation: The challenge of educational rights and responsibility. In *Derrida and Education*, ed. J. J. G. Biesta and D. Egéa-Kuehne, 186–208. Oxford: Routledge.

Number 10. 2012. Transcript: PM speech at coasting schools meeting. Available at: www.number10.gov.uk/news/coasting-schools/.

Ofsted. 2005. *2004/5 Annual report on curriculum and assessment*. Available at: www.geography.org.uk/download/GA_NKS3QCAreport.pdf (accessed 20 June 2012).

Ofsted. 2008. *Geography in schools changing practice*. Available at: www.ofsted.gov.uk/resources/geography-schools-changing-practice (accessed 20 June 2012).

Rawling, E. M. 2001. *Changing the subject: The impact of national curriculum policy on school geography 1980–2000*. Sheffield: The Geographical Association.

Sahlins, M. 1985. *Islands of history*. Chicago: University of Chicago Press.

Sahlins, M. 1995. *How 'natives' think: About Captain Cook, for example*. Chicago: University of Chicago Press.

Standish, P. 2001. Data return: The sense of the given in educational research. *Journal of Philosophy of Education* 35, 3: 497–518.

Stoker, B. 1897. *Dracula*. Hertfordshire: Wordsworth Classics.

Stoker, B. 1999. *Dracula*. Adapted by D. Calcutt. Oxford: Oxford University Press.

Villiers, A. 1967. *Captain Cook: The seaman's seaman*. London: Penguin.

Williams, G. 2008. *The death of Captain Cook: A hero made and unmade*. London: Profile Books.

Winter, C. 2009. Places, spaces, holes for knowing and writing the earth: The Geography curriculum and Derrida's *Khora*. *Ethics and Education* 4, 1: 57–68.

Chapter 13

Engaging with student-teachers on reflective writing

Reclaiming writing

Duncan Mercieca

Introduction

Reflective teaching and writing is now a fundamental aspect and practice of being a teacher. It is seen as 'an effective tool in democratizing teaching and learning processes' (Galea 2012, 245) that counter balances the 'positivistic technicist approach to teaching and learning that has overwhelmed the educational sector' (ibid.). The move towards greater accountability has led to an emphasis on measurement, and this gives rise to a search for that which can be measured. 'The most insidious danger', as Jennings and Kennedy (1996) argue, 'is that only that which can be measured will be considered worthwhile, thereby leading to a revision to the worst excess of behaviourism and a blinkered focus on behavioural objectives' (p. xi). Managerial discourses and market forces, particularly at a time of world financial crises, are more than ever pressing on educational aims. Political expediency has become the norm. Under such circumstances, there is the need for teachers to stand back and reflect upon their professional lives and interactions with children and others. It is in this light that the majority of teacher training schools are putting a lot of effort into training, nurturing and guiding student-teachers in becoming reflective practitioners. There seems the need for the 'search for meaning' to be at the heart of the process of becoming-teachers.

As I sit at my desk, I am surrounded by numerous files and bits of writings that our student-teachers have written as reflective writings during the course of four years. Working in Malta, over the last two years, as part of an ongoing research project, I have collected from some of our student-teachers, who have just finished their teacher training course, all the writings which they consider as reflective writing done throughout their four-year course. And I am amazed and flabbergasted at the volumes that each student-teacher got to my office: parts of assignments and tasks assigned; activities aimed specifically at encouraging reflection; and, of course, all those activities that involved working directly with children and their parents, in schools, and in carrying out lessons.

I gradually become more aware of the process of writing involved in reflective writings that our student-teachers carry out in the course of their training. For, apart from 'reflective conversations' that occur at different moments in the training of teachers, most reflective processes involve the act of writing. Having engaged with Derrida's ideas, I started to question the process of writing involved in reflective writing. Derrida's apprehension for writing has been a lifetime concern, with his concepts on writing scattered all across his work, while certain of his texts problematise the issue further.

Derrida cannot be reduced to a model of analysis often known as deconstruction. Jacques Derrida (1988, 3) warns us that '[it] is not a method and cannot be transformed into one' (p. 273). What Gert Biesta (2009) reminds us is that 'we should not aim to deconstruct anything, but rather engage in witnessing the *event* of deconstruction' (emphasis in original, p. 400). We need to give witness to 'those moments where conditions of possibility and impossibility "cross" each other and in their crossing provide a deconstructive opening . . . an entrance for the incoming of something new, something unforeseen' (ibid.). We do not make deconstruction happen – deconstruction occurs whether we like it or not, but we can acknowledge it and give witness to it.

This has been my driving question in reading my students' writings: do their writings allow for witnessing the event of deconstruction? Do their writings allow, give space or even create space for the impossible to cross the possible? What other models of writing could allow for more acknowledgement and witness of the possible and impossible crossing each other?

This chapter is divided into three parts. Each part explores the process that I engaged in, in my research. If I want to categorise this research project, it falls under the terms 'action-research'. Carr and Kemmis (1986) 'regard it as a form of "self-reflective inquiry" by participants, undertaken in order to improve understanding of their practices in context with a view to maximizing social justice' (quoted in Cohen et al. 2000, 227).

In the next section I put forth some ideas from Derrida that have challenged my ideas on writing. I give an idea about how these Derridian concepts helped me make strange the familiarity I am accustomed to in reading the student-teachers' reflective writings. In the last section, I show how my reading of Derrida calls for a political action on my part, calling me to take up my responsibility (my ability to respond) and act by trying out a different model of writing with the student-teachers.

Derrida on writing

Before engaging in some of the ideas developed in this chapter, it is important to remind ourselves that Derrida's writing style is itself his philosophy (see Rorty 1978). The way that numerous Derridian texts are presented to us readers, texts which often are difficult to read and 'understand' within the Western philosophical tradition, are playing this double articulation between the text and the concepts. Texts and concepts are in infinite play with each other, being both inseparable and mutually contaminating for each other. Since my initial reading of Derrida's text, this has always fascinated me: How does writing create one's philosophy? And how does one's philosophy create one's writing?

In 'Force and signification' (1978), Derrida is engaging with French structuralism. In particular he uses the text of Jean Rousset, *Forme et signification* (1989), to create his argument. One can immediately see Derrida's play with the words *form* and *force,* where he is using the latter to correct Rousset's idea of form. Rousset developed geometrical schemas for studying literary texts and Derrida argues that this process is one of reductionism. This reductionism 'appears to give exhaustive descriptions of the "structures" or "formal constants" underlying the texts' (Johnson 1993, 13). Derrida argues that these structures become ends in themselves, and rather than the text being under study, the structure is. Also the structures from their nature are spatial entities and are applied to the text. As Christopher Johnson (1993) argues, 'the nature of Rousset's method is indeed appropriately expressed in his choice of title, *Forme et signification*: his own forms (spatial, geometrical) are imposed upon different textual significations' (pp. 13–14). Derrida furthers his analysis of Rousset and argues that his approach is 'performist', the idea that organisms develop from miniature complete versions of themselves. Each small part reflects and resumes the whole, and the temporal dimension is therefore always of the present. This implies 'the idea that the totality of the literary work is contained in germinal form at its beginning, the end of the work being implicit in its origin' (p. 15). These are Derrida's two main concerns – structures and time, what Derrida calls the 'flatness' of structuralism (two-dimensions):

> the panoramagram, the very image of the structuralist instrument, was invented in 1824, as Littré states, in order to 'obtain immediately, on a flat surface, the development of depth vision of objects on the horizon'. Thanks to a more or less openly acknowledged schematization or spatilization, one can glance over the field divested of its force more freely or diagrammatically.
> (Derrida 1978, 5)

It is this removing of, or hiding of, the 'force' in order for things to seem simpler, ordered, systematic and clean, that Derrida wants to recuperate in structuralism. Derrida does this by wanting to think in terms of three-dimensions, rather than two. He wants duration (instead of the present time) and becoming (rather than geometrical structures) to play a part in flat structures, in order to give volume (that is the third dimension) to structures: 'in its demand for the flat and horizontal, what is intolerable for structuralism is indeed the richness implied by the volume, every element that cannot be spread into the simultaneity of a form' (p. 25).

The question that follows from this is: how do we do this? How to produce volume in flat structures? As often happens, we introduce opposites to help us overcome the linearity of things, to find some sort of (Hegelian) synthesis between the opposites. Derrida will take a different stance to this – he will suggest 'that it is necessary to seek new concepts and new models, an economy escaping this system of metaphysical oppositions' (p. 19). This *economy* takes us at the heart of the Derridian project which is summarised in the term 'logocentrism'. This term is relevant to this chapter, as in *Of Grammatology* (1976) Derrida examines the relationship between speech and writing. He argues that the latter is subordinate to the former: we think, speak and then maybe write what has been spoken. Logocentrism is the idea that the *logos* (speech) and not writing is central to language. The assumption is that speech is clear and transparent. We can understand the speaker and know what she is talking about – 'the subject is the "master" of language' (Usher and Edwards 1994, 121). But writing is seen as suspect and untrustworthy because it can be interpreted in various ways and have different interpretations from what the author meant and implied. However, writing for Derrida is able to escape the control of the speaker/writer/reader and we are in a position where language controls us.

This, obviously, 'plunges us into a realm of strangeness' (ibid.), as we have lost control of language. 'Grammatology', a term Derrida uses to refer to writing, can free our ideas of writing from being subordinated to our ideas of speech/writer/ reader. In this way, the logos is a presence, what Derrida refers to as the 'metaphysics of presence' – a centre or original guarantee of all meaning, which for Derrida has characterised Western philosophy since Plato. The 'metaphysics of presence' is motivated by a desire for a 'transcendental signified', a signified that transcends all signifiers, as meaning that transcends all signs. What happens is that we measure everything in relation to the logocentric, so writing is measured in relation to speech, or to give another example, woman is measured in relation to man, and so on.

The 'economy' that Derrida writes about that escapes this system of metaphysical oppositions, that is the logocentrism:

> can be announced only through a certain organization, a certain strategic arrangement which, within the field of metaphysical opposition, uses the strength of the field to turn its own stratagems against it, producing a force of dislocation that spreads itself through the entire system, fissuring it in every direction and through delimiting it.
>
> (ibid.)

In order to answer the question posed above: how do we do this? How to produce volume in flat structures? Derrida's answer in 'Force and signification' (1978) is to bring form and force in an economy, allowing for fissure to appear when doing so. Although Derrida wants duration and becoming to play a part in flat structures, in order to give volume, pure duration and pure becoming still need a 'certain organisation' – a form. Without a form these would never actualise. 'The point of articulation between force and form' (Johnson 1993, 23) is the 'inscription'.

Inscription is the line, the moment between force and form. The 'scribble' (see Derrida 1979) that engages in that automatic brings death! It brings death because the moment I scribble something down, I have not opted for the other thousand possible words and ideas that potentially could have been scribbled down. I did not choose these words and ideas. For Derrida following Kierkegaard, this is a moment of madness (Derrida) – the aporia of the infinite possible words has been summed up in some scribbling. Scribbling is violent – it leaves a mark, a scratch. This is painful. Derrida uses the term 'anguish' (Derrida 1978, 9), which from its Latin roots means 'narrowness' and 'difficulty'. Derrida uses Artaud's 'description of the painful experience in writing' (p. 22) and then Derrida argues that anguish is the condition from which all expression proceeds. It is as if infinite words and expressions are pressing on the writer – all wanting to be scribbled. It is in this light that Derrida (ibid.) argues:

> To write is only to know that through writing, through the extremities of style, the best will not necessarily transpire . . . It is also to be incapable of making meaning absolutely precede writing: it is thus to lower meaning while simultaneously elevating inscription.
>
> (p. 10)

Therefore, the inaugural moment[1] is writing and not speaking/thinking about something. It is writing, re-writing and re-re-writing that 'is, in a certain way, the condition of meaning and of the concept' (Johnson 1993, 28). The process of writing is that which constitutes the condition of sense, and not sense which is then written down.

Routinised writing

> Such 'reflective writing' is a very effective and worthwhile exercise. There are many ways of doing this, but the most effective one is to find *your own* system of how to write about your feelings and thoughts regarding your own professional and personal development as teachers. In the portfolio you are being given several reflective tasks which will help you to focus your thoughts and ideas and reflectively question your choices and learning experiences.
>
> (Professional Development Portfolio, undated, 7)

The Professional Development Portfolio starts off by stating that student-teachers need to find their own voice in how to write about feelings and thoughts, regarding their professional and personal development as teachers. Yet, when one goes through the portfolio, one cannot fail to observe that it is made up of numerous tasks, which the student-teachers have to fill under various subheadings every week, spread over their second academic year. Now, our School of Education has shifted from hard copies to online portfolios where student-teachers are also given word limits for certain online tasks, and an automated system will not allow the student-teachers to move forward if they have not inputted every part as expected.

The Professional Development Portfolio is just one example of the many reflective activities that student-teachers are asked to do. Similarly, when on teaching practice,[2] student-teachers are asked to reflect-on-practice (see Schön 1983, 1987, 1991), our primary students are given a *Reflective Questions* booklet (Cardona 2005) which 'is designed to assist you with your reflections as you write up your weekly self-evaluations during Teaching-Practice' (p. 1). Even if it is specifically stated in the introduction that the questions provided for each week should not be seen as a 'comprehension exercise' (p. 2), yet a closer look at the document does suggest so and also the student-teachers' answers suggest this. The following is an example of one of the questions suggested for the second week:

> The effectiveness of any classroom management depends on a teacher's attitudes and practical intelligence. Reflect on these basic principles:
>
> a. Have you established a friendly relationship with your students?
> b. What did you establish the relationship on?
> c. Do you consider yourself to have established a supportive and trusting relationship?
> d. What is your regard towards disruptive students?
> e. Can you honestly say that you have a positive regard towards disruptive students?
> f. Do you consider your approach to be an optimistic and no-nonsense approach?
> g. If you do, how did you set about establishing it?
>
> (p. 5)

From reading through the students' work, I found that when student-teachers are not given models of reflective practices, still most of them develop a very systematic approach to writing their reflections. The following excerpt is taken from a reflection diary that student-teachers are asked to keep during their teaching practices.

> How to improve:
>
> 1. I should repeat over and over again and remind students continuously about the present perfect, as it was difficult for the students to understand. The worksheet given for group work was not an ideal one. I should have provided a worksheet with various examples where children would decide if the examples were simple past and present perfect. Another thing which I could do is to have an exercise with examples copied on their copybooks. The examples will then be worked out as a whole class to make sure that everyone is following and understanding.
> 2. The worksheet which I have given today for group work should have been given another time, when children would have understood the concept better.

3. I could have put the slideshow on the classroom computers and shown the PowerPoint presentation from there. In fact I gave every child a copy of the PowerPoint on the USBs, so that they could see it again at home.
(Student-teacher, personal communication, June 2011)

This particular student-teacher, when reflecting-on-practice about the lessons she delivers, divides her reflections into three sections: Things I did wrong; How to improve; and What went well. A number of bullet points are written under each section. Similarly, when she is writing about particular children, she has another list of subsections: 'General overview of the child'; 'The child's abilities'; 'Support areas needed to be addressed'; and 'How to intervene with child'. Every bit is compartmentalised, split into sections and seems to fit nicely into place within a large picture. It is like when one finds a missing piece in a big jigsaw puzzle. The pieces fit nicely together. The moment one fills in a piece of writing it is as if a piece of the puzzle has been fitted in the large picture. What also becomes evident in this example is how the present is made manifest to us. With the student-teacher's writing we can come to know exactly how things are, what she did, what her intentions and actions are. We seem to be present during her lesson delivery. There is a clear end in the writing of the student-teacher. Every point mirrors her whole lesson, thus allowing the totality of the lesson to be permanently present in any one of the points written down. The beginning and end of the lesson can be seen through each point written down.

Structures, whether imposed by lecturers or by student-teachers themselves on themselves, seem to have taken over most reflective writing. And it is here that I question, in light of Derrida's arguments, whether structures of reflective writing have become ends in themselves? And if these structures are just promoting the present? Content seems to have second place. Form has taken over the force; or to explain it in another way, force has been channelled into paragraphs, subtitles and bullet points that seem to dilute, stifle or even kill this force.

It is not only the reflective writing which seems to be too structured and promoting the present, but also the way we teach and theorise reflective practice. One of the texts that we use with our student-teachers is by Anthony Ghaye and Kay Ghaye (1998). In this text we are presented with a model of reflection which has four characteristics: 'it is cyclical, flexible, focused and holistic' (p. 6). Then we are presented with four foci which are at the heart of this model:

Reflection on Values: self → others → action (which influences the self)
Reflection on Practice: political → professional → personal (which influences the personal)
Reflection on Improvement: construction → interpretation → validation (which influences the construction)
Reflection on Context: Partnership → culture → empowerment (which influences the partnership)

(p. 8)

Not that there is anything wrong with such structures of how to think and engage in reflective practices, but the concern is that we tend to follow to the letter these structures. This could be seen as the flatness of structure, where a certain kind of geometry and a certain conception of time are at play. From the above, it was evident for me that how we teach reflective practice to student-teachers and how they write their reflective practices seen within a Derridian framework may not give enough space for force and duration to manifest themselves. Rather, what this writing seems to be reinforcing is a logic of identity – through writing the student-teacher can arrive at the origin of herself and what it means to be a teacher. Writing is seen as that means through which we are able to master and control ourselves. What this writing leaves out or what it eliminates is the other of ourselves. We see ourselves as having a particular identity which excludes alterity. 'The otherness which is excluded and suppressed in order to maintain the myth of a pure and uncontaminated original presence is actually constitutive of that which presents itself as pure, self-sufficient, self-present, and therefore as totally different from this otherness' (Biesta 2001, 44).

In the next section I will 'reflect' about the second phase of my research, which is still developing as this chapter is being written.

Student-teachers writing the self

According to Richard Rorty (1978), 'for Derrida, writing always leads to more writing, and more, and still more' (p. 145). Probably this quote puts 'in a nutshell' (Caputo 1997) the ideas of this section. As part of my research, after I have read extensively the reflective writings written by my students, I wanted to take up Derrida's invitation of trying to come up with an economy that escapes as much as possible closure. As already pointed out previously, force still needs form. So I thought of shifting from reflective writing to narrative writing. From this year, while student-teachers still engage in reflective teaching and writing, I was able to create a study-unit for the student-teachers with the title of this section. What this study-unit does is to give spaces for writings to take place, hoping that Rorty's suggestion holds true. No formula of how to write is presented and any kind of writing is accepted. I will give just a brief description of the study-unit to situate the reader of this chapter. The study-unit is carried out after the student-teachers have a long period of being in schools, where they are mainly involved in teaching and working with students. During the course of the lectures, they are presented with different policy documents, ideas from philosophers, pieces of poetry and novels (in particular Kafka and Woolf), photos of past and contemporary educational settings, hear elderly people talking about their experience of schooling, read narratives written by teachers and watch movies of teachers. The student-teachers are encouraged to write their narrative of their recently finished teaching experience in relation to these. The aim is to stimulate the student-teachers to write about themselves, their ideas of teaching, the process of working with children, their families and the experience of teaching classes. They are asked to write events that they experienced in the light of these stimulations.

The aim of these stimulations together with the experience of their recently finished teaching practice is to help escape the idea that the self is transparent and can be seen or spoken of through writing by the student-teachers. Rather than seeing the self as transparent, clear and accessible to oneself, the idea is to see the self as multilayered and strange to oneself. The self is made up of various ideas and connections and the other of the self is given space to disrupt the identity that we have built or assume that we have. Not only that, but this process questions the idea of 'the self' of the student-teacher as something fixed which can be understood and known. This obviously questions the idea of agency that reflective practice seems to be putting forth. The student-teachers' experience and the stimulations give the possibility of the 'play of difference', which comes across through writing and re-writing. I am seeing this as a way in which difference is not reduced to sameness. Here writing is not seen as a representation of a thought-out process by the student-teacher, but rather the process of writing creates the student-teacher and her 'sense'-making of the teaching experience. This would provide depth and volume to the flatness mentioned earlier.

In no way does this mean that this process has worked for all – probably, the contrary. From reading the writings of the student-teachers it is evident that some student-teachers were struggling to engage in this experience of writing and re-writings. One student-teacher emailed me telling me that she is 'lost' as she does not know what she has to do. She writes 'I know that I have to write about my experience in relation to the various stimulations that we had, but HOW do I start writing? . . . can you please consider giving us clear guidelines in how to do this writing' (personal communication – email by student, March 2011). The fear of getting 'lost' seems to be at the heart of what this student-teacher is afraid to engage in, which is contradictory to the heart of the whole project, that is, of getting lost. I do not offer structures to my student-teachers, only exemplars (Woolf, Kafka, and many narratives of teachers) and a few suggestions. My first suggestion to the above student-teacher is: 'start writing'. 'When you don't know what to write just start writing'; 'Start writing about your feeling of "getting lost" and see where that takes you'; 'Not all writing takes you somewhere – but you are on the road'; 'Writing is a painful process'. A student-teacher reacted very vociferously to the latter phrase, saying to me 'why does writing need to be painful? The kind of writing that is being suggested opens up things that I don't want to deal with. It is not like the other reflective-practice writing – that closes up things' (personal note after lecture). This comment was very revealing to me. First, it is interesting that for her reflective-practice writing (as she calls it) closes down her experience. Yet she does not want, or is finding it difficult, to engage with another writing that opens things up. This could be painful for her. But, it seems that pain or anguish, as Derrida (1978) refers to it, is a fundamental part of writing and re-writing.

Although at this stage of my research I also feel lost on how to present this to the student-teacher, I do feel that this 'feeling lost', 'strangeness', is a driving force. Derrida's idea of aporia – to be caught in moments of uncertainty, to have all possibilities available – is fundamental here. Daniela Mercieca (2009, 2011) draws upon Klein to explain how the psyche is engaged in a constant move towards integrity, that the discomfort experienced in the unknown is anxiety-provoking.

> It is very difficult to produce an account which acknowledges contradictions, and describes the detail and diversity of events and analyses experience in terms which go beyond the unitary, rational subject. Defences are maintained to achieve integrity with an energy which is equivalent to the energy of the original repressed desire.
>
> (Mercieca 2011, 30)

She quotes a number of papers written by professionals, whose aim is to explore ways of reducing the uncertainty using systematic procedures. However, Mercieca (2009, 2011) suggests we attempt to befriend the contradictory state of being and to view it as part and parcel of who we are.

> I maintain that it is incumbent upon us to make sure that they do have a place. It is only through maintaining a healthy level of doubt that the complexities and contingencies of the situations which children present us can be received and listened to. It is only by allowing ourselves to be uncertain that we are open to shock and surprise. It is through being more tolerant of the feelings that accompany not knowing, rather than resisting that which we do not expect, that we can be more open to children. And it is this that will enable our continuous development of professionalism, as opposed to a 'restriction of the role of the professional practitioner to that of the technical operative' (Nixon 2004, 246).
>
> (Mercieca 2009, 177)

Conclusion

The School of Education I work for puts reflective practice at the core of the student-teacher experience, with particular focus given to written reflective practice. Using a Derridian framework, my action-research process, of which I have given highlights above, helped me question the taken-for-granted familiarity that I was engaged with when teaching reflected practice and reading reflective writings. Through reading Derrida and engaging with his various writing styles, I started to become more aware of the process of writing and its complexity. This helped me think about the possibility of offering such ideas to my students and also to open myself up to various writings which do not follow structures to the letter and allow for some force to be demonstrated through the writing.

During the course of this action-research I have been caught in moments of aporia and 'madness of deciding', particularly when I was trying out with student-teachers the new study-unit that asks them to write their narrative. My many moments of doubt, of not knowing exactly where I was going, of correcting myself as I developed this course, was a very strange feeling of uncertainty. Considering that performativity is fast becoming a characteristic even within universities (see Nixon et al 2001, Nixon 2001, 2003, 2004), where assessment and measurement of each study-unit is now in place, to carry out a study-unit that is fluid can have its consequences. Yet Derrida comes to me as a comfort and also as a provocation: a decision only takes place when one is caught in a moment of aporia. If one follows structures and procedures, then there is no decision. What I and my student-teachers seemed to be doing for some time now, as described above in 'Student-teachers writing the self', was mostly on my part to create structures of reflective practice and for the student-teachers to follow. What I am now trying to do is to provide a space for the student-teacher to escape these formulated structures and to allow their otherness to come across and disrupt the identity. This process has also disrupted my identity as a lecturer and researcher. Maybe the word 'disrupted' is not the best to use here. Rather, this process gave me the opportunity to let the other (the impossible) be made possible in my identity as a lecturer – challenging (at times violently) who I am as a lecturer. Not that the impossible is actualised, but that which cannot be foreseen is made present in what I do and influences my decisions. And while I already feel tired at the thought that next year (when this study will continue to explore possibilities of how I can help student-teachers write themselves as narrative) I will have to start over again, yet I feel that this openness to the other is a possible way forward that allows for the 'incalculable' for me and my students. This is nothing if not justice for Derrida. Therefore writing that is just!

Notes

1 Derrida always asks why there is something and not nothing.
2 In Malta, Teaching Practice for student-teachers is a six-week teaching block.

References

Biesta, G. J. J. 2001. 'Preparing for the incalculable': Deconstruction, justice and the question of education. In *Derrida and Education*, ed. G. J. J. Biesta and D. Egéa-Kuehne, 32–54. London: Routledge.

Biesta, G. J. J. 2009. Witnessing deconstruction in education: Why quasi-transcendentalism matters. *Journal of Philosophy of Education* 43, 3: 391–404.

Caputo, J. D. ed. 1997. *Deconstruction in a nutshell. A conversation with Jacques Derrida*. New York: Fordham University Press.

Cardona, A. 2005. *Reflective questions*. Available at: www.um.edu.mt/educ/downloads.

Carr, W. and S. Kemmis. 1986. *Becoming critical*. Lewes: Falmer.

Cohen, L., L. Manion and K. Morrison. 2000. *Research methods in education.* London: Routledge Falmer.

Derrida, J. 1976. *Of grammatology.* Baltimore: Johns Hopkins University Press.

Derrida, J. 1978. Force and signification. In *Writing and difference.* London: Routledge and Kegan Paul.

Derrida, J. 1979. Scribble (writing-power). *Yale French Studies* 58: 117–147.

Derrida, J. 1988. 'Letter to a Japanese friend', trans. D. Wood and A. Benjamin. In *Derrida and différance*, ed. D. Wood and R. Bernasconi, 1–5. Evanston Illinois: Northwestern University Press.

Galea, S. 2012. Reflecting reflective practice. *Educational Philosophy and Theory* 44, 3: 245–258.

Ghaye, A. and K. Ghaye. 1998. *Teaching and learning through critical reflective practice.* London: David Fulton Publishers.

Jennings, C. and E. Kennedy, eds. 1996. *The reflective professional in education: Psychological perspective on changing contexts.* London: Jessica Kingsley Publishers.

Johnson, C. 1993. *System and writing in the philosophy of Jacques Derrida.* Cambridge: Cambridge University Press.

Mercieca, D. 2009. Working with uncertainty: Reflections of an educational psychologist on working with children. *Ethics and Social Welfare* 3, 2: 170–180.

Mercieca, D. 2011. *Beyond conventional boundaries: Uncertainty in research and practice with children.* Rotterdam: Sense Publishers.

Nixon, J. 2001. 'Not without dust and heat': The moral bases of the 'new' academic professionalism. *British Journal of Educational Studies* 49, 2: 173–186.

Nixon, J., Marks, A., Rowland, S. and Walker, M. 2001. Towards a new academic professionalism: A manifesto of hope. *British Journal of Sociology of Education* 22, 2: 227–244.

Nixon, J. 2003. Professional renewal as a condition of institutional change: Rethinking academic work. *International Studies in Sociology of Education* 13, 1: 3–15.

Nixon, J. 2004. Education for the good society: The integrity of academic practice. *London Review of Education* 2, 3: 245–252.

Professional Development Portfolio. n.d. Malta: University of Malta.

Rorty, R. 1978. Philosophy as a kind of writing: Essay on Derrida. *New Literary History* 10, 1: 141–160.

Rousset, J. 1989. *Forme et signification.* Paris: José Corti.

Schön, D. 1983. *The reflective practitioner: How professionals think in action.* London: Temple Smith.

Schön, D. 1987. *Educating the reflective practitioner.* San Francisco: Jossey-Bass.

Schön, D. ed. 1991. *The reflective turn: Case studies in and on educational practice.* New York: Teachers College (Columbia).

Usher, R. and R. Edwards. 1994. *Postmodernism and education.* London: Routledge.

Index

Academies (England) 12, academies
    policy 144; faith-based 138–9, 144;
    and field 145–6
Accountability, accountability trap 85;
    and education 84; and legal
    regulation 91; mechanisms of 84, 88;
    and temporal regulation 90
Adorno, T. and Horkheimer, M. 86–7
Ainley, M. 77
Allan, J. 10, 21, 31
Anderson, N. 22
Aporia, 13, 75, 186–7, 192, 204,
    209–210
Assessment 7, assessment interview
    103–5, 110; assessment practices 9;
    and performativity 210; risk
    assessment 40, 92; and RPL 98, 100,
    103
Atkinson, W. 153, 157, 164–5
Ayers, A. 70

Baker, B. 26
Balibar, E. 171, 174–5, 177–8, 180
Ball, S. 139, 193
Barberis, P. 84
Bash, L. Coulby, D. and Jones, C. 46
Bates, R. 121
Bauman, Z. 40, 43.
BBC News 41
Bell, D. 47
Bentham, J 24, 36; and panoptican 24,
    36
Berneaur, J. 27
Besley, T. and Peters, M. 59
Best, S. 5; and Kellner, D. 6
Biesta, J. J. G. 186, 201, 207
Billig, S.H. 79
Blake, N. and Masschelein, J. 172, 175

Blake, N., Smeyers, P., Smith, R. and
    Standish, P. 171–2, 174–5, 186
Blaug, R. 85, 88–9
Bloom, B. 70
Bogard, W. 40. 45
Boud. D., Keogh, R and Walker, D.
    60
Bovens, M. 85
Bowles, S. and Gintis, H. 122
Boyne, R. 31, 37, 40
Brannington, J., Robbins, R. and
    Wolfreys, J. 186–7
British Sociological Association
    121
Brookfield, S. 99
Brooks, R. 153
Brown, P. 85
Brown, T. and Jones, L. 171
Brubaker, R. 118
Burchell, G. 31
Bureaucracy 86–7, 92, 99; and
    accountability 11, 84–85; and quality
    assurance 84, 87; street-level
    bureaucracy 85
Butin, D. 22

Callinicos, A. 14
Caputo, J. 185–6, 207
Cardona, A. 205
Carr, D. 77
Carr, W. and Kemmis, S. 201
Carson, D. 148
Carter, B. and Whittaker, K. 76
Casella, R. 42
Church of England 144
City Technology Colleges 144
Clarke, J. and Newman, J. 84
Clarke, R. 43

Classrooms, classroom politics 91; and interaction 140; management of 205; surveillance of 41–2
Cloke, P., Philo, C. Sadler, D. 194
Cohen, L., Manion, L. and Morrison, K. 201
Colonisation 8, 12, 93–4; colonisation in schools 89; and regulation 91; colonisation of the lifeworld 12, 99
Communicative action, application of 95; and methodology 101; and RPL 99; theory of 5, 11–12, 69, 72, 78–80, 85–6, 100
Competence, political competence 84; and RPL 98
Connell, R.W. 143–4; and Ashenden, D.J., Kesler, S. and Dowsett, G.W. 121
Cooper, B. 85
Cooper, D. 31
Couldry, N. 125
Crawford, K. 78
Critical pedagogy 171
Critical theory 70, 86, 171–80
Crotty, R. 78–9
Cultural capital 120, 125, 138, 140; and academies 144; and class 157; definition of 143; and exchange 156; and family 159; and habitus 155; and higher education 153; and parental influence 161–2, 165; and religious habitus 149–150
Curriculum, and academies 144; assumptions of 74; and Derrida 184; geography curriculum 187; health care curriculum 61, 104; and observation 42, and religious habitus 150; and social reproduction 121; and values education 76

Damasio, A. 77
Darling, J. and Nordenbo, S.E. 174, 181
De Certeau, M. 45
Deconstruction, and Bourdieu 131; definition of 184; and Derrida 171, 184; and education 171; and education research 173; and Marx 6; and Marxism 175; and pedagogy 179
Democracy 4; and accountability 85, 94; deliberative democracy 98, 102
Dewey, John 70, 77, 80, 180

DfE 144, 151
Discourse, christian discourses 146; communicative discourse 101; and control 37; and curriculum 76; disciplinary discourse 36; and Foucault 21; and genealogy 53; of inclusion 26; managerialist discourses 200; postmodernist discourses 174; and Rousseau 5; of structuralism 23; totalising discourses 192–3
Doll, W. 73
Doyle, A. 38
Dracula 191, 184, 194
Durkheim, E. 128
Duvenage, P. 88

Edgoose, J. 186
Egéa-Kuehne, D. 178–9, 186–7
Elliot 4, 14
Erlandsson, P. 60; and Beach, D. 60
Ewert, D.G. 98–9
Exworthy, M. and Halford, S. 86

Feeley, M. 41
Fejes, A. 11, 52, 60, 64–5; and Dahlstedt, M. 52, 65; and Nicoll, K. 60
Fenech, M. and Sumeson, J 22
Fernandez, L.A. and Huey, L. 46
Ferre, F. 70
Feyerabend, P. 71
Fleming, T. 99
Fowler, B. 5
Frankfurt School 69, 86
Fraser, N. 14
Freire, P. 3, 172, 181

Galea, S. 201
Gallagher, M. 42
Garrison, J. 178, 180
Gellel, A. 78
Ghaye, A. and Ghaye, K. 206
Giddens, A. 118
Giroux, H. 171–3
Gorard, S. 145
Governance 14; and Foucault 85; and Habermas 85–6; institutional governance 84; and learning 63
Grace, G. 139, 144–5
Gramsci, A. 181
Green, A. and Vyronides, M. 154–5
Green, E. 12, 138, 145, 146–7

Grenfell, M. 118, 131, 133
Groombridge, N. 47

Habitus 12–13, 117–19, 132–3,
    139–41, 144; habitus and academies
    146–8; habitus and practice, 122–4;
    religious habitus 149–50; researcher
    habitus 128–9, student habitus 142
Handal, G. and Lauvås, P. 60
Haggerty, K.D. and Ericson, R.V.
    37–9
Hall, N. 42
Harrington, A. 4
Heimans, S, 134
Henderson, D. 78
Hier, S. 37
Hirst, P. and Peters, R.S. 71
Hollande, J.A. and Einwohne, R.C. 46
Hope, A. 10, 35, 42, 45–8
Houlbrook, M.C. 99

Identity, corporate identity 148–9;
    identity cards 42; identity formation
    48; marginal identity 31; student
    identity 47; teacher identity 194,
    207–8, 210
Inclusion 3, 9; children with special
    needs 29; discourses of 26
Irwin, J. 13, 171–3, 177, 181

Jenkins, R. 127, 139, 143
Jennings, C. and Kennedy, E. 200
Johns, C. 64
Johnson, C. 202–3

Kauppi, N. 125
Kearney, R. 176
Kellner, D. 5
Kenway, J. 133
Kleanthous, I. 12, 155, 158; and
    Williams, J. 166
Koskela, H. 37–8
Krathwohl, D., Bloom, B. and Masia,
    B. 70
Kuehn, L. 39
Kuhn, T. 70
Kupchik, A. and Monahan, T. 41

Lakatos, I, 70
Lane, J. 133
Lareau, A. and Weininger, E.B. 154,
    167
Lather, P. 171–3, 175–7, 180–1

Learning; holistic learning 69, 76;
    learning conversations 60; prior
    learning 69, 98; and surveillance 43
Levine-Rasky, C. 153
Lewin, Kurt 124
Lingard, B. 117; and Rawolle, 126,
    132; and Rawolle, S. and Taylor, S
    125–6
Lipsky, M. 85
Lovat, T. 11, 69, 76 80; and Dally, K.,
    Clement, N. and Toomey, R. 76, 80;
    and Holbrook, A. and Bourke, S. 75;
    and Monfries, M. and Morrison, K.
    73; and Smith, D. 73; and Toomey,
    R. 76; and Toomey, R. and Clement,
    N. 76, 78–9
Lyon, D. 36–8, 40

Man, S., Nolan, J. and Wellman, B.
    46–47
Marginson, S. 126
Markus, T.A. 36
Martin, A.K., Gutman, L. and Hutton,
    P. 38, 46
Martin, J.L. 124
Marx, G. 40, 46–8
Marx, Karl 3, 5–6, 175, 180; Marx
    and Bourdieu 124; Marx and
    deconstruction 175; Marx and
    Foucault 21; Marxism 14, 23, 172,
    178; Marxian political economy 6;
    Marxism and praxis 175; neo-Marxism
    70, 122, 172–3
Mathieson, T. 38
Maton, K. 126
McCahill, M. and Finn, R. 43
McLaren, P. 171–3, 175, 180
McWhorter, L. 26
Mercieca, Daniela 209
Mercieca, Duncan 13, 200
Mezirow, J. 99
Miller, J. 22, 24, 27, 31
Ministry of Education (Sweden) 98
Moran, P. and Murphy, M. 99
Morris, M. 88
Murphy, M. 11, 85–6; and Bamber, J.
    14; and Fleming, T. 87, 98–9; and
    Skillen, P. 11

Newmann, F. 77
New Labour 144
New sociology of education 121
Nicoll, K. and Fejes, A. 64

Nixon, J. 209–10
Norris, C. 36; and Armstrong, G. 37

O'Cadiz, M., del Pilar, P., Torres, C.A.
  and Lindquist, P. 171, 181
Odhiambo, G. 84
Ofsted, 187, 193
Osterman, K. 77

Panopticism 35–48
Papadopoulos, Y. 85
Parents, and capital 157; middle-class
  parents 12, 153–4; parental influence
  153, 158; and social capital 159; and
  symbolic violence 160
Park, C. 76
Pederson, J. 102
Performativity 12, 174, 192, 196,
  performativity culture 193; school
  performativity 188; and universities
  210
Peters, M. 171, 174, 178–80; and
  Trifonas, P. 173–4; and Wilson, K.
  172–3
Phenix, P. 71
Pike, J. 44
Poster, M. 37, 39, 40
Power, 4, 6–7; disciplinary power 48;
  and genealogy 24; and knowledge 22,
  24, 65; and learning 60; and
  misrecognition 119; and
  normalisation 25; and panopticon
  36–7; 42–3; parent power 157,
  160–1; power of teacher-learner
  relationship 74; power relations 46–8,
  165–6; and reflective practice 63–4;
  and social theory 4, 8; and technology
  52–3, 60

Quality assurance 84–5, 89; new
  bureaucracy of 88; and political
  regulation 91
Quine, W.V. 71

Rajchman, J. 31
Rawling, E. M. 187
Rawolle, S. 124–6, 134; and Lingard, B.
  12, 117, 122, 126, 134
Reay, D. 139, 153–4, 157, 164–5; and
  Davies, J., David, M. and Ball, S. 154
Reed-Danahay, D. 133
Research methodology 117, 145; and
  Bourdieu 127–8

Rey, T. 147
Rizvi, F. and Lingard, B. 129
Robbins, D. 121, 140, 150
Rodriguez, L. and Craig, R. 22
Rolfe, G. and Gardner, L. 64
Rorty, R. 21, 23, 201, 207

Said, E. 134
Salter, B. and Tapper, T. 84
Sandberg, F. 11, 99, 103; and
  Andersson, P. 99, 103
Santoro, M. 118, 133
Scambler, G. and Britten, N. 86
Schooling, and accountability 89;
  instrumentalist notions of 80; and
  reproduction 121
School surveillance 34
Schön, D. 59, 204
Scott, C. 84
Selwyn, N. 40, 43
Shore, C. and Wright, S. 84
Simon, B. 42, 46
Small, N. and Mannion, R. 85
Smart, B. 29
Social capital 125, 153, 155–6, 159,
  161, 165
Spencer, J. 46
Spivak, G. 176–7
Standish, P. 192
Staples, W.G. 45
Stecher, F. and Kirby, R. 86
Steeves, V. 47
Stoker, B. 191
St Pierre, B. and Willow, W. 172, 181
Stronach, I. and Maclure, M. 171
Student resistance 45–48
Sullivan, M. 31
Sumner, J. 85
Symbolic violence 12, 124, 139–41; and
  academies 147; and christian ethos
  148; and education 142–4; and family
  156, 160, 165; and parental influence
  155, 157; and reproduction 142
Symeou, L. 154

Taylor, C. 56
Teaching, and askesis 56; biblical
  teaching 147–9; and Derrida 173;
  and Foucault 25; geography teaching
  187, 193, 196; medical knowledge
  23; reflective teaching 200, 204–5,
  207; student teachers 207; teaching
  of philosophy 178; values of 78

Teese, R. 121, 133
Thomas, A. 98
Thrupp, M. and Wilmott, R. 86
Travers, M. 84
Trifonas, P. 171, 173–5, 178–9, 181
Tyler, R. 70

Usher, R. and Edwards, R. 203

Van Manen, M. 73, 75
Veyne, P. 27

Wacquant, L. 118–19, 122, 129
Walsh, P. 86
Webb, J., Schiraton, T. and Danaher, G. 133

Weber, M. 86–7
Weiss, J. 47
Welton, M. 99
Williams, G. 191
Williams, J. 166
Willis, P. 46
Winter, C. 13, 184, 187–8
Woodward, I. and Emmison, M. 121
Wright Mills, C. 118, 133

Yar, M. 37
Young, M.F.D. 121
Young, R. 73

Zevenbergen, R. 166
Žižek, S. 172, 181